Learning to Study Critical Thinking

Jonelle A. Beatrice
Youngstown State University

IRWIN
CAREER
EDUCATION
DIVISION

Chicago • Bogotá • Boston • Buenos Aires • Caracas
London • Madrid • Mexico City • Sydney • Toronto

Senior developmental editor: Jean Roberts
Senior marketing manager: Lynn M. Kalanik
Project editor: Waivah Clement
Production manager: Laurie Kersch
Designer: Laurie J. Entringer
Cover photographer: © 1993 Carlos Alejandro
Art studio: Electronic Publishing Services, Inc.
Art coordinator: Heather Burbridge
Compositor: Carlisle Communications, Inc.
Typeface: 10/12 Century Schoolbook
Printer: R. R. Donnelley & Sons Company

Library of Congress Cataloging-in-Publication Data

Beatrice, Jonelle A.
Learning to study through critical thinking / Jonelle A. Beatrice.
p. cm.
Includes bibliographical references (p.) and index.
ISBN 0-256-15449-X
1. Study skills. 2. Critical thinking—Study and teaching (Higher) I.Title.
LB2395.B39 1995
378.1'7'02812—dc20 94–15557

Printed in the United States of America
1 2 3 4 5 6 7 8 9 0 DO 1 0 9 8 7 6 5 4

To my late parents and grandparents, whose lives remain a constant source of inspiration, and to Mark, Jared, and Blythe, who fill my life with light.

PREFACE

The dynamic rate of change taking place in our society raises questions about the role of education in preparing students for a future that is unpredictable. Teaching methods that attempt only to impart a required amount of traditional knowledge can no longer prepare students for the many changes that will occur in their vocations and their lives. Educators are now charged with the responsibility of developing *critical literacy*—the intellectual processes necessary for problem solving, decision making, goal setting, and lifelong learning. Thus, the focus in education must shift from teaching students *what* to think to teaching students *how* to think. In this way students will be given the tools they will need to become lifelong learners both in and out of the classroom.

Learning to Study through Critical Thinking offers a unique, holistic approach to teaching thinking. While some texts present critical thinking as a set of isolated skills to be learned, this text presents thinking as a process to be used. Thinking is presented as an integral part of all learning in college through application to actual course content and student experience. The focus of this text is on empowering students to take control of the highly individual process of thinking and learning.

Who Can Use This Book

Learning to Study through Critical Thinking can be used by any post–high school student who wants to develop or enhance the ability to think and learn. Regardless of age, course of study, or ability level, all students must develop the basic skill of learning to learn by learning to think. The examples and applications in the text cover many areas of study and will appeal to students in all career fields at any point in their education.

Benefits from Using This Book

Unlike most study skills texts, this text uses a holistic approach to infuse studying and thinking into the total post–high school experience. Its objective is to create independent learners who understand the process of learning and thinking and can apply that process in and out of the classroom.

Cognitive transfer is emphasized while students become involved and empowered in the process of their own learning. Students will understand how and why learning takes place. They will then learn to incorporate higher levels of learning and thinking skills into systems of study and problem solving.

Affective transfer is enhanced as students learn how to become more aware of and to direct their thinking process. Individual and cooperative activities throughout the text focus on the development of attitudes and dispositions associated with effective thinking. A framework is provided for learning and thinking in school and throughout life.

Skills That Will Be Taught

The text is divided into three parts that build on each other to create a complete picture of thinking and learning. Part I of *Learning to Study through Critical Thinking* lays the foundation for successful college learning. It establishes the need for lifelong learning skills, and it directs the student to take control of the learning situation. Time management and goal setting are introduced as means of enhancing and directing the ability to think and learn. Students will:

- Examine the differences between high school learning and college learning.
- Explore their motivation for being in school and their resulting approach to learning.
- Learn how to effectively budget their time according to their needs and how to set priorities.
- Learn how to set goals that are specific, realistic, and personally desirable.

Part II of *Learning to Study through Critical Thinking* creates the focal point of the text—how to think and how to learn. It introduces the principles of learning and thinking that serve as the basis for every technique presented in the text. Students will:

- Determine their learning style.
- Learn what memory involves.
- Select techniques for preparing to learn, processing information, and recalling information that are based on their learning style.

- Learn to identify the difference between fixed and dynamic learning tasks.
- Learn how to go beyond the memory level of learning by translating, interpreting, applying, analyzing, synthesizing, and evaluating information.
- Learn what good thinking involves.
- Learn how to identify obstacles to critical thinking in themselves and others.
- Learn how to enhance their ability to think creatively.
- Learn how to apply a problem-solving model to their creative and critical thinking processes.

Part III of *Learning to Study through Critical Thinking* uses the principles of learning and thinking to create systems for notetaking, reading, test taking, and writing.

- Learn mental and physical strategies for preparing to take notes, processing while they take notes, and recalling after they take notes.
- Learn mental and physical strategies for preparing to read, processing while they read, and recalling after they read.
- Learn mental and physical strategies for preparing to take tests, processing while they take tests, and analyzing errors after they take tests.
- Learn mental and physical strategies for preparing to write, processing while they write, and revising after they write.

Pedagogical Features

The following features were designed to promote transfer of chapter content and to involve the student in translating, interpreting, applying, analyzing, synthesizing, and evaluating their understanding of each chapter.

Conceptual Goal. Each chapter begins with a statement of its main concept. Students should be directed to focus on this concept to get the "big picture" as they work through the chapter. Applying these general concepts will lead to achievement of proficiency in the specific goals presented in each chapter.

Chapter Goals. Chapter goals are presented on the initial page of each chapter. These goals provide students with a purpose for reading, informing them of the skills they should strive to achieve, and establish the focus of each chapter.

Sharing Your Ideas. Throughout each chapter, group activities are suggested to reinforce material and involve students in the skills of cooperative learning and decision making.

Putting It All Together. A brief summary is provided at the end of the body of each chapter to help students review and consolidate chapter information.

Making the Connection. Students are asked to check their understanding of each chapter through a series of exercises that require them to translate, interpret, and apply what they have learned.

Thinking It Through. Each chapter contains a realistic student problem that is related to its content. This activity requires students to transfer what they have learned by applying critical thinking and problem-solving skills to a college learning situation.

Applying Your Skills. Several write-in activities are located at the end of each chapter. They provide students and the instructor with means of applying and evaluating chapter content that use the students' own text and course material.

Using Your Resources. Each chapter suggests that students make use of a campus resource that is somewhat related to the chapter's content. This activity provides students with a means of applying their thinking and learning skills both in and out of the classroom and will expand the repertoire of sources they can use for social and academic assistance.

Instructor's Manual. The *Instructor's Manual* accompanying *Learning to Study through Critical Thinking* contains suggestions for effectively using the text to promote critical thinking in the classroom. The manual includes a philosophy of teaching for thinking, a sample syllabus, a course flowchart, and a chart illustrating how to integrate course content with campus resources. Suggestions are given for enhancing the content of each chapter and for creating a climate for thinking in the classroom.

A C K N O W L E D G M E N T S

I would like to express my gratitude to those who have helped make this project a reality:

To Joan Sonnett, director of developmental education, Youngstown State University, who opened all the doors by providing me with my first opportunity to work in developmental education. Her ceaseless dedication to learning has inspired and directed my work. The content of this text is a compilation of all I have learned through her patience, love, and encouragement.

To Pat Shively, English teacher and journalist, Mineral Ridge High School, who pushed me through the open doors by placing my work in the right hands. Her confidence in me and my work caused this book to be written. Her ability to bring the content of this text to life in the classroom has served as a constant inspiration for my teaching.

To Diane Armbrecht, Youngstown State University, whose command of the elements of style helped me fine-tune my manuscript.

To Nancy Maruniak, Youngstown State University, who counseled me on my work as only a writer could.

To Joan Bevan, Tracey Lomker, and Denise Anderson, who patiently deciphered my notes and produced many of my charts.

To the dedicated faculty and staff of the Reading and Study Skills Program at Youngstown State University, whose significant contributions to my work and to the students at Youngstown State must be recognized.

To Sheri Zander, coordinator of the Writing Center, Youngstown State University, for her advice and support.

To Carol Long, former executive editor, IRWIN Career Education Division, for her patience, knowledge, and unique sense of timing.

To Jean Roberts, senior developmental editor, IRWIN Career Education Division, whose incredible patience, knowledge, and encouragement directed my work.

To the production team at Irwin, who turned the manuscript into a book: project editor Waivah Clement, designer Laurie Entringer, art coordinator Heather Burbridge, and production supervisor Laurie Kersch.

To the following reviewers, who offered invaluable advice on the development of this manuscript:

L. Jacquelene Burnett, Southern Illinois University at Edwardsville

Stephen B. Coble, Tennessee Technological University

Mary Susan Hall, DeKalb College

Mildred J. Stenehjem, Yakima Valley Community College

Charles B. Stevenson, Indiana University of Pennsylvania

To the entire staff of the IRWIN Career Education Division for their unsurpassed expertise and professionalism.

Finally, to my husband, Mark, and to my children, Jared and Blythe, who have believed in me and supported me throughout this project.

Jonelle A. Beatrice

TO THE STUDENT

You are your own teacher. Whether you know it or not, you have more knowledge about yourself than anyone else does. You know what is easy for you and what is difficult, what you enjoy and what you dislike. You even know better than anyone else why you're in school in the first place. While you're in school, your instructors and texts will present you with much valuable information, but the task of learning that information is yours. This book will put you in control of your own learning. It will make you more aware of your abilities, and it will give you the information you need to become the best teacher you ever had.

The way you think is a unique part of who you are. Because learning involves thinking, becoming aware of the way you think can guide you as you learn. This book will put you in control of your thinking process. It will help you understand what good thinking involves, and it will improve your ability to think in and out of the classroom.

The ability to think is the most important skill you can gain from your education. After your instructors are gone and school becomes a fading memory, that skill will help you continue to learn throughout your life. No matter what career path you choose, how many times you change vocations, or how much your chosen vocation changes in a lifetime, the ability to think will remain your most effective key to success.

C O N T E N T S

PART II

Principles of Learning

PART I
ADAPTING TO COLLEGE

C H A P T E R

1 College Learning

Focus on how to learn as well as what to learn in college.

Chapter Goals

After you read this chapter, you will be able to:

- Identify factors that may keep you from accomplishing your goals for school and a career.
- Explain the differences between learning in high school and learning beyond high school.
- Understand your definition of what it means to be educated.
- Assess your motivation for learning and determine how this affects your approach to studying.
- Identify and explain your response to educational discord.

What is your definition of learning? If you think about your past experiences in school, chances are you think of learning as something that was done to you by the teacher. Your definition might include some reference to memorizing instead of thinking, reciting facts instead of understanding them, knowing *what* to learn instead of knowing *how* to learn. As a result, you may now be the proud owner of a head stuffed full of somewhat meaningless information.

"Hey, so what," you say. "I'll get my diploma, graduate, and get a real job." It's important to remember, however, that after landing a real job, you must be able to keep it. There you'll be, ready to impress your boss with your ability to . . . recite the preamble to the Constitution? . . . produce a time line of the history of Western civilization? . . . recall lists of famous geological formations? In addition to these unsettling thoughts, Richard Paul, author of *Toward a Critical Society,* reports that "few high school students (according to one study, only 16 percent) have the same vocational plans after they graduate as when they entered, and that within five years of university graduation only a minority of students have jobs in the area of their collegiate major."

The American anthropologist Margaret Mead summed up the situation when she said, "We are now at a point where we must educate our children in what no one knew yesterday, and prepare our schools for what no one knows yet." This chapter will help you prepare for your future by asking you to identify your current views about education and to analyze how they affect your methods for learning. Next, you will be asked to determine whether the methods you now use are adequate to prepare you for your future career and for the many changes that will occur throughout your life.

Why Good Students Fail

Imagine yourself the lone passenger in the cockpit of a small private plane cruising high above the clouds. You consider yourself experienced in flying since you have been in airplanes many times. Your pilot is both personable and experienced, making you feel relaxed and confident. Suddenly you sense that something is wrong. It could be because your personable and experienced pilot has just let out a bloodcurdling scream. As she clutches her chest and takes her last labored breath, she collapses over the steering device. Your efforts to revive her fail. What would you do? Would your first reaction be to take the wheel and try to navigate the plane even if you didn't know how? Would you try to radio for help? Perhaps it would be easier to just give up and bail out.

Let's change the scene a little. Imagine yourself a student who has spent many years in school and has come to know what to expect. Your teachers, for the most part, have been willing to help you by selecting much of the content to be learned. Because of this, you have become rather used to the way things operate. As you begin yet one more year of education after high school, you sense that something is wrong. The bloodcurdling scream in this example is coming from *your* mouth! You feel yourself sinking fast as your grades dive toward the bottom of a deep pit. What should you do? Would your first reaction be to try to figure out another way of learning, even if you weren't sure how? Would you know where to go and whom to see in order to get help? Perhaps it would be easier to just drop the class or leave school altogether.

Although the above situations differ, your response to both should be the same: *Take the controls! Radio for help! Don't bail out!* Most of the students who fail in college fail because they do not follow these three directives: They do not take control of their own learning, they do not ask for assistance, and they stop trying. The author Robert Sternberg, in his book *Intelligence Applied: Understanding and Increasing Your Intellectual Skills,* lists a number of reasons that students fail to realize their full potential. As you read those reasons, identify the ones you see in yourself.

Also, think about how many of the items on Sternberg's list could be the result of not taking control, not asking for help, or just giving up.

Obstacles to Full Realization of Intelligence

1. Lack of motivation.
2. Inability to control impulses.
3. Difficulty in completing problems and following through.
4. Failure to begin tasks.
5. Fear of failure.
6. Procrastination.
7. Excessive self-pity.
8. Excessive dependence.
9. Blaming others for your difficulties.
10. Wallowing in personal difficulties.
11. Becoming easily distracted.
12. Spreading yourself too thick or too thin.
13. Too little or too much self-confidence.
14. Inability to wait for rewards.
15. Lack of balance between critical thinking and creative thinking.

High School versus College

Why do students, who have been in school much of their lives, have difficulty in taking charge of their own learning and in asking for help? One very good reason is that they've never had to do it before. Regardless of what kind of school they're attending, college is different from any learning situation most students have ever encountered. Unfortunately, unless students realize this fact, they may simply bail out, feeling that somehow they lost a few brain cells between the time they left high school and the time they started college.

Table 1–1 lists a few of the major differences between high school and college. As you read through them, notice that one of the most important differences is the shift in responsibility. The person in charge of selecting what to learn, how to learn it, when and where to learn it is no longer the teacher but the student.

Major Differences

What to Learn. As a high school student, you may never have had to make decisions about what to learn from lectures and textbooks. Your teachers most likely selected information for you and told you to learn it for

TABLE 1–1 Differences between High School and College

Area of Difference	*High School*	*College*
What to learn	Teacher selects and presents material.	Student must decide what is important.
How to learn	Teacher includes practice as part of instruction.	Student is responsible for method of learning.
Level of learning	Emphasis is on memorization of content.	Emphasis is on applying content.
Volume/pace	Amount of material and speed of presentation are regulated by student's understanding.	Amount of material and speed of presentation are regulated by necessity to cover material in a term.
Amount of freedom	School structure and rules dictate personal time.	Student has complete personal and academic freedom.
Resources	Some support services are offered outside the classroom.	Vast array of opportunities and support services is available beyond the classroom.

a test. Now, as a college student, you are expected to know how to select what is important from several hundred pages of text and class notes.

How to Learn. Can you recall the class review sessions that were held in high school the days before a test? You may have been given study guides, had practice quizzes, or played games for review of content. Your teacher may have organized these review sessions according to the type of test you would be taking. As a result, you may not be aware of techniques to use in order to organize and review content according to the type of exam you will be taking.

Level of Learning. When you recall what and how you learned in high school, do you remember memorizing facts in order to repeat them on exams? Did you ever try to deeply understand or apply any of this information to your life? How would you go about learning if you suddenly found that memorizing no longer worked? Many college students get a jolt when they take their first exam and find that hours of memorizing earned them an F. An often heard response is, "That jerk tested us on material he never gave us." What happens in these instances is that information was given in the form of ideas to be understood and applied, and instead was memorized with little comprehension.

Volume/Pace. The amount of information received in one day of college may be equal to the amount received in one week of high school. Yes, you read that correctly! Perhaps you had better read it again and think about what it means with regard to the amount of work you have to do in one term. What a change from the days when your teacher taught it until you got it!

Amount of Freedom. "Free at last, Free at last, Thank God Almighty, Free at last." Along with Martin Luther King, Jr., a recent college freshman expressed this sentiment when describing her newfound independence. A major factor leading to the downfall of many college students is that they perceive themselves as having a great deal of freedom. They are unaware that for every one hour they are in class, they should be spending two hours studying the material outside of class. They think of college as a part-time project instead of a full-time job.

While you were in high school, teachers dictated how you used your time. In college there is no one to tell you what to do and when to do it. You have gone from being in school eight hours a day to being in class three hours a day. This abrupt change can spell trouble for students who are not organized, who tend to put things off, or who do not realize that going to college requires an immense amount of time and energy.

Resources. When you need to "radio for help," you have to know where to call. Your college provides services to help you deal with any problem that arises. All you have to do is find out where they are and how they can help. In high school you were used to having a counselor or school nurse down the hall from your classroom; you may not feel comfortable seeking out help located in a building across campus. You may also miss the chance to receive help because you are unaware of the many resources available. Do you know, for example, that most colleges have drug and alcohol abuse programs, medical services, psychologists, career counselors, financial aid specialists, tutoring services, campus ministries, credit unions, escort services, handicapped services, and minority and multicultural student services, to name a few? Do you also know that you're paying for these services through your tuition? Since you're paying, be sure to get your money's worth.

At the end of each chapter in this book you will find an activity called "Using Your Resources." It will ask you to visit and learn about services at your college that can make you more successful in and out of the classroom. Use this activity to help you take control of your learning.

The Role of the Teacher

Because of the differences between high school and college, you must begin to change your ideas about teachers and their role in your education. In the past, your teachers have been much like pilots in total control of your destiny. They have charted your course by selecting what was important for you to learn from textbooks and class sessions. You relied on them to tell you what to know for a test. They may even have taken the time for practice sessions in class. If there was difficulty with specific content, your teachers may have repeated it until understanding was achieved. Many students enter college with the same expectations of their instructors. Because these expectations are not met, students may feel their instructors are unskilled. When this happens, it is usually because the student does not understand the role of the college instructor.

If high school teachers can be compared to pilots, then college instructors can be compared to tour guides. They are expert travelers who know the lay of the land. They may plot your general course and point out some areas of interest, but don't expect them to take you by the hand and lead you around. It is up to you to do your own sightseeing along the way. In other words, do not rely on them to tell you what to learn or how to learn it; that is up to you. Understand that they are laying a foundation for learning with each lecture. You must build on that foundation using your own knowledge, knowledge from outside sources such as your textbook and from any other materials you choose to include.

The Role of the Student

In college your role as a student must also change. Take the controls! You must decide what information from lectures and texts is important and then determine how to learn this information. You must also figure out how much time all of this is going to take and when you will have that time. Finally, so you don't have to bail out, you must find out whom to call and where to go when you are overwhelmed. If you are already overwhelmed, have no fear; that's where this text comes in. In this text you will learn how to determine *what* is important in the classroom. You will become an expert in analyzing course content and your various professors.

When deciding *how* to learn, you will know the principles of learning and how they relate to you and your course work. You will know *when* to learn through your knowledge and application of the principles of time management. If you need to "radio for help," you will be aware of *where* to call. Through the activities in this text you will gain a working knowledge of the locations and functions of the various support services your school has to offer.

Thus, in order to successfully make the change from high school to college, you must first realize that you need to change roles from passenger to pilot. Then, before you "take the controls," you must learn what taking the controls means.

What Is an Educated Person?

The first step in taking the controls is determining where you want to go and how you plan to get there. Planning your destination as you begin college will help you decide the best route to follow. Otherwise, you may graduate and find that you've not become educated in the manner you had hoped. You may find yourself with a degree but not really educated. Is that possible? How can you have a degree and still not be educated? Is a diploma a guarantee of ability, or is it just a certificate that you have been exposed to information? Can you get a college degree without actually learning? These questions, which many students never ask, are vital in determining your route in college. Your views about what it takes to be educated will determine how you go about learning.

A student can take two general approaches to the task of learning: a surface approach or a deep approach. Students who take a surface approach tend to be somewhat passive in their view of education. That is, they see learning as something done to them. Their task is to take what is provided and deposit it in their brain for later recycling on an exam. This mode of learning has also been referred to as the bulimic approach: The student binges by cramming and memorizing large quantities of facts that he or she purges or spits out at exam time. You may be a surface learner if you find that you try to remember everything from your texts and from lectures or if you find that you try to memorize and recite information exactly as it is stated. This mode of learning may be efficient for short-term use, such as taking an exam; however, information stored in this manner is often difficult to retrieve. It is also difficult to make later use of information you may really not understand.

Students who take a deep approach view learning as an active process of seeking understanding. Instead of memorizing information, they try to put it in their own words. Deep learners often apply what they learn by relating it to their own lives. Deep learners look for the main point of an entire lecture rather than trying to memorize it as a list of facts. They read and think about the information presented, and they try to relate that information to their own experience. Because this mode of learning requires higher-level thought processes, the information is usually retained for later use. How do you view education and learning? According to the above descriptions, do you feel you are a surface learner or a deep learner?

Motivation for Learning

Evidence suggests that students in higher education approach learning not only according to their view of education but also according to their motives or reasons for being in school. For example, if your goal at school is to become qualified for a specific job, then the route you take will probably focus on completing the classes you need in order to become qualified for that job. Learning in those classes may not be as important to you as just getting them listed on your final transcript. This is what Australian researcher John Biggs calls *instrumental* learning: learning to become qualified for a specific job as easily as possible. If your goal is to get high grades, Biggs classifies you as an *achievement*-oriented learner. In this instance, the high grade on your transcript may be more important to you than the actual learning that did or did not take place. Some students, however, are actually in college to become as competent and informed as possible. Grades or jobs do not motivate these students as much as the love of learning. Biggs terms these individuals *intrinsic* learners.

Sharing Your Ideas

How do you classify yourself? Are you an instrumental learner who wants to become qualified for a specific job? Are you an achievement-oriented learner who strives for high grades and recognition? Are you an intrinsic learner who simply likes to learn? In order to help you to determine your primary motivation for learning, complete the following sentence:

The most important reason I have for attending this institution is:

____

Review responses as a class in the following manner:

1. Have each student share his response.
2. As a class, analyze whether the response focuses on instrumental, achievement, or intrinsic reasons for learning.
3. Seek agreement or disagreement from the student whose response is being analyzed.
4. Use the following criteria to assist you in your analysis:
   Instrumental learners
   Responses focus on getting a job.
   Achievement learners
   Responses focus on winning approval, usually in the form of grades.
   Intrinsic learner
   Responses focus on learning for the sake of self-improvement.
5. Survey the total number of instrumental, achievement, and intrinsic learners. Can you draw any conclusions from your results? ■

Motivation and Approaches to Study

Why is it important to determine your ideas about being educated and your motivation for learning, whether instrumental, achievement, or intrinsic? Studies have found that a student's ideas about being educated and her motivation for learning determine whether she approaches learning in a deep or surface manner.

Students whose motivation for learning is job related or *instrumental,* according to a study done by John Biggs, tend to take a surface approach to study. Those who are motivated by grades or are *achievement*-motivated learners tend to take the approach (whether surface or deep) that will result in the highest grade. Biggs found evidence that *intrinsic* students, who learn for the sake of self-improvement, most often take a deep approach to learning. According to the information you gained from the preceding activity, are you instrumental, achievement, or intrinsic in your motivation for learning? Based on John Biggs's findings, what approach to learning are you most likely to take?

Now that you know how you approach learning, you may want to ask yourself why. What causes students to become more focused on getting good grades or a good job than on actually learning? Is this something you decide yourself, or do the expectations of others have something to do with it? What role do your parents, your college, and society in general have in determining why you are in college and what you need to gain from it? Are you the first one in your family to attend college? Do you or your parents expect you to get good grades because college is an investment? Does your college require you to achieve a certain grade point average? When you begin to look for jobs, will prospective employers care more about your grades than about what you've learned? Could your current method of learning have negative effects on your job after graduation?

These are questions you need to ask as you begin college. You might begin to realize that because of outside pressures you are going about learning in a manner that could cause you to graduate without the skills you will need to function in a rapidly changing job market. You may find that you're likely to graduate and be unable to function because everything you memorized has been forgotten, is no longer current, or was never fully understood.

Understanding your approach to learning might also save you from experiencing educational discord. This is a condition that causes you to feel angry and confused about school. It makes you feel an uncontrollable desire to commit wild and violent acts on your textbooks. You may have hallucinations of demonic instructors who are never pleased with your performance. Illogical lectures may invade your dreams on a nightly basis. You may also become a raving maniac when it is time to study. These symptoms occur because no one bothered to tell you about that part of education known as the hidden curriculum.

The Hidden Curriculum

The Hidden Curriculum is the title of a book that educator Benson Snyder wrote in 1970. In this book Snyder explains that every class has two plans you can follow: the formal one that the instructor expects you to follow and the hidden one that you eventually realize you can get away with. You may find that even though your math instructor assigns 20 problems a night, you can actually get away with working only the last few without immediate negative consequences. Suppose you take a course with nightly assigned readings. After taking the first test and talking with a few friends, you come to realize that reading the text is not necessary for a good grade. What would you do?

It is this education decision making that can cause you to have mixed feelings about how to learn. Your motivation for learning will determine exactly how you choose to learn and how you feel about it. If you are an achievement learner who is motivated by grades, you will probably have no trouble ignoring the text if reading it is not necessary for a good grade. As an instrumental learner who just wants to get a degree and make money, your response will be the same. What would an intrinsic learner do in this case? On one hand, reading the text is not necessary. On the other hand, it must have been assigned for some reason and intrinsic learners are motivated by learning for self-satisfaction. Chances are, most intrinsic learners would feel torn and confused. They have indirectly been asked to choose between what they feel they should do and what they know they can actually get away with.

You must develop your own game plan or method of dealing with educational discord when it occurs. You must learn to select and weigh that which is important to your individual motivations or goals and that which is important in your course work. Sooner or later everyone comes to the realization that, at times, something may have to be neglected. Knowing what can be pushed aside with the least academic risk and personal concern is part of learning how to deal with the hidden curriculum. Instrumental learners may push too much aside with little concern, while intrinsic learners will suffer over having to omit anything from their studies.

It is important that, as a student, you "take the controls" by determining why you are in college and then deciding how you need to go about learning in order to reach your goals.

Putting It All Together

Many factors may contribute to failure in making the transition from high school to post–high school education. The greatest difficulty many students have is in taking a more active role in their learning. In college, much of the responsibility for learning shifts from the teacher to you. In order to "take the controls," you must analyze how you view education and your purpose for attending college. Knowing what it means to be educated and what you want to get out of college will determine how you go about learning.

Because much of your education to this point has focused on memorization, you may view learning as the process of storing facts. You may feel that your role in college is to memorize as much as you can in order to graduate and get a decent job. However, a successful person must know how to use information and continue to learn throughout life. This could alter the way you approach learning.

Your emotional response to the way you study is also tied to your purpose for learning. There is a hidden curriculum in most courses that may force you to make decisions about learning. Some decisions may be contrary to the way you want to learn. Knowing this can help you understand your reaction to various courses and help you decide how to take control of your learning experience.

Making the Connection

Check your understanding of the concepts presented in this chapter by completing the following activity. If you are unable to recall information in a particular area, go back and review that material before completing the rest of the exercises in this section.

1. Write one or two sentences to summarize what you recall about each of the following topics:

   Why good students fail ____________________

   ____

   ____

   The differences between high school and college ____________________

   ____

   ____

   An educated person ____________________

   ____

   ____

   How views of education affect learning ____________________

   ____

   ____

   How motivation for learning affects method of study ____________________

   ____

   The hidden curriculum ____________________

   ____

   ____

2. List one new idea you've gained about education and learning in college as a result of reading this chapter. ____________________

   ____

   ____

3. Describe one change you plan to make in the way you go about studying or learning in college. ____________________

   ____

   ____

Thinking It Through

Read the following passage. Then answer the questions by applying what you've learned about motivation for learning, approaches to study, and the hidden curriculum.

> Mr. Jones planned to become an electrical engineer. He chose a school with a solid reputation in electrical engineering. Although his instructors said that much reading and understanding were required in order to become a good electrical engineer, Mr. Jones found he was able to make straight A's as a result of hours of memorizing information gained through lectures. He soon stopped reading his texts. Mr. Jones felt successful as a learner because his grade point average remained high. His goal, to land a good job with a noted company, required an outstanding academic record.
>
> Mrs. Smith, also an electrical engineering student, realized that she was being asked by her instructors to memorize and return large quantities of information on exams. Refusing to submit to a surface approach to learning, she studied and understood ideas in a deep manner. However, when asked to spit back information exactly as it was stated in her notes, Mrs. Smith had difficulty. As a result, her grade point average was not as praiseworthy as Mr. Jones's.

1. What do you see as Mr. Jones's problem(s)? ______________________

____

____

2. What do you see as Mrs. Smith's problem(s)? ______________________

____

____

3. Would you describe Mr. Jones as an instrumental, achievement, or intrinsic learner? Why? ______________________

____

4. Would you describe Mrs. Smith as an instrumental, achievement, or intrinsic learner? Why? ______________________

____

5. Describe how these students' motivation for learning causes them to approach learning the way they do. ______________________

____

____

6. Which student's approach do you feel is better? Explain your selection. ____________________
____
____
____

Applying Your Skills 1 *Self-Assessment*

Instructions: The skill areas listed below are those in which you will need to become proficient in order to take control of your learning in college. As you begin this text, you may find that you need improvement in many of the areas. Don't be discouraged! You may not yet have had the opportunity to develop and use these skill areas. This assessment will give you an idea of the areas in which you are already strong and the areas on which you will want to focus as you use this book.

Assess your current level of achievement by circling the number that most closely reflects your behavior. When you have completed all the items, add up your score for each area and mark it by placing a dot under the proper skill area on the graph found on the final page of this exercise. When you have completed this text, take this assessment again using a different color of ink. Compare your results and evaluate your progress.

1 = Never
2 = Rarely
3 = Sometimes
4 = Frequently
5 = Always

Campus Orientation

1. I make use of the special academic services available to students in need of assistance in math, writing, reading, and general tutoring.	1	2	3	4	5
2. I take part in social events at my institution.	1	2	3	4	5
3. I know how to find what I need at my school.	1	2	3	4	5
4. I belong to a club or organization at my institution.	1	2	3	4	5
5. I take advantage of college services pertaining to my physical and mental health.	1	2	3	4	5

Time Management

1. I prepare a study schedule at the beginning of each term.	1	2	3	4	5
2. I know when and where I study best and take this into account when preparing my study schedule.	1	2	3	4	5
3. I allow for leisure time daily on my study schedule.	1	2	3	4	5
4. As an assignment is given, I write the due date on my calendar.	1	2	3	4	5
5. I also use my calendar to schedule the time it will take to complete an assignment.	1	2	3	4	5

Goal Setting

1. I have set long-term personal goals for the next five years of my life.	1	2	3	4	5
2. I have set long-term professional goals for the next 5 to 10 years of my life.	1	2	3	4	5
3. I set short-term academic goals for each class I take in school.	1	2	3	4	5
4. When setting goals, I take into account my strengths, weaknesses, and values.	1	2	3	4	5
5. I have used professional resources in selecting my career.	1	2	3	4	5

Memory and Learning

1. I use techniques to focus my attention before trying to learn.	1	2	3	4	5
2. I am aware of the best methods for organizing and storing information because of the way I learn.	1	2	3	4	5
3. I space my learning over short periods and take frequent breaks.	1	2	3	4	5
4. I know when I should memorize and when I should understand content.	1	2	3	4	5
5. I know why forgetting occurs and how to prevent it.	1	2	3	4	5

Critical Thinking/Problem Solving

1. I try to understand and apply information from texts and lectures instead of using memorization.	1	2	3	4	5
2. I often develop new ideas from information gained from texts or lectures.	1	2	3	4	5
3. I mentally question material as I read or as I listen to a lecture.	1	2	3	4	5
4. I am able to make myself consider both sides of an issue before making a decision.	1	2	3	4	5
5. I have a consistent system of analyzing problem situations.	1	2	3	4	5

Notetaking

1. I read assignments before going to class.	1	2	3	4	5
2. As I listen to lectures, I try to focus on topics and subtopics.	1	2	3	4	5
3. I know what to do if I get lost or confused while taking notes.	1	2	3	4	5
4. I review my notes as soon as possible after class and add anything I may have left out.	1	2	3	4	5
5. I use a system for studying my notes daily that includes labeling and reciting them in my own words.	1	2	3	4	5

Reading

1. I prepare my mind for reading by looking through a chapter and thinking about the content before I read it.	1	2	3	4	5
2. As I read a chapter, I use more than highlighting to organize and store important information.	1	2	3	4	5
3. I divide long or difficult chapters into smaller chunks in order to read and comprehend the material better.	1	2	3	4	5

4. I often stop to summarize sections and put information together in order to get the main idea of the entire chapter.	1	2	3	4	5
5. I have a method for regularly reviewing my text and for comparing information with my class notes.	1	2	3	4	5

Test Taking

1. In order to prepare for a test, I make up practice questions.	1	2	3	4	5
2. I have techniques that enable me to feel calm and confident during the testing situation.	1	2	3	4	5
3. Before I begin a test, I look carefully through it in order to properly pace myself.	1	2	3	4	5
4. As I take a test, I read carefully and underline key words.	1	2	3	4	5
5. After taking a test, I analyze my errors in order to determine specific sources of problems.	1	2	3	4	5

Writing

1. I brainstorm to select a topic before I write.	1	2	3	4	5
2. I create an outline to guide my thoughts as I write.	1	2	3	4	5
3. I use my outline to create a thesis for my paper.	1	2	3	4	5
4. When writing a paper I include an introduction, a body, and a conclusion.	1	2	3	4	5
5. I write two drafts and carefully proofread my work.	1	2	3	4	5

Plotting Your Progress

Complete the graph below by adding up your score for each area of the self-assessment and entering it as a dot to show the correct number of points received. Draw a line from dot to dot in order to graph your strengths and weaknesses. To measure your improvement, take the self-assessment again after you have completed this text and plot your scores on the graph in a different color. How many areas were you able to improve on?

	Campus Orientation	Time Management	Goal Setting	Memory and Learning	Critical Thinking/Problem Solving	Notetaking	Reading	Test Taking	Writing
25									
24									
23									
22									
21									
20									
19									
18									
17									
16									
15									
14									
13									
12									
11									
10									
9									
8									
7									
6									
5									
4									
3									
2									
1									

Applying Your Skills 2 *Early Learning Survey*

Instructions: To determine your view of education and how you acquired it, complete the survey below.

1. Think about your most positive educational experiences at school. List as many as you can under each level.

   Preschool ____________________

   ____

   Elementary ____________________

   ____

   Middle ____________________

   ____

   High ____________________

   ____

2. Try to recall your most negative experiences in school. List as many as you can under each level.

   Preschool ____________________

   ____

   Elementary ____________________

   ____

   Middle ____________________

   ____

   High ____________________

   ____

3. Describe how you think these experiences affected your views of learning and of yourself.

   ____

   ____

   ____

   ____

   ____

4. Complete the following statement in order to formulate your personal definition of learning:

   To me, school and learning mean ________________________________

   ____

   ____

Applying Your Skills 3 *Hidden Curriculum Analysis*

Instructions: The hidden curriculum is discovered when you find that there is a difference between what your instructor requires and what you actually have to do *in order to be successful* in a course. It does not mean failing to fulfill course requirements and receiving *low grades.* To analyze the hidden curriculum in your courses and your reaction to it, complete the information below for each course you are taking.

Course

1. ________________________________
2. ________________________________
3. ________________________________
4. ________________________________

Attendance Requirement

1. ________________________________
2. ________________________________
3. ________________________________
4. ________________________________

Actual Attendance Required for Good Grade

1. ________________________________
2. ________________________________
3. ________________________________
4. ________________________________

Your Actual Attendance

1. ______________________________
2. ______________________________
3. ______________________________
4. ______________________________

Amount of Homework Required Each Night

1. ______________________________
2. ______________________________
3. ______________________________
4. ______________________________

Amount of Homework That Can Be Done and Still Recieve Good Grade

1. ______________________________
2. ______________________________
3. ______________________________
4. ______________________________

Amount of Homework You Do

2. ______________________________
3. ______________________________
4. ______________________________

Type of Learning Required (deep understanding or surface memorization, or both)

1. ______________________________
2. ______________________________
3. ______________________________
4. ______________________________

Type of Learning That Can Be Done and Still Receive Good Grade

1. ____________________
2. ____________________
3. ____________________
4. ____________________

Type of Learning You Do

1. ____________________
2. ____________________
3. ____________________
4. ____________________

Reasons for Fulfilling or Not Fulfilling Requirements

1. ____________________
2. ____________________
3. ____________________
4. ____________________

Applying Your Skills 4 *Using Your Resources*

Instructions: To know where to "radio for help," you will be asked to visit various school resources throughout this text. Keep this information so that you can refer to it when you need help outside the classroom.

Complete the information below after touring your school's library.

Location: ____________________

Hours of operation: ____________________

Contact person: ____________________

Phone: ____________________

Services offered: ____________________

____

____

____

Personal comments:
Briefly discuss how you could use this resource.

____

____

____

____

Applying Your Skills 5 *Library Research Project*

Instructions: To combine the information you gained from the tour of your campus library with information from this chapter and to apply what you've learned, use your library to research various views on what makes an educated person. Use the guidelines below to assist you.

1. Decide on the topic or key word you will use to research this information. If the word *education* is too broad a category, you might try "philosophy of education," "view of education," or "theory of education."

   ____

2. Use one periodical (magazine or journal) and one text as references.

   ____

3. Write a one-paragraph summary of each source. The summary should contain a topic sentence stating the main point of the author and a few sentences to support or add details to the topic sentence. For example: "Joe Smith believes that to get a good education, one must first master the basic skills of reading, writing, and arithmetic. For instance . . ." Do not state your opinion.
4. Footnote the source below each summary, using the following format:

   Periodical: Author, "Title of Article," *Title of Periodical,* Volume, Date, Page(s).

   Book: Author, *Title of Book* (Place of Publication: Publisher, Date), Page(s).

C H A P T E R

2 Time Management

Combine knowledge of study needs with principles of time management to improve your ability to think and learn.

Chapter Goals

After you read this chapter, you will be able to:

- Identify how time management affects your ability to achieve your goals.
- Determine your personal study needs.
- Apply the principles of time management to your course work.
- Make a daily "To Do" list to break big jobs into small ones.
- Create a weekly schedule that combines the principles of time management with your study needs.
- Devise a term calendar to record assignments for each course you are taking.

It's not the load that breaks you down,
It's the way that you carry it.

Three chapters to read, notes to study, a test tomorrow, my job, my family—help! Have you ever felt you had so much to do that you would never get it all done? How did you handle this feeling? Many students choose to bail out and do nothing at all. Others choose procrastination or the wait-and-see approach. I'll wait to do this assignment and see if it completes itself. Some worry themselves to exhaustion without doing anything constructive.

Other students who have the same load to carry—three chapters to read, notes to study, a test tomorrow, a job, a family—know how to take control and manage to get it all done without losing their mind. How do they do it? Do they possess some magical power?

Good time management does not happen by accident, nor is it magically bestowed on a select few. It is the result of good planning and steady, consistent progress toward completion of a project or goal. And because managing your time forms the base for all that you do in college, you must learn when to study before you learn how to study. Efficient use of time can make it possible for an average student to achieve far more than he ever imagined. On the other hand, inefficient use of time can cause a genius to become incapable of reaching his or her potential.

This chapter will uncover the mysteries of time management and give you the skills needed to use time effectively. By applying the principles of time management to your life, you can learn to skillfully carry your workload and to improve your ability to think and learn.

Determining Your Study Needs

Managing your time effectively requires combining knowledge of your personal study needs with the principles of time management. A survey has been provided on pages 29–30 to help you determine your study needs. It asks you to analyze when and where you are best able to concentrate. Before you complete this survey, however, read the information below for suggestions on finding your best time and location for study.

When to Study

If possible, study when you are best able to concentrate. "Morning people," who are fresh and alert at sunrise, can get a jump on the day by scheduling study in the early hours. "Night owls," who have more energy and ability to focus in the evening, can study late into the night. Once you have determined your best time, plan to study for your most difficult course during that period.

You are probably taking some courses that require long periods of intense concentration. When writing papers or reading difficult material, you will want to work without losing your train of thought. Plan to study for these courses when you have uninterrupted time available.

All courses have certain tasks that can be done in short periods. You can increase your ability to complete work by making good use of waiting time. Use time before classes, in the doctor's office, during cooking, and so on, to review and recite notecards or to organize material for later study.

No matter what time you select to study, be sure to get enough rest. Studying at your best time will do you no good if you end up too tired to concentrate. Most people need seven to eight hours of sleep to function well.

Where to Study

Think of studying as a job, and decide that when you are on the job you cannot be disturbed. This means that you must create one or more study areas at home, at the library, or in the dorm that are free from distractions. Your ability to think and learn depends on your ability to concentrate. You must be aware of those things that physically and mentally distract you.

It is important to have regular places to study. If you give yourself a desk or card table that is used for no purpose other than study, you will begin to focus the minute you sit down. Make your study area look like a work area. Include the proper tools for study, such as good lighting, several pens and pencils, paper, and a dictionary.

If you find yourself thinking about other things when you study, you must create ways to stay focused mentally. One way is to prepare your mind before reading or studying by thinking about the topic and remembering what you already know about it. Break your studying up into small chunks, and reward yourself after successfully completing each chunk. As you read and study, you might find yourself thinking about other things you have to do. To clear your mind of these mental distractions, keep a blank sheet of paper on your desk. Write down whatever pops into your head as you study. During your study break, attend to the items on your list.

Every student has different learning needs. Some students are bothered by things they can see. These students must be in an environment free from clutter in order to concentrate. Other students are bothered by sounds and must have absolute silence when they study. A few students have a hard time just sitting still long enough to read a few passages. The Study Needs Assessment below will help you identify your best time and place for study. The Learning Styles Inventory provided in Chapter 4 will give you additional information about what distracts you. It will provide several suggestions that will improve your ability to devote your full attention to learning.

Study Needs Assessment. Complete the survey below to help you determine your study needs.

1. At what time(s) of day do you feel you are best able to concentrate?

   ____

2. At what time(s) of day do you feel you are least able to concentrate? ______________________________

3. List the courses you are taking in order from those that require the most concentration to those that require the least.

   1. ____
   2. ____
   3. ____

4. ______________________________
5. ______________________________

4. Compile a list of periods during the day when you have waiting time.

____

____

____

5. List specific study tasks from your courses that you can work on during waiting time.

____

____

____

6. List things that distract you mentally or physically.

Mental Distractors	*Physical Distractors*
______________	______________
______________	______________
______________	______________
______________	______________
______________	______________
______________	______________

7. What area at home can you use only for study? ______________

____

8. Where can you study at school? ______________

____

9. List the items you will need in your study area to help you study properly. ______________

____

____

Principles of Time Management

Once you have determined your best time and place for study, you must combine that information with the general principles of time management shown in Table 2–1. Applying these 11 principles will enable you to make good use of your time and to enhance your ability to think and learn.

TABLE 2-1 Principles of Time Management

1. Be consistent.
2. Schedule sufficient time.
3. Review as soon as possible.
4. Study difficult subjects first.
5. Study at your best time.
6. Study similar subjects several hours apart.
7. Allow for review time before class.
8. Take a brief break each hour.
9. Take a long break every two hours.
10. Distribute study evenly over the week.
11. Allow for leisure time daily.

Principle 1: Be Consistent

If possible, study the same subjects at the same times each day. Set aside a specific block of time for each subject: for example, study math 8 to 9 and Business Communication 9 to 10. By doing this, you will train your mind to focus on a specific task each day at a specific time.

Students often have the impression that if they don't have "homework" in a specific subject, they don't need to set aside time for it. In college you must understand that you have "homework" in each subject every day, whether it's directly assigned or not. During scheduled study time you should read and review current and past material, go over the day's lecture notes and review past notes, and prepare study aids on material that is difficult for you to understand. You will learn specific techniques to help you do this throughout this book.

Principle 2: Schedule Sufficient Time

The usual rule for determining how much study time to devote to a class is two-for-one: two hours of study for every one hour you are in class. This means that if you are in English class three hours a week, you should spend about six hours a week studying English. If you are carrying a course load of 12 hours, then you should be spending about 24 hours a week studying. If a course is difficult for you, you may need to devote even more time than two hours for every one hour you are in class.

In many instances, because of other commitments such as jobs and family, the two-for-one rule becomes unrealistic. Use this rule only as a guide. Some classes may require more time than suggested; others may require less. If you find that your other commitments are interfering with your ability to devote as much time to your studies as you need, then you must reevaluate your priorities. List all of your commitments in order of their importance to you. Decide what you can change, what you are willing to give up, and what you must keep.

Sharing Your Ideas

Work with a partner to discuss your commitments and evaluate your priorities.

1. Discuss with your partner the responsibilities you have in addition to school.
2. After your discussion, write your commitments below in the form of a list. Be sure to include school.
3. Number your list in order of importance to you.
4. Discuss with your partner how you may be able to change some of the things on your list to give yourself more time. Write those changes on your list.
5. Have your partner help you decide whether there are things on your list that you can give up for now. Scratch those items off your list.

You now have a list of priorities that should determine how you use your time. If you find that you still do not have enough time for all of your responsibilities, work through this activity again and make additional changes. ■

Principle 3: Review as Soon as Possible

Studies of memory have shown that forgetting begins to occur directly after a task has been completed. After about one hour, recall of information can drop as much as 50 percent. At that rate, it takes little time to forget much of what was presented in a lecture. Therefore, the best time to review information is directly after receiving it.

Schedule at least 15 minutes as soon as possible after each class for reviewing your lecture notes. If you review your notes directly after each class (or as soon as possible) and during regularly scheduled study periods, you will be able to retain much of what you learn.

Principle 4: Study Difficult Subjects First

When given the choice of what to study and when to study it, most people choose to study their easiest, most enjoyable subjects first and to save the most difficult subject for last. This is actually the reverse of what you should do. By studying your most difficult subject first, you are able to give it the time and attention it needs while you are fresh and able to concentrate. If you put off studying difficult material for several hours, chances are you will be tired and unable to give it your full attention.

Getting into the study mode is sometimes a problem. Some students accomplish this by briefly studying an enjoyable subject first. Once they are focused and ready to get down to work, they find it easier to begin their most difficult subject. This can be an effective way to schedule study.

Principle 5: Study at Your Best Time

Now that you have completed your Study Needs Assessment and determined the time of day you concentrate best, use this information to schedule study and to schedule classes. If you find it difficult to concentrate early in the morning, it is not wise to schedule study or classes at that time. Often, you have no control over the time you can schedule your classes, but if you do, schedule them for your best periods of concentration rather than your worst.

Principle 6: Study Similar Subjects Several Hours Apart

Consider the type of studying you must do for each of your classes. Do you have courses that involve a lot of reading? Do you have courses that involve writing or solving mathematical problems? Different courses require different learning tasks, and you may find it refreshing to alternate tasks as you study. Reading for many hours at a time can become quite tedious and confusing. Instead, study subjects that involve math or writing between subjects that involve heavy reading.

Principle 7: Allow for Review Time before Class

When you study the principles of memory in Chapter 4, you will better understand why it is necessary to prepare your mind for learning. If you spend a little time thinking about the subject of a lecture *before* it begins, you will not have to spend time trying to get focused *while* the lecture is taking place. By taking a few minutes before class to review your previous notes and think about the topic, you will be ready to learn new information when the lecture begins.

Principle 8: Take a Brief Break Each Hour

Sometimes you may be tempted to try to get your studying over with all at once. You may say to yourself, "If I could just work for five hours, I could get a lot accomplished." Actually, after one hour of study your mind probably needs a rest. Pushing yourself beyond your ability to work productively gains you nothing.

Here's a good strategy to follow: Study for one hour, then take a 10-minute break. During this break, take care of things that distracted you during your study time, reward yourself with something to eat or drink, stretch, or do something wild and crazy to relieve stress. Do not get involved in a television show or a conversation. Your purpose is to rest briefly and then get back on task.

Principle 9: Take a Long Break Every Two Hours

Most people cannot concentrate effectively on a task for more than two hours. After two hours of study, therefore, take at least a one-hour break. Taking time away from periods of intense concentration will help you be more productive when you return to your work.

Principle 10: Distribute Study Evenly over the Week

Some students, in an attempt to free themselves for a weekend of partying, schedule all of their studying during the week. This is as foolish as trying to eat everything you need for a week so you won't have to bother eating on the weekend. Sooner or later you'll become so stuffed that nothing more can be digested. Use the weekend to even out your load. You do not have to devote your entire weekend to studying. Two hours of study on a Saturday and two hours on a Sunday are not much, but they can eliminate four hours of study during the week when your time is very limited.

Principle 11: Allow for Leisure Time Daily

Indulging in guilt-free leisure time each day is a necessity. Leisure time helps reduce stress. If you do not take this time, you may become too stressed out to concentrate. Plan activities for this time that you enjoy. No thinking about school is allowed! If you have properly planned your study time using the principles of time management, you will have plenty of time to complete your work. You can now rest assured that each activity has a time and a place. Your leisure time and place belong to you.

Putting It on Paper

Students who keep their mind on their work succeed. Students who keep their work on their mind go crazy. Which type of student are you? The best way to keep your mind on your work and not on all the things you have to do is to "put it on paper." Once you have scheduled all your work in written form, you no longer have to carry it around in your mind.

Putting things down on paper is an effective way to deal with procrastination. While some students have no problem beginning work as soon as it is assigned, others tend to delay their work until they are down to the wire. If you procrastinate, it could be because you are fearful of a task, indecisive, overwhelmed, have misjudged your workload, or lack enough information to begin. In any case, procrastinating prevents you from taking control of your learning. The suggestions below will show you ways to plan your work and make steady, consistent progress toward its completion.

A "To Do" List

If you had to think about every word on every page of every book you had to read before finishing your education, you would probably feel too overwhelmed to begin. Instead, you read steadily each day and it all gets done over time. This is how you must approach your assignments. Instead of thinking about everything you have to do for each class before the end of the term, break big tasks into small ones as soon as they are assigned. Then think about what you can do steadily each day.

One way to accomplish this is to make a list each night of things you have to do the following day. Figure 2–1 illustrates a daily "To Do" list. To make one, use a notecard or a piece of paper that you can carry with you. Write home, school, and job tasks that you want to accomplish the following day. List items in order of importance, and cross them off as they are completed. Items left at the end of the day should receive priority on the next day's list. If you find that you continue to put off doing something, try to break it into smaller parts. Remember that even a little progress is better than none at all.

Sharing Your Ideas

Work with a partner to make a "To Do" list.

1. Discuss the home, school, and job tasks that you would like to complete today.
2. Write your tasks on a piece of paper in order of importance. First list items that must get done today. Then list items that could wait until later.
3. After class, cross off tasks as you complete them.

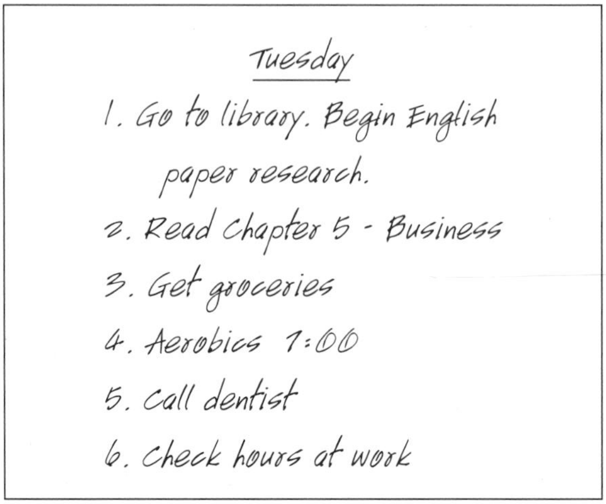

Tuesday
1. Go to library. Begin English paper research.
2. Read Chapter 5 - Business
3. Get groceries
4. Aerobics 1:00
5. Call dentist
6. Check hours at work

FIGURE 2–1
A daily 'To Do" list

4. Bring your list to the next session of class, and have a class discussion on the advantages and disadvantages you found in keeping a "To Do" list. ■

The Weekly Schedule

Creating a general written schedule that contains time slots for all that you do can reduce the stress in your life and make it easier to think and learn. When you plan for all you have to do, you will find that you no longer constantly feel worried that you should be doing one thing or another. Seeing your schedule on paper also helps you realize that there are enough hours in the day to do both what you need to do and what you want to do.

Figure 2–2 shows an example of a completed weekly schedule. A blank schedule is provided for you on page 44. Read through the following steps, and refer to Figure 2–2 when you complete your own weekly schedule at the end of this chapter.

Step 1: Schedule Fixed Time. The first step in creating a weekly plan is to schedule everything you cannot change. Think about a typical week. What time slots are fixed and cannot be used for studying? Examples of fixed slots could include class time, meetings, family responsibilities, or your job. Be sure to write in breakfast, lunch, dinner, the names of all your classes, family time, errand time, cleaning time, time for your job, church, and clubs. If you work shifts, plan a typical week and adjust as needed.

Step 2: Consider Your Study Needs. Use the information from your completed Study Needs Assessment to think about your study time. After filling in fixed times on your schedule, see what time slots are open for you to plan study time.

FIGURE 2–2

Weekly schedule

	Monday	Tuesday	Wednesday	Thursday	Friday	Saturday	Sunday
7:00	Wake up →	→	→	→	Sleep →	→	→
7:30	Breakfast →	→	→	→	↓	↓	↓
8:00	Travel →	→	→	→	Breakfast	↓	↓
8:30	Prep. math →	→	→	→	↓		
9:00	Math →	→	→	→	Study	Breakfast →	→
9:30	Class				Math xxxx		
10:00	Review-M →	→	→	→	Study	Chores	Chores
10:30	Prep. English →	→	→	→	Business	↓	↓
11:00	English →	→	→	→	Break	Study	Church
11:30	Class				↓	Math xxxx	↓
12:00	Business →	→	→	→	Study	Study	Free
12:30	Class				English	Business	Time
1:00	Review-B →	→	→	→	Free	Free	
1:30	Lunch	Lunch	Lunch	Lunch	Lunch	Lunch	Lunch
2:00	↓	↓	↓	↓	↓	↓	↓
2:30	Travel →	→	→	→	→	→	Study
3:00	Free →	→	→	Job	Job	Job	Business
3:30	Time →	→	→	↓	↓	↓	Free
4:00	Study →	→	→	↓	↓	↓	Time
4:30	Math xxxx	xxxx	xxxx	↓	↓	↓	↓
5:00	Study →	→	→	↓	↓	↓	↓
5:30	Business			↓	↓	↓	↓
6:00	Dinner	Dinner	Dinner	Dinner	Dinner	Dinner	Dinner
6:30	↓	↓	↓	↓	↓	↓	↓
7:00	Study →	→	→	↓	↓	↓	↓
7:30	English			↓	↓	↓	↓
8:00	Chores	Chores	Chores	↓	↓	↓	Study
8:30	↓	↓	↓	↓	↓	↓	Math xxxx
9:00	Free	Free	Free	Study	Free	Free	Study
9:30	Time	Time	Time	Math	Time	Time	English
10:00	↓	↓	↓	Free	↓	↓	Free
10:30	↓	↓	↓	Time	↓	↓	Time
11:00	Bed	Bed	Bed	Bed	↓	↓	Bed
11:30					↓	↓	
12:00							

Subject	Hours of Study Per Week
M = Math	11
E = English	7
B = Business	8
xxxx = Break (10 min.)	

Step 3: Apply the Principles of Time Management. Begin to fill in study time on your weekly schedule. Be sure to write what you are studying at each time, for example: "Study Math," or "S-Math" if you want to abbreviate. As you fill in study time, remember to apply the 11 principles of time management shown in Table 2–1.

After you complete your schedule, you may want to color-code it for easier use. Use a different color for each course to shade the time slots devoted to it throughout the week. This will help you see, at a glance, what you need to do and when you need to do it.

Step 4: Compute Total Hours of Study. At the bottom of your weekly schedule is a place to write the name of each course you are taking and how much study time you have scheduled for it. Add up the number of study hours you have planned for each course, and write the total on the proper line. During the term you may want to alter your study time for certain classes, especially if you are having difficulty with a course.

Step 5: Display and Use Your Schedule. Place your weekly schedule in your study area where it can easily be seen. Refer to it often, and soon studying will become a natural part of your life.

It is common to feel, at first, that scheduling your life in such a regimented fashion is unpleasant and impossible. You may find yourself thinking that there is no way you can know what you're going to be doing today or tomorrow. If this happens, tell yourself that being a student is a full-time job that will affect your entire life and that a major part of the job is staying organized. You must begin to build your life around your education instead of building your education around your life.

Remember that leisure time should be included in your schedule and that time slots in your schedule can be traded. If on a certain day you really want or need to do something during a time slot scheduled for study, exchange your leisure time for study time that day.

The Term Calendar

An additional aid that you might use to keep your assignments organized is a term calendar. You may have many long-term assignments and due dates for papers, projects, or exams. Instead of trying to keep the dates in your head or in separate locations, put them all in one place.

When making a term calendar, use a calendar that you designate only for this purpose. This will keep to a minimum the amount of information written on it. When test dates and assignment due dates are given, write them down on the calendar. At the same time, plan when you will begin to study for the tests or work on the assignments and write down those days on your calendar. Figure 2–3 illustrates how a student was able to plan in

FIGURE 2–3
Term calendar

Week #	Sunday	Monday	Tuesday	Wednesday	Thursday	Friday	Saturday
Jan. Week 1	2	3	4	5 Classes Begin	6	7	8
Jan. Week 2	9	10	11	12	13 Select Topic - English Research paper	14	15 Outline/Thesis English Paper
Jan. Week 3	16 English Paper - Library	17	18 English Paper - Library	19	20 English Paper - Library	21	22 English Paper - Library
Jan. Week 4	23 Study: Math & Business Test	24 Write Paper - First Draft	25 Write Paper - First Draft	26	27 Revise paper	28 Revise paper	29 Study: Math & Business Test
Jan./Feb. Week 5	30 Study: Math & Business Test	31 Study: Math & Business Test	1 BUSINESS TEST Study: Math Test	2 MATH TEST	3 Type Paper	4 Proof Paper	5 Type Paper Changes
Feb. Week 6	6	7 ENG. PAPER DUE	8	9 Study: Business Test	10	11	12 Study: Business Test
Feb. Week 7	13 Study: Business Test	14	15 Study: Business Test	16 BUSINESS TEST	17 Study: Math Test	18	19 Study: Math Test
Feb. Week 8	20 Study: Math Test	21 Study: Math Test	22 MATH TEST	23	24	25 Begin English Essay - Topic	26 Outline English Essay
Feb./Mar. Week 9	27 Write First Draft Essay	28 Write First Draft Essay	1	2 Revise Essay	3 Revise Essay	4 Revise Essay	5
March Week 10	6 Type Essay	7 Proof Essay	8 Correct/Type Essay	9	10 ENGLISH ESSAY DUE	11 Study: Math & Business Test	12 Study: Math & Business Test
March Finals Week	13 Study: Math & Business Test	14 MATH TEST Study: Business Test	15 BUSINESS TEST	16	17	18	19

advance for a paper and several exams. A blank calendar is provided for you on page 46. When you complete it, post it in your study area along with your weekly schedule.

Putting It All Together

Time management forms the base for all that you do in college. Using time wisely will help you control stress and skillfully carry your workload, thus increasing your ability to think and learn. By scheduling your commitments on paper, you will be able to give each part of your life the time and attention necessary to succeed.

Making the Connection

Check your understanding of the concepts presented in this chapter by completing the following activity. If you are unable to recall information in a particular area, go back and review that material before completing the rest of the exercises in this section.

1. Write one or two sentences to summarize what you recall about each of the following topics:

   Your study needs: where and when to study

   ____

   ____

   ____

   ____

   ____

   The principles of time management:

   Consistency ______________________________

   ____

   The two-for-one rule ______________________________

   ____

   Immediate review ______________________________

   ____

   Studying difficult subjects ______________________________

   ____

   Your best time ______________________________

   ____

   Studying similar subjects ______________________________

   ____

   Review time before class ______________________________

   ____

   Study breaks ______________________________

   ____

Distributing study ______________________________

____

Leisure time ______________________________

____

A "To Do" list ______________________________

____

A weekly schedule ______________________________

____

A term calendar ______________________________

____

2. List one new idea you've gained about time management as a result of this chapter. ______________________________

   ____

3. Describe one change you plan to make in the way you schedule time daily, weekly, and for the term.

   Daily: ______________________________

   Weekly: ______________________________

   Term: ______________________________

Thinking It Through

Read the following passage, and then answer the questions by applying what you've learned about time management.

Bill is a 25-year-old full-time student with a family and a job. To keep his scholarship money, he must go to school from 8 A.M. until noon each day. Because Bill has a wife and a baby, he must also work full-time. His job at a service station begins at 3 P.M. and ends at 11 P.M.

Lately, his wife has been complaining that she feels lonely and neglected. Bill has been thinking about quitting school to spend more time with his family, but he knows that if he does, he will lose his scholarship money.

1. Based on information from the passage, what do you see as Bill's specific problem(s)? ______________________________

2. List possible solutions, using what you have learned about time management. ______________________________

Applying Your Skills 1 *A Weekly Schedule*

Instructions: Use the four steps below to complete the weekly schedule form on page 44.

Step 1: Schedule fixed time.
Step 2: Consider your study needs.
Step 3: Apply the principles of time management.
Step 4: Compute total hours of study.

	Monday	Tuesday	Wednesday	Thursday	Friday	Saturday	Sunday
7:00							
7:30							
8:00							
8:30							
9:00							
9:30							
10:00							
10:30							
11:00							
11:30							
12:00							
12:30							
1:00							
1:30							
2:00							
2:30							
3:00							
3:30							
4:00							
4:30							
5:00							
5:30							
6:00							
6:30							
7:00							
7:30							
8:00							
8:30							
9:00							
9:30							
10:00							
10:30							
11:00							
11:30							

Subject ______________ Hours of Study per Week ______________

______________ ______________

______________ ______________

______________ ______________

Applying Your Skills 2 *Term Calendar*

Instructions: Complete the term calendar provided. Write in long-term assignments and test dates that you have at this time. For each date that you include, plan a time to begin study or work and write it on the calendar also. Keep your calendar up-to-date by adding assignments as they are given.

Week #	Sunday	Monday	Tuesday	Wednesday	Thursday	Friday	Saturday
Week 1							
Week 2							
Week 3							
Week 4							
Week 5							
Week 6							
Week 7							
Week 8							
Week 9							
Week 10							
Week 11							

Applying Your Skills 3 *Using Your Resources*

Instructions: To know where to "radio for help," you will be asked to visit various school resources throughout this text. Keep this information so that you can refer to it when you are in need of help outside the classroom.

Schedule a conference with one of your instructors. Following your meeting, complete the information below.

Name/course taught: ______________________________

Office location: ______________________________

Office hours: ______________________________

Phone: ______________________________

Suggestions for course success:

____

____

____

____

Personal comments:

Briefly discuss how you will use the information you received in this conference.

____

____

____

C H A P T E R

3 Goal Setting

Set goals to direct your efforts as you think and learn.

Chapter Goals

After you read this chapter, you will be able to:

- Set goals that are specific and measurable.
- Set realistic goals by identifying your abilities, interests, and priorities.
- Use knowledge of your abilities, interests, and priorities to establish personal, educational, and career goals.
- Identify the difference between being motivated from within and being motivated by outside rewards.
- Set long-term and short-term goals.
- Set deadlines for your goals and monitor your progress.

The day you've waited for all year has finally arrived—two weeks of vacation from work and school. With no destination in mind, you throw some clothes into a suitcase and jump into your car to get away from it all. As you hit the road, you begin to wonder if you packed the right things. Just where are you going? How far can you afford to drive? Will there be a place you can enjoy *and* afford? Should you head for the beach? The mountains? The desert? North? South? East? West? How will you know when you get where you want to be?

Few people take a vacation without planning where they are going and how they are going to get there. To do otherwise would be a waste of money and time. Yet, when it comes to making more important and long-lasting personal, school, or career plans, some people never think about where they are going and how they are going to get there. Are you traveling the road of life without a map, or have you plotted a course for your future?

This chapter will tell you how to give direction to your future through goal setting. You will analyze your abilities and interests so you can set realistic goals. You will learn how to determine what you value so you can set goals that are important to you. You will determine specific priorities so you understand where to focus your energy. You will learn how to plan the steps necessary to reach your short- and long-term goals. Finally, you will learn how to monitor your progress and make changes in your plans if changes are needed. Your goals will be your road map to success. They will direct your efforts as you think and learn in and out of the classroom.

Dreaming Dreams and Setting Goals

Do you ever daydream about the future? What is it that you dream? If you were magically granted the power to make your dreams come true, where would you be and what would you be doing? Dreams about the future are just dreams when they include no real course of action and are so impossible that they do not take into consideration your abilities, priorities, and interests. However, daydreams can be useful if you use them to help you develop goals.

A goal is more specific than a dream. It is an outcome that you try to achieve through a detailed and realistic course of action. Goals must take into account your abilities, interests, and priorities. You can set personal goals that concern your private life, educational goals that relate to school, and career goals that refer to your job.

Short-term goals can be set for something you want to achieve in a year or less. You can set short-term goals every day by making a "To Do" list of things you want to accomplish that day. You can set short-term goals each school term to help you reach desired grades. On the other hand you can set long-term goals for things that will take several years to accomplish. Earning a degree is an example of a long-term goal. A long-term goal may include a number of short-term goals. Earning a degree requires taking and passing many courses. Each course passed is one of many short-term goals that will eventually lead to a degree.

When you are setting goals—short-term or long-term goals; personal, educational, or career goals—be sure you are goal setting instead of dreaming. This chapter will present a six-step goal-setting plan that will help you establish and achieve your goals. You will learn how to (1) set goals that are specific and can be measured, (2) consider your personal abilities and interests, (3) determine the difference between what you want and what others want for you, (4) evaluate your priorities, (5) create a plan of action, and (6) measure your progress and make changes if necessary.

Set a Goal That Can Be Measured

Your goals must be specific so that you can make detailed plans and determine when those goals have been reached. When goals are too general, it's hard to tell what you're aiming for. For instance, if your goal is "to have a good life," how will you know when you have one? What determines "a good life"? How will you go about getting one? How long do you think it will take?

If you can describe *what* your goal includes and if you can plan *how* and *when* you will reach that goal, it is probably a specific goal. A way to rephrase the goal in the example above to make it more specific is to ask yourself *what* "having a good life" includes. Perhaps to you it includes getting an education, having a home, and raising a family. These are all goals that can be measured. Next, you need to determine *how* and *when* you can get an education, a home, and a family. Thus, to make a goal measurable, you must be able to state what you want and how and when you plan to get it.

Sharing Your Ideas

Work with a partner to set a measurable personal, school, or career goal.

1. State your goal. ______________________________

   ____

   ____

2. Share your goal with your partner. Discuss what your goal includes, how you plan to achieve it, and when you plan to achieve it.
3. List the what, how, and when of your goal.

   What my goal includes ______________________________

   ____

   ____

   How I plan to reach my goal ______________________________

   ____

   ____

   When I plan to reach my goal ______________________________

   ______________________________ ■

Consider Your Abilities and Interests

If you found a magic lamp whose genie granted you only one wish, what would you wish for? Money? Happiness? What do you really want? Most students ask themselves this question time and time again when trying to determine what they want to do with their lives. After achieving everything they thought they wanted, some people find that it wasn't what they wanted at all. In a sense, they made the wrong wish.

To prevent this from happening to you, when setting goals you must ask not only "What do I want?" but also "Who am I?" Only when you have a good understanding of your abilities and interests will you understand what will bring you fulfillment. You must think about what you like to do, not just in school, but in life. What do you do well? Sometimes you may close the door on your natural abilities or gifts and focus instead on pursuits that others want you to undertake. If this happens, you may end up working at a job that you find dull and tedious. As a result, you won't do it well.

To consider your abilities and interests when setting goals, complete the following activity as a class.

Sharing Your Ideas

1. Fill in the chart that follows by listing things you did during each period that made you feel successful or happy. These things do not have to be related to school in any way. For instance, during ages 5–10 you may have felt proud when you learned to ride a bike.

Ages 0–4	*Ages 5–10*
______________________	______________________
______________________	______________________
______________________	______________________
______________________	______________________
______________________	______________________

Ages 11–15	*Age 16 and Above*
______________________	______________________
______________________	______________________
______________________	______________________
______________________	______________________
______________________	______________________

2. Read your list to a partner. Working together and using information from this list and from your personal experience, create another list entitled "Things I Do Well."

Things I Do Well

____

____

____

____

____

____

____

____

These are natural abilities on which you should focus when setting goals. For example, if working with your hands is something you do well, you should consider setting career goals that involve this type of activity.

3. List things you were asked to do during the following periods that made you feel frustrated or unhappy. For example, maybe you disliked having to read in front of the class during ages 5–10. Again, the things you list do not have to be related to school.

Ages 0–4	*Ages 5–10*
____________	____________
____________	____________
____________	____________
____________	____________
____________	____________
Ages 11–15	*Age 16 and above*
____________	____________
____________	____________
____________	____________
____________	____________
____________	____________

4. Read your list to a partner. Working together and using information from this list and from your personal experience, create another list entitled "Things That Are Difficult for Me."

Things That Are Difficult for Me

____

____

____

____

____

____

____

____

These are areas of weakness that you need to take into account when setting goals. For example, if you have difficulty with math, accounting may not be a realistic career goal for you. If the goals you set include areas that are difficult for you, be prepared to seek help from others and to take more time reaching your goal. ■

Decide What You Want

What is it that *you* want? Our society seems to value material things—the more the better. As a result, you may feel that for your life to have meaning or for you to be successful, you must have money so that you can buy more "things." Your parents may want you to join the family business, so you may be taking classes for that reason. What did you wish for when the genie granted you one wish? Was it money because you feel that money would make you happy? Was it happiness because that is what you value above all else?

Often, it is difficult to determine the difference between what you want and what others want for you. A goal must be something *you* want if you are to stay motivated enough to reach it. Working toward something you desire is rewarding because it makes you feel good. Motivation that comes from within puts you in control. This is called *intrinsic motivation.* If you set a goal to exercise every day because this will make you feel better about yourself, you will be more likely to reach your goal than if someone else tries to make you exercise every day.

When goals are established because of what others want for you, your motivation comes from outside rewards or pressure. This is called *extrinsic motivation.* With this kind of motivation, you are not in control and you will find working toward the goals less rewarding. For this reason, you must be sure the goals you set are your own.

Sometimes it may be necessary to use both intrinsic and extrinsic motivation to reach a goal. For instance, suppose you decide that you want to complete your education. This is a goal you set for yourself (intrinsic). However, you are having difficulty with a course you dislike. You must find a way to motivate yourself with some type of reward or pressure (extrinsic) to make it through the course so that you can reach your goal. You decide that a tutor is necessary. Because you dislike the tutoring sessions and the work involved, after each session you reward yourself with something you like—a workout in the gym.

There can never be enough outside reward or pressure to help you reach a goal that is not yours in the first place. But if you are finding it difficult to achieve a goal you set for yourself, extrinsic rewards may help you get back on track. The activity that follows will help you analyze some personal, career, and educational goals to determine whether they belong to you or to someone else.

Sharing Your Ideas

1. Work individually to complete the chart that follows. Put a check under each goal that you have and that your parents or other people important in your life have for you.

Goal	*My Goal*	*My Parents' Goal for Me*	*Another's Goal for Me*
Educational Goals			
A college degree			
Technical training			
Good grades			
New knowledge/skills			
Other: ________________			
Career goals			
Any job			
A local job			
A secure job			
A high-paying job			
An interesting job			
An important job			
A creative job			
Other:________________			
Personal Goals			
Helping others			
Improving appearance			
Being more reliable			
Traveling			
Buying a home			
Marrying			
Having children			
Other:________________			

2. Compare your goals with the goals others have for you. List the goals you share with your parents or other persons important to you. These goals should be easiest for you to achieve because when you work to achieve them, you will be motivated from within and you will receive motivation from others.

   Goals That I Share with Others

   ____

   ____

   ____

   ____

   ____

3. List the goals that are yours alone. Because these goals are things you desire, you will be motivated from within to achieve them.

   Goals That Are Mine Alone

   ____

   ____

   ____

   ____

   ____

4. List the goals that others desire for you. These goals will be the most difficult for you to achieve because your only source of motivation will be rewards or pressure from others.

   Goals That Others Have for Me

   ____

   ____

   ____

   ____

   ____

5. Share the results of this activity by reading your three lists to a partner.
6. With your partner, discuss ways of dealing with the difficulties that occur when other people in your life do not share your goals. ■

Evaluate Your Priorities

Life is full of choices. Anytime you have worked hard to reach a goal, you've probably had to give up certain things along the way. Think of the last goal you worked toward. What did you have to give up to achieve it? In setting a goal for yourself as a student, you must rank that goal in order of its importance in your life. If you find that other commitments or desires are interfering with your progress toward your goal as a student, you must reevaluate your priorities. In other words, you must ask yourself, "What am I willing to give up in order to make my goal as a student a reality?"

To evaluate your priorities, first make a list of commitments or desires that are interfering with the pursuit of your goal as a student. Add that goal to your list. Table 3–1 illustrates such a list. Next, analyze the items on your list and decide whether there is anything about them that you can change. For instance, perhaps a car pool could change the amount of time you spend in the car. Housework could become a family chore. Meals might be made simpler. After making such changes, decide which items you are willing to give up and which items you feel you must keep. Number the remaining items in order of their importance to you. Those at the top of your list should receive most of your time and energy.

TABLE 3–1 A Priority List

Two children under 10
Driving children to and from school each day
Driving children to and from activities each day
Housework
Meals
Part-time job on weekends
Goal as a student: Complete technical school

Sharing Your Ideas

Work with a partner to create your own priority list.

1. Discuss with your partner the commitments that are interfering with the pursuit of your goal as a student.
2. Make a list of those commitments and add your goal as a student.

3. With your partner, decide whether you can make any changes in your list to simplify your commitments. If so, make the changes.
4. Discuss with your partner items you are willing to give up and items you must keep.
5. Number the remaining items in order of their importance to you. ■

You have now identified some of your abilities, interests, and priorities. In doing so, you have probably learned something about who you are and the kind of goals you have. Since ideas don't work unless you do, however, you need to determine how to make your goals happen.

Whether your goals are short-term, such as getting a certain grade in a course, or long-term, such as becoming an office manager, you need a plan. And when your plan doesn't work, you need to be flexible enough to try something else.

Create a Plan

You must devise specific steps to take in order to reach each of the goals you set. Failure to do so is like drawing yourself a map without marking any streets or roads: You may know where you're headed, but you'll have no idea how to get there. Therefore, for each of the goals you set, you must create a plan that contains instructions telling you what you have to do in order to reach that goal. It is also a good idea to put those instructions within a certain time frame. If you give yourself a deadline, even if you have to change it, you are defining a starting point and an ending point for your plan. Both are necessary in reaching goals.

TABLE 3–2 Short-Term Goal: An A in Accounting

Step	Deadline
1. Talk with instructor for tips	First week of class
2. Make study schedule/calendar	First day of class
3. Read/review assignments	Daily from 7–8:30P.M.
4. Make study cards/review them	Daily from 8:30–9P.M.
5. Review notes directly after class	Daily from 1–1:30P.M.
6. Attend all classes	Daily
7. Analyze errors on exams	After each test
8. Talk with instructor	If problems occur
9. Arrange for a tutor	As soon as problems arise

TABLE 3–3 Long-Term Goal: To Become an Accountant

Step	Deadline
1. Talk to advisor for information	First term of classes
2. Plan courses leading to major	First term
3. Maintain good grades (see short-term goal)	Each term
4. Join professional organizations	Each year
5. Look for summer job related to accounting	Year two
6. Volunteer for community-related work	Fall/annually
7. Register with Career Services	First term
8. Begin building résumé and portfolio	First term
9. Request/complete applications	Fall, year four
10. Schedule interviews	Winter, year four
11. Follow up interviews	Winter, year four

Begin creating your plan on paper. First, write your goal at the top. Be sure to state it in specific, measurable terms. Next, list the specific steps that you must take to reach your goal. Beside each step, write when (the specific day, month, or year) you plan to take it. By giving yourself specific steps and deadlines, you will be able to check your progress each week and to cross off items as you accomplish them. Tables 3–2 and 3–3 illustrate a short-term and a long-term goal broken down into steps and deadlines.

These examples illustrate the steps you must take to reach your short-term and long-term goals:

1. State your goal in specific, measurable terms.
2. List the steps you must take to reach your goal.

3. Beside each step, write a deadline for taking it.
4. Check your progress each week, and mark off the items that you have accomplished.

Make Changes and Begin Again

As you can see, it takes a lot of planning to reach a goal and even the best plans sometimes don't work out. When this happens, it's easy to feel defeated and to give up. This is when you must be taught one of life's great lessons—you can learn much from your failures. You will never be able to control all that happens in your life, but you can control your reaction to what happens to you. In the event of a failure, instead of focusing on your difficulties, decide what new course of action you must take and create a new plan using what you learned from your failure.

Putting It All Together

Goals give direction to your efforts as you think and learn. For goals to be achieved, they must be realistic, important to you, and specific. This means that you must become aware of your abilities, interests, and priorities and that you must be able to determine the specific steps necessary to reach your goals. A six-step plan for setting and reaching goals in this manner is to (1) set goals that are specific and can be measured, (2) consider your personal abilities and interests, (3) determine the difference between what you want and what others want for you, (4) evaluate your priorities, (5) create a plan of action, and (6) measure your progress and make changes if necessary.

Making the Connection

Check your understanding of the concepts presented in this chapter by completing the following activity. If you are unable to recall information in a particular area, go back and review that information before completing the rest of the exercises in this section.

1. Write one or two sentences to summarize what you recall about each of the following topics:

   The difference between dreams and goals ______________________

   ____

   ____

   How to set goals that can be measured ______________________

   ____

   ____

   How to determine your abilities and interests ______________________

   ____

   ____

   ____

   The difference between intrinsic and extrinsic motivation ____________

   ____

   ____

   How to determine your priorities ______________________

   ____

   ____

2. List one new idea about goal setting that you've gained as a result of this chapter. ______________________

   ____

   ____

3. Describe one change you plan to make in the way you go about setting and working toward goals. ______________________

   ____

   ____

   ____

Thinking It Through

Read the following passage, and then answer the questions by applying what you've learned about goal setting.

Lora can never manage to get things done. She participates in a choir and does aerobics three times a week. She also has a part-time job and a boyfriend, and she is going to school full-time to become a legal assistant. Lora enjoys going to school, but she hates the work that has to be done after class. Much of it seems like meaningless busywork to her.

Lora's parents are pleased that she is taking classes at the local community college but keep pressuring her to go into nursing like her sister. Her boyfriend wants her to quit school and get a full-time job so they can save money and get married. Lora is not doing well in school and has very little time or energy to devote to anyone or anything.

1. Based on information from the passage, what do you see as Lora's specific problem(s)? ____________________

____

____

____

2. Create a solution for Lora that involves evaluating her priorities.

____

____

____

____

____

____

____

____

____

____

____

____

____

Applying Your Skills 1 *How Do You React?*

Instructions: Read the list of personality traits below. Circle all of those that you possess.

outgoing	shy
happy	gloomy
sloppy	neat
careless	careful
quiet	loud
organized	disorganized
calm	nervous
kind	cruel
rough	gentle
pleasant	grumpy
thoughtless	thoughtful
picky	easygoing
ambitious	lazy
crazy	serious
social	private

If you circled several traits that are opposites, chances are that you are somewhat flexible in your reaction to various situations. This is an important characteristic to have when setting goals. Being flexible lets you learn from your mistakes and devise other plans without being overly concerned about failure.

Applying Your Skills 2 *Educational Goals*

Instructions: For each course you are taking, decide on changes you need to make in the way you study. Devise a study goal for each course. Under each goal, write the steps necessary to achieve it. Beside each step, write when you plan to take it.

Goal: ____________________

Steps	*Deadlines*

Goal: ____________________

Steps	*Deadlines*

Goal: ____________________

Steps	*Deadlines*

Applying Your Skills 3 *Career Goal*

Instructions: Use the information you have gained from the activities in this chapter to select a career you might consider. Talk with a career counselor and other knowledgeable people or use what you know to list the steps you should take from the present through graduation in order to obtain a job in the field you have selected. Beside each step, write down when you hope to take it.

Goal: ______________________________________

Steps	*Deadlines*
______________________	______________________
______________________	______________________
______________________	______________________
______________________	______________________
______________________	______________________
______________________	______________________
______________________	______________________
______________________	______________________
______________________	______________________
______________________	______________________
______________________	______________________

Applying Your Skills 4 *Personal Goal*

Instructions: Use what you've learned about your abilities, interests, and priorities to set a personal goal. Write your personal goal on the goal line. Then list the steps you will take to reach that goal. Beside each step, write when you hope to take it.

Goal: ______________________________________

Steps	*Deadline*
______________________	______________________
______________________	______________________
______________________	______________________
______________________	______________________

Applying Your Skills 5 *Using Your Resources*

Instructions: To know where to "radio for help," you will be asked to visit various school resources throughout this text. Keep this information so that you can refer to it when you are in need of help outside the classroom.

Complete the information below after meeting with a career counselor.

Name: ______________________

Office location: ______________________

Office hours: ______________________

Phone: ______________________

Services offered:

Personal comments:

Briefly discuss how you will use the information you received at this meeting.

P A R T

II Principles of Learning

C H A P T E R

4 Memory and Learning Styles

Pair your learning style with the principles of memory to improve your ability to think and learn.

Chapter Goals

After you read this chapter, you will be able to:

- Analyze the processes that must take place for memory to occur.
- Devise methods for focusing your attention in order to prepare to learn.
- Devise methods for processing information that needs to be stored.
- Devise methods for recalling information that has been stored.
- Determine methods to use in storing information for deep or surface learning.
- Identify your learning style and apply appropriate study techniques.

You should now be aware that learning in college is quite different from learning in high school. As a college student, you have the monumental task of selecting important information from hundreds of pages of text and class notes. You also have to learn this information in such a way that you can recall it five weeks later for an exam and then use it months, perhaps years, later when you are on the job. This is not as impossible as it sounds if you first understand how memory works and then learn to apply that understanding directly to the courses you take.

This chapter will enhance your learning capabilities in all of your courses. Effective strategies for focusing your attention and for storing and retrieving information will be presented. Because every person learns differently, you will assess your learning style and discover which strategies will work best for you.

What Memory Involves

Before this chapter addresses what should take place when you learn, let's see what actually does take place when you are asked to remember something. To determine your current system for remembering information, complete the following activity as a class.

Sharing Your Ideas

In order of seating, have each person in your class recite his first and last name and briefly tell one thing about himself. (Use only 15–20 students if the class is large.) Be aware that after this has been done, everyone will be asked to write, from memory, the information that each person presented. You may do whatever is necessary to help you remember as information is given, including taking notes. You may not, however, use your notes when trying to recall the information. Use the following steps to complete this activity:

1. Each person in the class will slowly tell his first and last name and one additional bit of information about himself.
2. After the last person has taken a turn, everyone should put all notes away and, on a blank sheet of paper, number from 1 to the total number of students in the class.
3. Three items must be written alongside each number in order to receive 3 points: first name, last name, and personal comment made.
4. After a brief period each person will again recite his information and you will grade your own paper while this is done.
5. Each item should be given 3 points for fully correct information, 2 points for two correct items, 1 point for one correct item, or 0 points for no correct information.
6. Add your total score, and discuss the following as a class:
   - What methods were used to remember the information?
   - Would other methods have worked for you?
   - Why did you select your method?

Chances are, the people who scored the highest on this activity know how to best focus their attention in order to store material so that they can recall it. However, what worked for them might not have worked for you, and what worked in this situation might not work in another. The true art of memory is knowing how to best focus your attention and store information according to the task involved. ■

The Three Stages of Memory

If you analyze what occurred during the group activity when you successfully remembered information, you will find that the information you remembered passed through three stages. First, you had to *prepare* to obtain the information to be stored by focusing your attention on it. Next, you had to *process* and store the information by holding it in your mind. Finally, after focusing to obtain the information to be stored and after processing it in order to store it properly, you had to *recall* or retrieve it.

When you perform these three stages well, you are able to recall information; when you do not, you have difficulty remembering. If you are unable to remember something, you must ask yourself whether the difficulty is a result of a problem in the preparation stage, the processing stage, or the recall stage.

Most students seem to think that their memory problems are with recall. "I have a hard time recalling what I read" is a common complaint. Most likely, the difficulty is not with the recall stage but with focusing attention in the preparation stage or with storing information in the processing stage. The recall stage usually gets blamed because memory problems become more evident when it is time to recall information. You could be drawing a blank because you are having difficulty in finding information you stored or because that information never made it to the recall stage. We have all experienced times when we thought we were having difficulty in recalling information that we really never stored. Read the following examples, and notice how the three stages of memory function.

Suppose you're at a large formal gathering at your school. The room is packed with hundreds of people you've never seen before. A friend introduces you to Norman Young. As the introduction is made, you are thinking about how much longer you have to stay in your uncomfortable clothes. You mindlessly shake Norman's hand and move on.

The next day you see Norman in your class and want to borrow his notes from a lecture you missed. You think to yourself, "What is that guy's name? I can't remember!" Actually, it would be impossible for you to remember his name because you never really learned it. You did not *prepare* to learn by focusing your attention. Thus, the information was not *processed* or held in your mind at all. The result, of course, was a blank when the *recall* stage came along.

To see how this entire process can work well, let's go back to that large, boring gathering at your school. As you scan the room looking for an exit, you happen to see a very interesting-looking person you would like to meet. When you finally make your way across the room, you introduce yourself and extend your hand. Your eyes are locked on this wonderful human being in front of you as you are told, "My name is Pat Perfect." "Pat Perfect," you say to yourself over and over. "This is perfect! The person of my dreams is *really* perfect!" You get Pat's phone number, 222-6824, which you realize is really 222-MUCH. Later that evening, as you think about how this perfect Pat person is too much, you dial 222-6824 and ask for Pat.

How were you able to recall Pat's name and number so easily? When you approached Pat, your attention was very focused and you were prepared to remember because you had a purpose. When the information was

FIGURE 4–1
The three-stage memory process

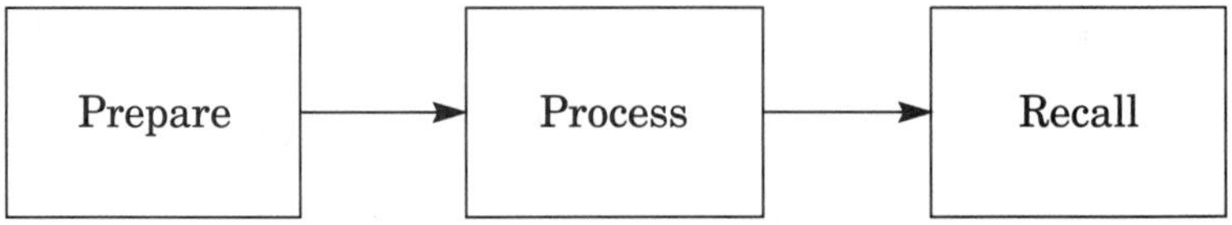

given, you not only repeated it over and over again, but you associated it with the word *perfect.* By processing the information in this way, you caused it to be stored. Later, when you had to dial the phone number, you were able to think about how you had stored it and recalled that "perfect Pat is too much." Thus, you were aided in your recall of Pat Perfect, 222-6824.

This three-stage memory process, illustrated in Figure 4–1, can be applied to every learning task you encounter, in or out of the classroom. It will be specifically applied later in this text to reading, notetaking, test taking, and writing in the form of a system called PPR (prepare, process, recall).

For memory to take place, information must pass through the same three stages for everyone. However, the techniques you choose to help you prepare, process, and recall will depend on how you learn best. The inventory below will help you determine your learning style. After each item, select the choice that best describes you by circling the letter *V, A,* or *K.* If more than one choice strongly applies, then circle more than one.

Learning Style Inventory

1. If I have to learn how to do something, I learn best when I:
   (V) Watch someone show me how.
   (A) Hear someone tell me how.
   (K) Try to do it myself.
2. When I read, I often find that I:
   (V) Visualize what I'm reading in my mind's eye.
   (A) Read out loud or hear the words inside my head.
   (K) Fidget and try to "feel" the content.
3. When I am asked to give directions, I:
   (V) See the actual places in my mind as I say them or prefer to draw them.
   (A) Have no difficulty in giving them verbally.
   (K) Have to point or move my body as I give them.
4. If I am unsure about how to spell a word, I:
   (V) Write it in order to determine if it looks right.
   (A) Spell it out loud in order to determine if it sounds right.
   (K) Write it in order to determine if it feels right.
5. When I write, I:
   (V) Am concerned about how neat and well spaced my letters and words appear.

(A) Often say the letters and words to myself as I form them.
(K) Push hard on my pen or pencil and can feel the flow of certain words or letters as I form them.

6. If I had to remember a list of items, I would remember best if I:
   (V) Wrote them down.
   (A) Said them over and over to myself.
   (K) Moved around and used my fingers to name each item.
7. I prefer teachers who:
   (V) Use the board or overhead projector while they lecture.
   (A) Talk with a lot of expression.
   (K) Use hands-on activities.
8. When trying to concentrate, I have a difficult time when:
   (V) There is a lot of clutter or movement in the room.
   (A) There is a lot of noise in the room.
   (K) I have to sit still for any length of time.
9. When solving a problem, I:
   (V) Write or draw diagrams in order to see it.
   (A) Talk myself through it.
   (K) Use my entire body or move objects to help me think.
10. When given written instructions on how to build something, I:
    (V) Read them silently and try to visualize how the parts will fit together.
    (A) Read them out loud and talk to myself as I put the parts together.
    (K) Try to put the parts together first and read later.
11. To keep occupied while waiting, I:
    (V) Look around, stare, or read.
    (A) Talk or listen to others.
    (K) Walk around, manipulate things with my hands, or move / shake my feet as I sit.
12. If I had to verbally describe something to another person, I would:
    (V) Be brief because I do not like to talk at length.
    (A) Go into great detail because I enjoy talking.
    (K) Gesture and move around while talking.
13. If someone were verbally describing something to me, I would:
    (V) Try to visualize what she was saying.
    (A) Enjoy listening but want to interrupt and talk myself.
    (K) Become bored if her description got too long and detailed.
14. When trying to recall names, I remember:
    (V) Faces but forget names.
    (A) Names but forget faces.
    (K) The situation in which I met the person better than the person's name or face.

Scoring Instructions: Add the number of responses for each letter and enter the total below. The area with the highest number of responses is probably your primary mode of learning. Because most people learn through a mixture of all three styles, read all of the learning suggestions given and select those you feel will work best for you.

Visual	*Auditory*	*Kinesthetic*
V = _____	**A** = _____	**K** = _____

Learning Suggestions

Visual Learners

Visual learners learn best by seeing. The following suggestions will enhance the visual learner's ability to focus on, store, and recall information:

1. Your study environment should be clutter free, away from windows and movement.
2. Highlight and write as you study. Use different colors to select and organize.
3. Always write down what you need to remember. This includes using notes as reminders and using a calendar to list due dates and dates to begin assignments.
4. Make class notes visual with drawings, spacing, symbols, and so on.
5. Make use of text visuals such as charts and pictures. If you have to recall them from memory, practice reproducing them on a piece of paper.
6. Use study cards with written information organized into outlines, drawings, or diagrams. Review them by writing to reproduce the information.
7. Make your recall cues as visual as possible. Use capital letters, colors, illustrations.
8. Recall information for exams by visualizing text pages, notes, or study cards.
9. When solving problems, draw or illustrate the problem and solution.
10. If permitted, make notations on test questions. Underline key words, or draw what you find difficult to understand.

Auditory Learners

Auditory learners learn best by hearing. The following suggestions will enhance the auditory learner's ability to focus on, store, and recall information:

1. Have a quiet place to study. If you cannot eliminate background noise, conceal it by quietly playing classical music or an environmental sound track.
2. Recite aloud as you study.
3. Attend all lectures. Copying another's notes is not as effective for you as hearing the material.
4. In addition to taking notes, use a tape recorder to record lectures. Always ask the instructor for permission to tape a lecture. As you review your notes after class, use the tape for those parts of the lecture that were difficult to understand. Play lecture tapes in your car to make good use of commuting time.
5. Study in groups or with a friend. Explain information in your notes to another person. If you find a study group distracting, have a person you can call on a regular basis to discuss class content over the phone.
6. Talk to yourself. Describe diagrams and practice answering test questions out loud.
7. Recite study cards into a tape recorder, and play the tape back for repeated practice.
8. When solving problems, talk yourself through each step.
9. Recall information during exams by hearing yourself recite in your head.
10. Chunk test questions, and recite each part to yourself in your head.

Kinesthetic Learners

Kinesthetic learners learn best by doing and moving. They often have difficulty sitting still for long periods. The following suggestions will enhance the kinesthetic learner's ability to focus on, store, and recall information:

1. Use as many of your senses as possible when you study: see, hear, touch, taste, smell.
2. Move around when you study. Put as much as you can on study cards. Lay study cards out on the floor in various locations, and practice reciting them as you move around the room.
3. Carry study cards with you everywhere, and use them whenever you have to wait.
4. Study in small, frequent chunks. Give yourself breaks and rewards.
5. Use a timer, and decide on an amount of time you feel you can effectively sit and work. Underestimate, and work up to longer periods if possible. When the timer sounds, take a break and do something physical.

6. Set a goal as to the amount of information you will cover, such as five pages. When you reach your goal, take a break.
7. For surface learning, use a mnemonic device called the method of place. When you have to recall items on a list, imagine them as placed in sequential locations in your home and associate them with those places. For example, if you have to remember the names of the presidents of the United States, begin in your kitchen. Wash Washington in the sink, bake Adams's apple in the oven, and so on. To trigger recall for a test, imagine yourself walking to each area.
8. Study with other kinesthetic persons. Their gestures and activities may give you additional input.
9. When solving a problem, move around and manipulate items to represent parts of the problem.
10. When taking exams, try to "feel" how you stored information by remembering what you did physically as you studied.

Principles for Preparing, Processing, and Recalling

For each stage of the memory process, general principles can be applied to prepare, process, and recall. Your use of some or all of them will depend on the material to be learned, as well as your interest, background, purpose, and style of learning. Although we all learn differently, to remember information we must all address each of the three stages. As you read about the general strategies given for each stage, think about those you already use successfully and identify those you could learn to use in order to better prepare, process, and recall.

Stage One: Preparing to Remember

Focusing your attention on what you want to remember is like preparing your mind to accept new information. You actually need a way of telling your brain, "Hey, be ready in there! Something important has to be stored." There are three general principles for preparing to remember (see Figure 4–2):

1. Establish a purpose.
2. Eliminate distractors.
3. Activate prior knowledge.

Principle 1: Establish a Purpose. Remember Pat Perfect? You had a strong desire to learn that person's name. Norman Young, on the other hand, was unimpressive. You thought you had no purpose for learning his

FIGURE 4–2
Stage one: preparing to remember

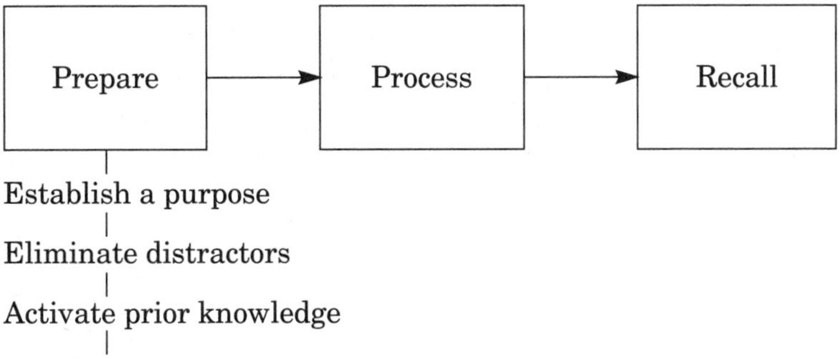

name, so you didn't. How do you feel about the content of your textbooks and class lectures? Are you as excited and impressed with them as you were with Pat Perfect? Perhaps that's too much to ask. It is necessary, however, to remember how the memory process fails when your attention is not focused because you see no purpose for remembering.

Think about how you feel when your instructors begin a lecture or when you begin to read. Do you start each task mindlessly, or are you focused? You need to walk into each lecture with a purpose: an intent to listen for what you feel is the most important information so that you can record it. You must establish the topic of the lecture and determine whether your focus should be on remembering specific details or gaining a general understanding of the material. The PPR notetaking system presented in Chapter 7 will help you establish a purpose for taking notes.

Before reading a chapter, you must decide whether you need to remember details or gain general background knowledge from your reading. In looking through the chapter, you should also determine what it covers and what you should intend to remember. A specific system for achieving this will be presented in the PPR reading system in Chapter 8.

Principle 2: Eliminate Distractors. When you are trying to focus your attention, you can become distracted in two general ways: physically and mentally. Physical distractors are the things in your environment that you can see, hear, touch, taste, or even smell. What distracts one person may not bother another, depending on his style of learning. When people who learn best by hearing are trying to concentrate, they are often bothered by sounds. People who learn best visually are more distracted by things they can see. Once you are aware of what distracts you, you can structure your learning environment with that in mind.

Whatever your style of learning, the best way to limit distractors is to establish an area used exclusively for study. That area could be a desk or even a card table. The place you select should be as free from distractors as possible. It should have good lighting and a stock of study supplies. By using a consistent place to concentrate, you will condition your body and mind to begin to focus immediately whenever you're there.

Suppose you're in your study area, free from physical distractors, when your mind begins to wander. You begin to think about other things you have to do or want to do. This is mental distraction. One of the best ways to avoid it is to get plenty of rest, exercise regularly, and eat properly. When your body is healthy, every part of it, including your brain, functions better.

No one, however, can concentrate for hours without a break. For each hour you study, you need at least a 5- to 10-minute break. Even with a break between hours, after two hours of study, hang it up. If you don't, you'll blow a fuse. Several short sessions of learning are more effective than one long session. This means no cramming!

If you apply all of these strategies and still find that things pop into your mind when you're trying to concentrate, try keeping a sheet of paper handy for use as a distractor list. Write down the things that are distracting your attention. Get them out of your head and onto paper. Then, during your study break, attend to them.

Principle 3: Activate Prior Knowledge. To best illustrate what has to happen in your brain to prepare it for learning, let's go inside your head.

Imagine that your brain is like a spaghetti factory and that a huge mass of cooked spaghetti is sitting inside your head. Strands of spaghetti represent memory traces containing general information about different topics that you've learned throughout your life. Smaller strands with related information cling to the larger strands. These smaller strands represent new information that you've been able to learn and tie into the old information. For you to learn or store information, you must either make a completely new strand of spaghetti for an idea entirely new to you or connect a smaller strand to one already established.

Now, let's go outside your head and see what you have to do to get production rolling. When you begin to listen to a lecture or to read a book, all that spaghetti up there is sitting in one massive clump. If you try to send information into your brain at this point, it has no direction. It may fall on top of the spaghetti heap, it may get lost in the pile, or it may fly completely over the mass.

What you need to do is to alert the proper strand and let it know you're going to be throwing in something it has to catch. To do this, you must determine the topic of the lecture or book and ask yourself what you already know. This immediately brings the proper strand to attention inside your head. Then, when you begin to read or to hear the lecture, the information has direction and ties into the proper memory strand. For instance, before reading a chapter on investments, you might begin to think about anything you've read, heard, or actually experienced in the area of investments. This will alert the memory strands that store investment information. When you begin to read about investments, the material will then tie right in to what you already know.

What happens when you begin to read a book or hear a lecture on a subject completely new to you? You may have thought to yourself: "This book might as well be written in a foreign language," or "Am I the only person in here who is completely lost?" This occurs because there is nothing in your brain (no strand of spaghetti) to activate or to tie into. You must somehow begin production of a completely new strand or memory trace. If you find yourself in a class where most of the material is new to you, you will have to put in some time doing extra work. You can:

1. Read at a slower pace.
2. Get more background information from another source.
3. Discuss the material with other class members or the instructor.
4. Get a tutor.

All of these strategies will help you build the background you need in order to tie in the new information being presented.

Stage Two: Processing Information

Once you are prepared to learn, your brain is ready to process and store information (see Figure 4–3). This requires a physical change in your brain that will either tie related information into an established memory strand

FIGURE 4–3
Stage two: processing information

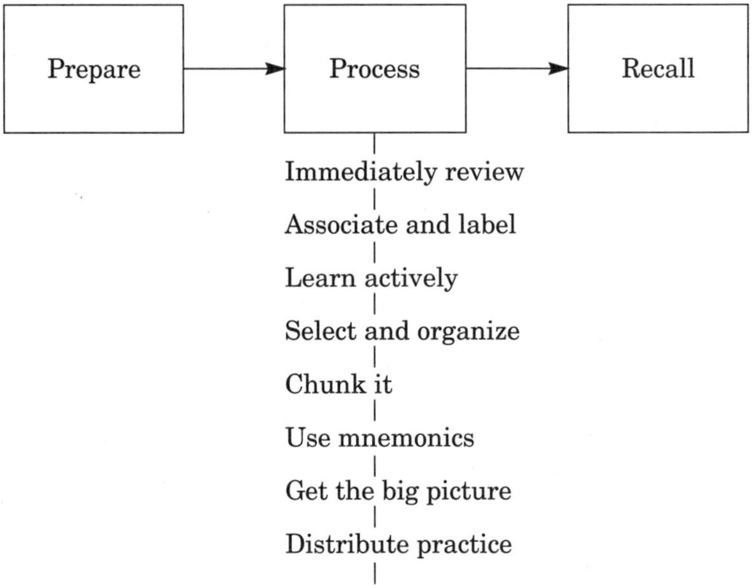

or manufacture a completely new strand. For our purposes, it is not necessary to know much about the physical change itself. Be aware, however, that information must be processed in this manner for about 15–30 seconds in order to be stored. Shorter periods may be sufficient for uncomplicated information that you can tie into established strands, while longer periods are needed if a new memory strand must be made.

Thus, to effectively store information, you must use strategies that will help you hold it in your mind long enough to cause a physical change to occur. If information is to be easily recalled later, it must be stored in an organized fashion and sent to the correct location or memory strand. Your ability to recall information is directly related to the manner in which you store it. You can't get out what you don't put in.

Following are some general storage principles you can use:

1. Immediately review.
2. Associate and label.
3. Learn actively.
4. Select and organize.
5. Chunk it.
6. Use mnemonics.
7. Get the big picture.
8. Distribute practice.

These principles will enable you to hold information in your mind long enough to produce strong, effective memory strands. Later in this text, each of the principles will be specifically applied to reading, notetaking, test taking, and writing through the PPR systems.

Principle 1: Immediately Review. A physical change in your brain, once made, may never reverse itself, erasing the information entirely, but that information can fade and become difficult to recall. Imagine that each new memory trace you made is like a path across a field of tall grass. If you walk that path frequently, it remains; if you do not, it quickly becomes overgrown.

As a student, you must immediately review everything you hope to recall. Studies of memory loss have shown that recall drops below 50 percent within one hour of learning. Therefore, you need to review your class notes as soon as possible each day to maintain a high level of recall. You should also review information in your texts as soon as possible after reading them. Studying in this manner helps keep recall at a high level by making stronger, clearer memory traces. The longer you wait and the less frequently you review, the faster your memory traces will fade. Walk the path every day.

Principle 2: Associate and Label. Read through the list of words below, and take one minute to try to learn them in their proper order. Cover the list with your hand, and write as many of the words as you can recall.

hig	hig
ritimit	ritmit
elephant	elephant
skeeging	skeeping
lacooba	lacooba
Malcolm X	malcom X
pidalogy	pidalogy
CD player	CD pleyer
milidelphia	mildelphi

Which of the words were easy for you to remember? What did you do to help you store the others?

Chances are, you were able to easily recall those words that had meaning for you. You simply tied them into memory strands that were already established. To store the nonsense words, you may have tried to associate them with words you already knew, for example, *hig* with *pig* or *milidelphia* with *Philadelphia*.

It is easier to store and retrieve if you tie information into an already established memory trace. The best way to do this is to relate to the new material you are learning. When you read or study your notes, pause frequently to think about how this information connects with what you already know and to put the information into your own words. By doing this, you tie the new information to information that you've already stored. This is deep learning.

To help you recall where you've stored information when you need to retrieve it, use labels or key words as you do when you use a computer. By giving your class notes, study cards, and text content labels or file names, you will be able to call information up when you need it. You are telling your brain which memory strand to activate.

Principle 3: Learn Actively. If you find yourself mindlessly reading your textbooks and then unable to recall information, try visualizing while you read. The wilder your visualizations, the better. You could also draw diagrams, take notes, recite content aloud, or use your fingers and toes to recall lists. The more senses you involve in your learning, the stronger the memory trace.

Once you have determined your learning style, you should use methods that focus on your learning strengths. Students who learn best by seeing should use visual techniques. Students who learn best by hearing should use strategies that involve listening to the material to be learned. Students who learn best by doing should use a lot of physical, hands-on activity as they learn.

Principle 4: Select and Organize. How successful would you be if you were asked to learn everything on this page well enough to close the book and reproduce the page from memory? Luckily, no one would ever ask you to do that. However, many students go about learning as though they may have to reproduce entire pages or paragraphs. Do you use a highlighter as you read? If so, take a look at a few pages of a text in which you marked a lot of important information. Can you really learn all of that by just reading through it? Look at your notes from a recent lecture. Are you writing down every word in the form of sentences and paragraphs?

Underlining or highlighting is a way of selecting what is important from your reading. It is not effective, however, if you select too much information. The same problem occurs in notetaking. Students often feel it necessary to take down every word of a lecture for fear of missing something. When they study their notes, they read over every word that was said. You can't remember it all.

Taking good notes and successfully marking a textbook require two steps. The first step is to select what is important, and the second step is to organize it. In the first example below, key words and phrases in a paragraph of text have been selected and underlined.

Studies of Learning

> In studies of learning, it has been found that breaking up or distributing practice is better than practicing in one session for a long period of time. When practice is broken up, blocks of practice are alternated with blocks of rest. When learning time is computed, distributed practice has been found to be more efficient.

In the next example, the information selected from the paragraph has been organized into a more visual form. Which example would be easier for you to store?

Studies of Learning

Practicing in One Session	*Distributed Practice*
Long periods	Blocks of practice and blocks of rest
Less efficient	More efficient

Principle 5: Chunk It. The PPR (prepare, process, recall) notetaking and reading systems will show you when and how to select information from your texts and notes and to organize it into charts, outlines, diagrams, maps, or summaries. When you are determining how to organize information, divide or chunk it into small sections. It is much easier to learn information in several small chunks than in one large mass.

When you are trying to remember long lists of such items as names, dates, numbers, or places, chunk the lists into groups of seven or less. Think about how difficult it would be to remember a phone number, say 410-675-3120, if it looked like this: 4106753120. The numerals in phone numbers are chunked for easier storage and recall. This strategy can also work on a larger scale. It may be more efficient to divide a chapter into small readings or to study a large volume of information in chunks or parts.

Principle 6: Use Mnemonics. Mnemonics (ni-mon-iks) are little tricks used for memorizing information. It is important to note the word *memorizing.* The mnemonic devices presented below will help you store information at a surface level. They will not aid in deep understanding. They can be successfully used to store information that does not change and requires no understanding beyond what is given. Anything you might have to recall exactly as stated, such as the planets of the solar system, can be memorized with mnemonics.

A mnemonic device that is often helpful in remembering a list is to remember the first letter of each item on the list. The name *Roy G. Biv* is actually the first letter of each color of the rainbow: red, orange, yellow, green, blue, indigo, violet. The word *homes* can help you remember the great lakes—Huron, Ontario, Michigan, Erie, and Superior—in much the same manner.

You can also make up complete sentences, rhymes, or songs to help you memorize information. Most music students know that "Every good boy does fine" is used to remember the notes, E, G, B, D, and F. "Thirty days hath September, April, June, and November . . ." is a rhyme used to remember the number of days in each month of the year. What mnemonic devices have you used as an aid to memory?

Principle 7: Get the Big Picture. To best demonstrate this principle, complete the following activity: Look at Figure 4–4 for approximately five minutes. Then close your book and reproduce the figure from memory. Do whatever is necessary to help you remember what it looks like.

When you have completed your drawing, compare it with the original. Did you have difficulty remembering what to draw? How did you try to store the content of the illustration? If you tried to memorize individual parts, it was probably quite difficult for you to store and retrieve them. If you looked

FIGURE 4–4

SOURCE: From Graham Gibbs, "Changing Students' Approaches to Study through Classroom Exercises," in *Helping Adults Learn How to Learn,* ed. R. M. Smith. Copyright 1983 by Jossey-Bass, Inc., Publishers. Reprinted by permission.

at the entire picture and tried to make it meaningful, you may have been able to see a person sitting on a horse. Even if you saw something else, by studying the picture as a whole, you probably had an easier time storing and recalling.

Compare your approach to learning in this activity with the way you approach learning in your courses. Do you try to put information together by summarizing what you hear in lectures or read in texts, or do you memorize details and never really understand how they fit together? By looking at the big picture when you learn, you are deeply understanding the information. You are also storing the details of that information together on a memory strand for easier recall. Because the details are stored together, remembering one detail can trigger recall of the whole.

Principle 8: Distribute Practice. Imagine that the content of each class you attend can be condensed into a stick of beef jerky that you can later eat to help you recall. At the end of each session, your instructors simply distribute the jerky and you go merrily on your way. You can use two methods to handle this daily distribution of jerky: You can take it back to your study area and let it pile up, or you can chew on it a little each day. Let's suppose you prefer to let your beef jerky remain in a pile until the night before the big exam. Although it may take you hours, you then have to cram all of that beef jerky into your system and hope you can digest it. This, of course, is similar to the cramming many students do when they reserve studying until the night before an exam. How much easier it would be to bite off a little each day.

You can distribute practice on a smaller scale when you are attempting to learn material. It is more efficient to space out your study so that you practice material several times throughout the day. Try this: After taking notes in a class, review them as soon as possible. In the evening, as you review them again, construct several study cards on which selected information is organized more visually. Take these cards with you everywhere, and review them several times throughout each day. If you distribute your learning in this manner, studying for a major exam is not like sitting down to a feast of beef jerky but like having a light, easily digestible snack.

Stage Three: Recalling Information

Suppose you are going to use a computer to continue work on an assignment you began last week. You turn the computer on in preparation to continue your work. Next, because you have stored the information you need, you must retrieve it from the computer's memory. You type in a file name, the computer searches, and soon you see your material on the screen.

Your goal as a student should be to store and retrieve information much as a computer does. When it is time to recall information, you can use a cue

Figure 4–5
Stage three: recalling information

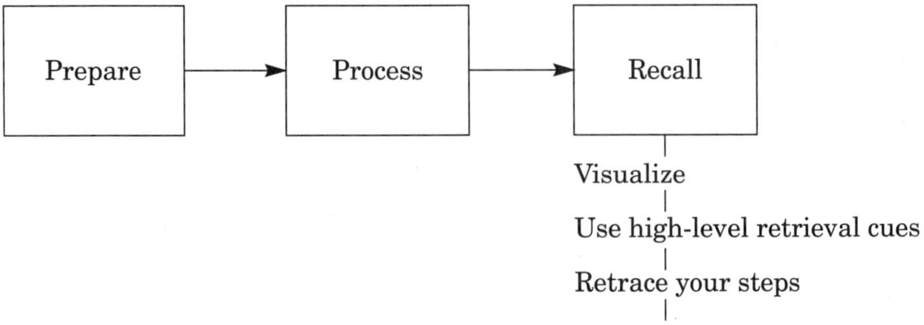

that allows you to search for and find the proper memory strand. Successful recall depends on the use of proper storage techniques.

If you are having difficulty in recalling information, there are several possible reasons: You never focused your attention in the preparation stage and thus did not store the information; you did not use the proper techniques in storing the information; you did not go over the information on a regular basis, so your memory trace has faded; or you are not finding the correct file or memory trace.

All but the last of the above reasons can be corrected by using the information in this chapter on preparation and storage techniques. If you have done all you can to properly prepare and store information and you still can't recall it, you can use three strategies to help you find the correct memory trace (see Figure 4–5):

1. Visualize.
2. Use high-level retrieval cues.
3. Retrace your steps.

Principle 1: Visualize. If you stored information by getting the big picture, all of the information is tied together on one memory strand. Bringing back one part of it should trigger recall of the whole. If you selected and organized the information on a chart, diagram, or outline, you should be able to see, in your mind's eye, the topic you need to recall. Focusing on that topic is like locating the primary memory strand. Often, this is enough to help you recall the information you tied in if you stored it using proper storage principles.

Suppose you created the diagram in Figure 4–6 as a study device for an English class. By first recalling the main topic, "Parts of a Research Paper," you can then recall the minor topics: "Introduction," "Body," and "Conclusion." Next, focusing on each minor topic will help you recall the information stored under each.

FIGURE 4–6
Study device for an English class

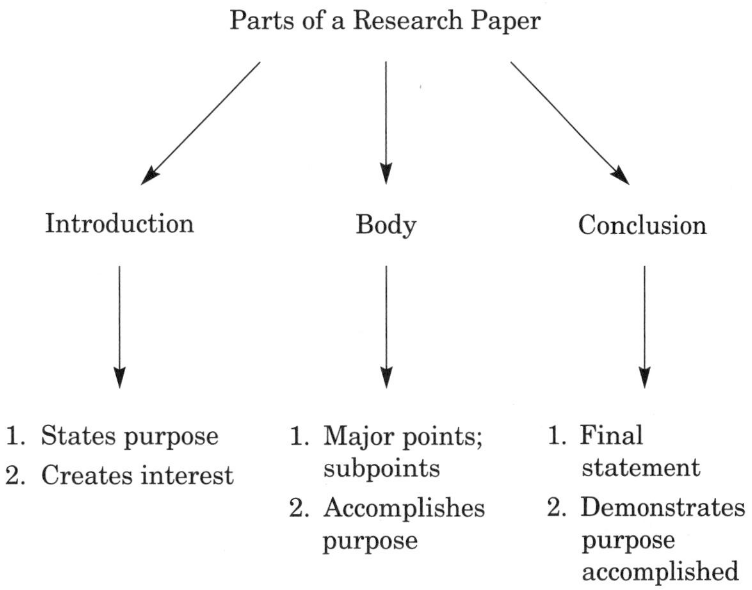

Principle 2: Use High-Level Retrieval Cues. You have already learned that you should label what you store in order to be able to call it up when you need it. Using a cue that is too broad or general could make recall inefficient and difficult. As an example, think about the topic "pollution." How much information about pollution do you have stored in your brain? Unless you tell your brain what you need to know about pollution, you could be retrieving stuff for years and not hit on the needed bit of information.

If you give yourself more information about what you need to recall, such as the causes and effects of pollution, you will have a better chance of finding what you need. Five general patterns into which all information can be organized are illustrated in Table 4–1. Using one of these patterns with your topic label will make it easier for you to recall what you need.

TABLE 4–1 Patterns of Organization

1. Definition or example—information is defined or is given as an example.
2. Time order—information is given in a specific order.
3. Simple List—information is given as list.
4. Cause/effect—information tells what happened and why.
5. Comparison/contrast—information identifies similarities and differences.

These patterns will be explained further in Chapter 7, which will deal with high-level retrieval cues as part of the notetaking process. By using the patterns to categorize and label information you are developing both a more efficient means of retrieval and a higher understanding of the material you store. The PPR notetaking and reading systems will help you categorize and label your notes and texts in this manner.

Principle 3: Retrace Your Steps. Imagine that you've lost your car keys. You know you had them last night when you came home from that party. Where did you put them? What would you do to find them? Most people would retrace (either physically or mentally) their movements from the last time they remembered having their keys until now.

Imagine that you're taking an exam and the same thing happens. You try to recall something you know you stored and you draw a blank. What do you do to find it? Don't panic. Retrace your learning steps. See yourself in your study area. Remember the card, text, or notebook where the information appeared. See the way the information was organized. How did it look? Next, try to recall the storage technique you used. With what did you associate? How did you label? Did you learn actively? Did you use a mnemonic device?

If you are unable to retrace the steps you used while storing information in your study area, try to go back to the actual class in which the material was first presented. See yourself in your usual seat. Where was your instructor standing? What was she saying? Was she writing on the board or using an overhead projector? With what were you associating when you stored this information? What did you write in your notes? Retracing *how* you stored—the time, place, and method—can often help you find *what* you stored.

Matching Methods to Learners

Which of the principles of memory do you already use to prepare, process, and store? Chances are, you have already determined that some techniques work for you and others do not. As mentioned, the true art of memory is knowing how to best focus attention and store information according to the task involved. Strategies that work in one instance may not work in another. The strategies you choose to employ should be determined by the learning task (surface or deep), your interest (high or low), your background (previous experience or lack of experience), your purpose (remember specifics, gain general background), and your learning style (visual, auditory, kinesthetic).

If you lack interest or background, you must use several strategies, instead of just one, to enable you to focus on the material for a longer period. If you need to learn deeply, you must use techniques that help you understand the material: association, selecting and organizing with charts and diagrams, labeling with high-level retrieval cues, and getting the big picture by summarizing what you learn. Mnemonic devices can be used to store information that you can memorize at a surface level and do not have to understand.

Putting It All Together

For memory and learning to take place, a student must prepare to remember, process, and recall information. Failure to properly pass information through each of these three stages will result in difficulty in remembering.

General principles can be applied to any learning situation for each stage of the memory process. When preparing to remember, you should (1) establish a purpose, (2) eliminate distractors, and (3) activate prior knowledge. To hold information in the mind long enough to process it and thus cause a physical change in the brain, you can (1) immediately review, (2) associate and label, (3) learn actively, (4) select and organize, (5) chunk the information, (6) use mnemonics, (7) get the big picture, or (8) distribute practice. Finally, to recall what has been stored, you can (1) visualize, (2) use high-level retrieval cues, or (3) retrace your steps in learning the material. Which principles you should apply and how you should apply them depend on the material to be learned and on your style of learning.

Because each person learns differently and because the methods you select should be compatible with your learning style, you need to be aware of how you learn best. After you have determined that you learn best visually (by seeing), auditorily (by hearing), or kinesthetically (by doing), you can adopt specific ways of approaching each of the general principles for preparing, processing, and recalling so as to capitalize on your learning strengths.

Making the Connection

Check your understanding of the concepts presented in this chapter by completing the following activity. If you are unable to recall information in a particular area, go back and review that information before completing the rest of the exercises in this section.

1. Write one or two sentences to summarize what you recall about each of the following topics:

   What memory involves ______________________________

   ____

   ____

   The three stages of memory ______________________________

   ____

   ____

   Principles for preparing to remember ______________________________

   ____

   ____

   Principles for storing information ______________________________

   ____

   ____

   Principles for recalling information ______________________________

   ____

   Matching methods to learning style ______________________________

   ____

   ____

2. List one new idea you've gained about memory and learning as a result of this chapter. ______________________________

   ____

   ____

3. Describe one change you plan to make in the way you learn and study course content to improve preparation, storage, and recall. ______________

   ____

   ____

Thinking It Through

Read the following passage, and then answer the questions by applying what you've learned about memory and learning.

Joe, a visual learner, is studying to become an accountant. As a high school student, Joe was attentive in class and read assignments. He would briefly look over material the night before a test and thus be able to do an average job. He realized, however, that college would require more work.

During his first semester in college, Joe attended all classes and took notes on information he felt he would not be able to remember. He usually read assignments briefly, but didn't think he needed to mark or organize text material in any manner. The night before a test, he would go over his notes and try to briefly reread text assignments.

When Joe took his first finance test, he went blank for the first time in his life. He panicked and tried to quickly answer the multiple-choice items. None of them made sense to him. He felt that he was being tested on information that the instructor had never presented. He quickly marked any answer that sounded familiar.

Joe did not receive a passing grade on this test. He looked at his grade, felt disgraced, and threw the test away. He knew he must have done something wrong but did not know what changes to make to prevent repeating his mistakes.

1. What do you see as Joe's specific problem(s)? Give examples from the story that tell you this. ____

____

____

____

____

2. What specific methods should Joe use to remedy his problem(s)? Why?

____

____

____

____

____

____

____

____

Applying Your Skills 1 *Preparing: Focusing Your Attention*

Instructions: Select material that you need to learn from a course you are currently taking. Describe three specific techniques based on the three principles given below that you would use to prepare to remember. Using your course material, give actual examples of each technique.

Course: ____________________

Subject of material: ____________________

Principle 1: Establish a purpose.

(Why are you learning this material, and what do you need to remember?) ____________________

____

Principle 2: Eliminate distractors.

(What is going to interfere with your concentration, and what will you do to change it?) ____________________

____

____

Principles 3: Activate prior knowledge.

(What do you already know about this material?) ____________________

____

____

Applying Your Skills 2 *Storage: Constructing a File*

Instructions: Using the course material selected for Applying Your Skills 1, describe three principles of learning you would use to process this material in order to store it in your memory. Remember to give actual examples using the material and to select methods that are appropriate to the learning task and to your learning style. Choose from the following principles: immediately review, associate and label, learn actively, select and organize, chunk it, use mnemonics, get the big picture, and distribute practice.

Principle 1: ____________________

____

____

Principle 2: ____

____

____

Principle 3: ____

____

____

Applying Your Skills 3 *Retrieval: Locating the File*

Instructions: Using the course material selected for Applying Your Skills 1 and 2, describe the principles of learning you would use to recall the information selected from your text or notes. Be sure to give actual examples based on the techniques you used to store the material.

Principle 1: Visualize.

____

____

____

Principle 2: Use high-level retrieval cues.

____

____

____

Principle 3: Retrace your steps.

____

____

____

Applying Your Skills 4 *Using Your Resources*

Instructions: In order to know where to "radio for help," you will be asked to visit various school resources throughout this text. Keep this information so that you can refer to it when you are in need of help outside the classroom.

Complete the information below after touring your school's learning center or tutorial service.

Location: ______________________________

Hours of operation: ______________________________

Contact person: ______________________________

Phone: ______________________________

Services offered: ______________________________

____

____

____

____

Personal comments:

Briefly discuss how you could use this resource.

____

____

____

____

____

C H A P T E R

5 LEVELS OF LEARNING

Use the PYRAMID of learning to help you think as you learn.

Chapter Goals

After you read this chapter, you will be able to:

- Analyze your current level of learning.
- Compare and contrast fixed and dynamic content and identify appropriate learning techniques for each.
- Identify ways to memorize, translate, interpret, apply, analyze, synthesize, and evaluate information.
- Determine the levels of learning required in your current course work.
- Analyze tests to determine their level of questioning.

If you properly processed the information from the preceding chapter, you will recall that learning takes place in three stages and that various principles of learning should be applied within those stages. You will also recall that the methods you choose for applying these principles should depend on your ability to match your learning style with the learning task involved.

This chapter will show you how to take a closer look at the learning task. It will help you analyze your current courses to determine the type of material you can surface-memorize and the type of material you must understand at higher levels. Seven levels of learning will be introduced, and you will learn when and how to use them. In this way you will be able to select storage techniques that match both the level of learning required and your learning style.

Flip-Top Brain Syndrome

Heavily armed with a fluorescent highlighter, the student approaches his victim, the savage text. Coming upon a difficult passage, he draws his weapon. "Take that," he says, and with one lethal yellow line he polishes off an entire army of words with the deadly golden marker. "Gotcha!" he yells. But does he really have it? Has he actually captured the information, or has his weapon merely stunned something that will return to haunt him on an exam?

Settled in her seat in the classroom, the student anxiously awaits the wise instructor. As he lectures, she frantically copies each word while trying to relieve a painful writer's cramp. Later, in her room, she will read over those words of wisdom again and again so that she can memorize them for the exam. Does she truly own this material, or will she be convicted of stealing it when she repeats her notes word for word on an essay exam?

These two students display symptoms of flip-top brain syndrome—a condition resulting from the belief that learning means memorizing. One of its primary symptoms is throwing up masses of memorized information on exams. Students who become infected with flip-top brain syndrome, as illustrated in Figure 5–1, passively flip open their brain during a lecture or during reading and try to cram in as many facts as they can without really understanding them. Then, on exams, they simply recycle the information exactly as it was stated in their notes or in their texts.

FIGURE 5–1
Flip-top brain syndrome

Flip-Top Brain

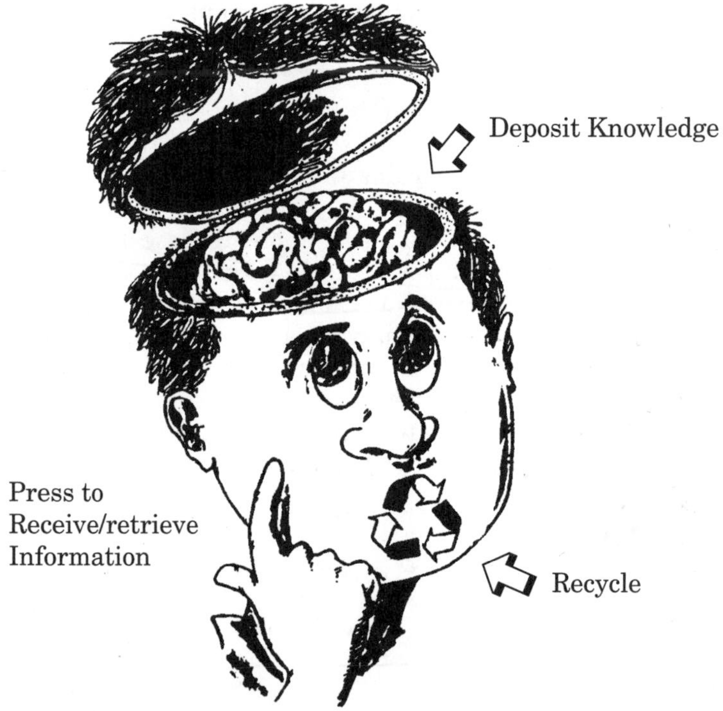

Students with this condition, like the students in the examples above, think that highlighting a text automatically causes the material to be understood. Such students take and "learn" lecture notes in much the same manner; they take down lectures exactly as these are given, and they read their lecture notes again and again with little understanding.

If you are currently using these techniques to study and are getting good grades, you may be wondering, "What's the big deal? It's not gonna kill me." Actually, flip-top brain syndrome can be deadly to your career. If you are able to land a job but are unable to function in it by using what you've learned or by continuing to learn as new information becomes available, your job will be history.

Although having flip-top brain syndrome can be fatal to your career, it doesn't have to be. To cure this ailment, you must realize that not all information can be stored exactly as it is given. Some information can be memorized word for word, but other information must be thought about and understood.

Fixed versus Dynamic Content

Most courses require that you memorize a number of facts. For example, in history courses you are often asked to remember dates and the events they represent. You may be asked, not to understand why or how these events occurred, but simply to know when they occurred. Information such as this (dates, lists of terms, states and their capitals, multiplication tables) is material that remains constant. You can be sure that 2 + 2 will equal 4 today, tomorrow, and in the distant future. Such unchanging material is called *fixed,* and fixed content can be memorized word for word.

Most courses, however, require not only that you learn a number of facts but also that you be able to understand and use them. In history courses, if you are asked why or how something occurred, you must recall basic fixed facts such as who, what, when, and where and then use these facts to come up with ideas. Information that does not stay the same because it relates to ideas is called *dynamic.* Fixed content, then, relates only to facts, while dynamic content uses facts to come up with ideas on and understandings of events, concepts, and theories.

Sharing Your Ideas

Complete the following activity as a class to help you distinguish between fixed and dynamic content.

Read through the list of learning tasks below. For each of these tasks, decide whether it involves only memorization of fixed facts or whether it involves the use of fixed facts to understand dynamic ideas. On the line provided after each item, write the word *fixed* for a task requiring only facts and the word *dynamic* for a task requiring thorough understanding.

1. Learn the names of all the bones of the body. __________
2. Run a computer program. __________
3. Discuss the causes and effects of the Civil War. __________
4. Copy a diagram of an electric current. __________
5. Repair a computer. __________
6. Add a column of numbers. __________
7. Prepare an income tax form. __________
8. Locate major cities and countries on a map. __________
9. Explain a definition in your own words. __________
10. Wire a fuse box. __________
11. Name all of the U.S. presidents in order. __________
12. Design a working model of a volcano. __________
13. Graph the findings of a survey. __________
14. Recite the Gettysburg Address. __________
15. Weigh the advantages and disadvantages of an issue. __________

Now that you have completed this activity, think about the courses you are taking. How much information in those courses is fixed, and how much is dynamic? ■

The PYRAMID of Learning

You should now begin to realize that most learning in college and in real life requires not only the memorization of facts but also the ability to put them to use at higher levels. The PYRAMID shown in Figure 5–2 illustrates seven levels of learning: memorize, translate, interpret, apply, analyze, synthesize, and evaluate. As each level is explained, you will learn step-by-step how and when to climb the PYRAMlD for deeper understanding.

Level 1: Memorize

The first and lowest level of the PYRAMID occurs when you memorize information. Notice that it is the base for all of the other levels and that it is the only fixed level. It can be used only for information that does not change.

FIGURE 5–2
PYRAMID of learning

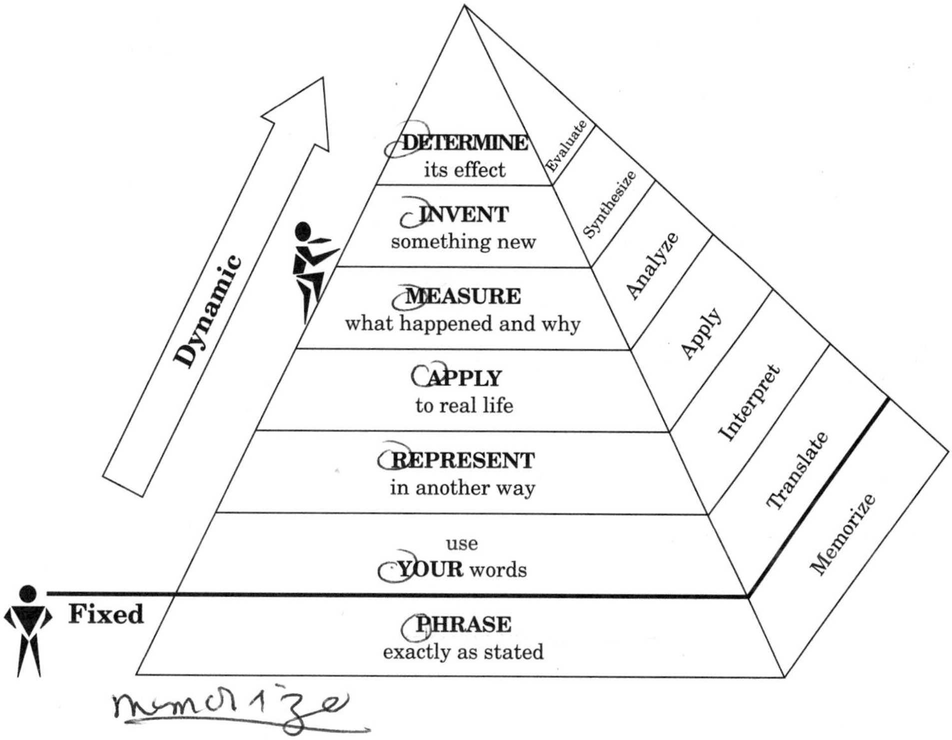

How to Memorize. You are probably already a pro at this level. The letter *P* in the word *PYRAMID* stands for *phrase* exactly as stated. Thus, in order to learn at this level, all you need to do is store information in the same form that you receive it. No deep understanding is needed. Mnemonic devices (presented in Chapter 4) are effective for memorizing. Using rhymes, making a word or sentence from the first letter of each item in a list, or making up a song about the material can help you store it at the memory level. Flash cards can also be used to help you recite and repeat information again and again exactly as it was given.

When to Memorize. The only time this level should be used is when you need to remember facts with little or no real understanding. Examples include basic math functions such as addition and multiplication, dates and names in a history class, parts of the body for an anatomy class, poems or recitations that you must learn word for word. Words that signal the need to memorize are: *name, list, recall, identify, reproduce, quote,* and *recognize.*

Level 2: Translate

The best way to go from fixed to dynamic learning is to put information into your own words. The letter *Y* in the word *PYRAMID* stands for *your words.* In order to put material into your own words, you must first understand it. Thus, even though "translate" is only one small step away from "memorize" on the PYRAMID, it is a giant leap toward understanding.

How to Translate. When reading, instead of highlighting someone else's words (memory level), read and summarize in your own words. You can write such summaries in the margin of your text or say them out loud. When studying your lecture notes, recite them in your words. Make study cards with material rephrased instead of repeated exactly as given. The PPR (prepare, process, recall) Systems discussed in later chapters will show you exactly how to translate when you read and take notes.

When to Translate. You should translate all material that you want to store beyond the memory level of the PYRAMID. This will force you to understand it. Although it is usually too difficult to translate an instructor's words into your words during a lecture, you should translate them soon after each lecture. As you read, you should periodically stop after each section or difficult paragraph and try to summarize the material in your own words. Unless your instructor wants you to be able to repeat information word for word the way it is given, you must translate it. Words and phrases often used to signal the need to translate are: *retell, rephrase, state in your own words, summarize,* and *restate.*

Level 3: Interpret

The third level of the PYRAMID calls for you to represent what you know about something in a different way in order to illustrate your understanding. The *R* in the word *PYRAMID* stands for *represent* in another way. Graphs, charts, diagrams, and illustrations are often used to interpret information.

How to Interpret. When reading, if you come upon a passage that you have difficulty in understanding, try changing the information to a picture or a diagram. Figure 5–3 shows how a paragraph of text can be interpreted through an illustration for better understanding.

The same idea can be applied to lecture notes. Instead of trying to recall information in the form of sentences, it's often easier to turn the ideas from your notes into labeled diagrams and illustrations, especially if you're a visual learner. The PPR Systems will demonstrate how to make detailed charts, diagrams, maps, and other visual forms of study.

When to Interpret. You may want to interpret information if it is difficult to store in its current form. If you find that after trying to put material into your own words, you still have difficulty with storage and

FIGURE 5–3
Interpreting a text passage

Homeostasis
Homeostasis occurs in humans when our body adjusts to maintain a constant body temperature. If body temperature falls below normal, a sensor in the brain sends nerve impulses to blood vessels and makes them adjust to reduce heat loss. If body temperature continues to fall, nerve impulses are sent to muscles. This causes shivering, a process that provides heat.

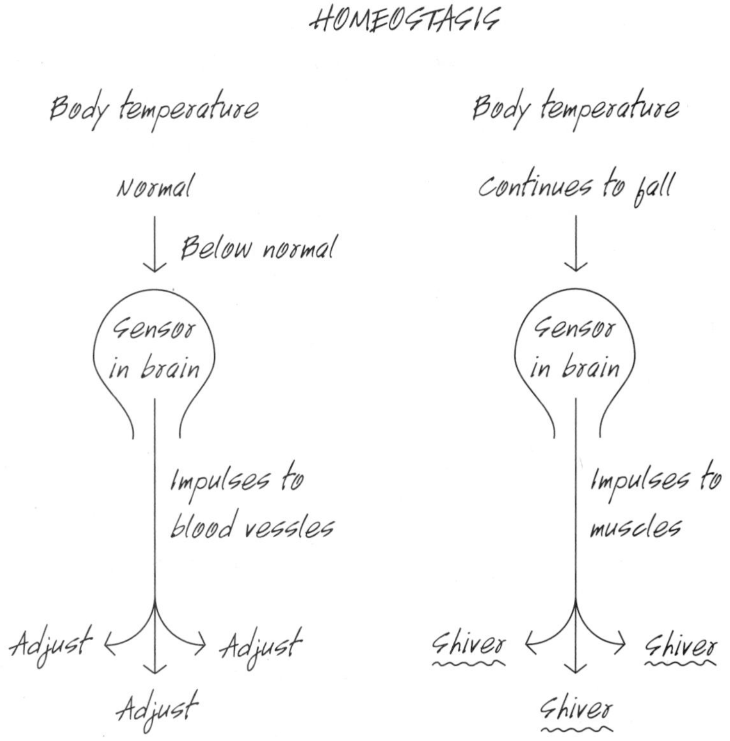

recall, try interpreting the information as a chart or diagram. Charts are especially helpful when you are trying to compare and contrast ideas or when you need to learn the same type of information for several topics. Outlines are a form of interpretation often used to represent major topics and subtopics. Diagrams or maps are helpful when you are trying to learn how things are related or how procedures flow. Words and phrases that may signal the need to interpret are: *relate, rearrange, compare, give your understanding, and describe in another way.*

Level 4: Apply

The most important goal at this point of your education should be to use what you're learning. The *A* in the word *PYRAMID* stands for *apply* to real life. Even though you may think several times a day "I'm never gonna use this stuff," much of what you learn will someday be of use to you. You especially need to be able to apply what you know so that when you graduate you can get *and* keep a job.

How to Apply. To begin applying or using what you've learned, you must be able to think of ways that the information in your texts and your lecture notes could be put to use. A good way to apply information from your texts and lecture notes is to create your own examples or to use that information in your own life. For instance, if your health instructor is explaining how cold germs can be transmitted from one person to another by hand-to-hand contact, you could apply that information to your own life by washing your hands frequently. After reading about how to build, repair, or do something, actually try it. When studying information that can't be directly applied at the moment, make up imaginary examples to illustrate a point. Write these examples in your notes or on a study card.

When to Apply. As a college student, you should begin trying to apply much of what you learn to your chosen vocation and to your life. As you listen to lectures or read your texts, you should begin to ask yourself, "How can I use this information now in my life?" "How can I use this information later as a butcher, baker, candlestick maker, and so on?" Words that may signal the need to apply are: *use, do, construct, apply, simulate,* and *make.*

Level 5: Analyze

When you analyze something, you take it apart and look at it closely to better understand it. Analysis requires you to think about things in an organized way so as to figure them out. That is why the letter *M* in the word *PYRAMID* stands for *measure* what happened and why. If you were asked to analyze the results of a football game, you would probably think about who won, who lost, and what caused the outcome. When you analyze information in a course, you do just the same thing: You figure out what makes things work the way they do.

How to Analyze. To figure out why one football team won and the other team lost, you would have to look at all the statistics of the game. You would take the entire game apart and look at the key plays. Then you would compare one team's performance with that of the other team.

To analyze information in your courses, you must take ideas apart and look closely at all of their components in much the same manner. One way to do this is to look at your notes or text and ask, "Why is this so?" Try to figure out all of the ideas involved, which ones are the most important, how each works individually, and what effects they may have on one another.

You can do this by putting information into categories, comparing the ways in which things are alike, contrasting the ways in which things are different, and considering the effect that one thing may have on another. The "Thinking It Through" activities provided at the end of each chapter of this text will give you practice in analyzing information.

When to Analyze. Analysis requires some basic knowledge about the topic in question. Before you can look at all the parts of something, you need to know what parts there are and how they work. You will want to analyze information in your courses when you need to have a good enough understanding of the content to answer the questions "How?" and "Why?" Other words or phrases that may signal the need to analyze are: *categorize, classify, group, compare, contrast, dissect, deduce,* and *determine.*

Level 6: Synthesize

Although many students never reach the sixth level of the PYRAMID, "synthesize," it is a desirable goal. Someone who synthesizes information takes all that she knows about a topic and creates something new. Thus, the *I* in the word *PYRAMID* stands for *invent* something new. When you graduate, if you understand enough about your chosen vocation to create new ways of doing things or new products, you will be a valued employee.

How to Synthesize. Synthesis requires a thorough knowledge of your subject. Once you have achieved this, you can begin to get creative and to experiment with what you know. You might try to come up with an improved design for a product or to devise a better way of doing something. For example, suppose you are an auditory and kinesthetic learner and you're having difficulty in storing and recalling. You know that you must involve your body in learning and that you learn best when you hear information. You could devise a new way to study in which song and dance movements are used to store and recall content.

When to Synthesize. Begin to practice using what you know in order to create new ideas now, during your college career. After gaining a good working understanding of something, you could begin to ask yourself, "How can this be improved?" or "How can I use this to do something in a better way?" Words that can be used to describe synthesis are: *devise, compose, formulate, hypothesize, design, create, imagine,* and *invent.*

Level 7: Evaluate

The highest level on the PYRAMID is reached when you are able to make a judgment or decision about something in order to determine its value or worth. The *D* in the word *PYRAMID* stands for *determine* its effect. To do this well, you must have a clear understanding of the topic, be able to think in an organized manner, look at all sides of the topic, and be able to give good reasons for your point of view. Chapter 6 will assist you in thinking in an organized, effective way in order to evaluate your ideas and those of others.

How to Evaluate. You already use evaluation outside the classroom every day of your life. When you say things like "cool," "awesome," "disgusting," and "sick," you're deciding whether something is good or bad, right or wrong, beautiful or ugly. The key to effective evaluation, however, is being able to look clearly at all sides of something before coming to a conclusion.

In the classroom you must learn to evaluate what your instructors say and what you read. You need to decide whether you are going to agree with everything you are told or to disagree when you have ideas and information that are different from those being presented. To do this, you must be an active learner and ask yourself such questions as these: "Does this fit into my understanding?" "How can this be proved?" "Why do I agree or disagree?"

When to Evaluate. An educated person should be a good thinker, and a good thinker evaluates most of what he or she accepts as knowledge. You should question all sources of information, including your text authors and your instructors: Who are they? Are they experts in their field? Is their information current? Is their information from a reliable source? Does their information conflict with something else that you know or have heard? Even when you agree with the information, you should judge or evaluate how it can be of use to you. Words or phrases that are used to describe evaluation are: *judge, decide, prove, justify, assess, recommend, give your opinion,* and *tell why.*

A Climb up the PYRAMID

Let's put to use what you've read about the PYRAMID of Learning. Although you will not have to take everything you learn through each level (how far you go will be determined by your purpose and your instructor's requirements), in this example we will take information through each of the stages from "memorize" to "evaluate."

Suppose the instructor of your Critical Thinking class asks you to learn the PYRAMID at each level from memory to evaluation. Below are the steps you could take at each level.

Memorize. The only fixed information in this learning task is to name the seven levels of the PYRAMID. You could take the first letter of each level and remember MTIAASE. If you have difficulty in storing this way, you could make up a sentence whose words begin with these letters, such as "*M*y *T*errific *I*nstructor *A*lways *A*pplies *S*tupid *E*xamples." The mnemonic PYRAMID has already been utilized to help you remember what each level means. Can you think of other ways to memorize the levels of the PYRAMID?

Translate. To translate each level of the PYRAMID, go through the seven levels and try to explain them in your own words. Does this make it easier for you to remember?

Interpret. One way to interpret the PYRAMID would be to draw or illustrate it in another way. Perhaps you would prefer to make a table for each level that would look something like this:

Level Name	*Explanation*	*How to Use*	*When to Use*
Memorize	Phrase as stated.	Repeat as given, or use mnemonics.	Static, rote memory, no understanding.

What other way can you create to interpret this information?

Apply. To apply the information from the PYRAMID, you could use the various levels in your course work. You might translate information by putting it in your own words as you study. You could make diagrams or illustrations in order to interpret or further explain material that is difficult to understand. How can you apply the levels of the PYRAMID as you read and take notes?

Analyze. If you tried to analyze the PYRAMID, you would look closely at each level and compare the levels with one another. You would see how each level is the same as the others, how each is different from the others, and what effect each has on the others. For example, to show how translating differs from interpreting, you would point out that one uses your words to understand material, while the other uses such methods as illustrations and charts. You might ask yourself when you would translate information and when you would interpret information. What is the difference between apply and analyze? When would you use each?

Synthesize. To synthesize the PYRAMID, you might create new names for each level or design a completely different type of arrangement in order to illustrate its use. You could use the ideas presented in the PYRAMID and construct a design whose levels and descriptions apply especially to accounting or computer students. If you were redesigning the PYRAMID, what would you call each level and how would you describe it?

Evaluate. Your evaluation of the PYRAMID should contain your opinion of its worth. Remember that you need to give good reasons for your judgment by telling what led you to your conclusions. Because you need to be able to look at all sides of any topic when judging, you should look at the PYRAMID's advantages and disadvantages. What do you see as the advantages to using the PYRAMID in your learning? What do you see as the disadvantages?

Putting It All Together

To be able to put your education to use after graduation, you need to deeply understand what you are learning. Although some information never changes and can be rote memorized, most of what you learn in college consists of ideas and therefore must be understood at higher levels. The seven levels of the PYRAMID of Learning (memorize, translate, interpret, apply, analyze, synthesize, and evaluate) can help you store information so that you can understand and use it. Storing information at any of the levels beyond memorization will enable you to use what you've learned in college and to continue to learn as information changes throughout your lifetime.

Making the Connection

Check your understanding of the concepts presented in this chapter by completing the following activity. If you are unable to recall information in a particular area, go back and review that material before completing the rest of the exercises in this section.

1. Write one or two sentences to summarize what you recall about each of the following topics:

   Flip-top brain syndrome ______________________________

   ____

   Fixed versus dynamic content ______________________________

   ____

   The PYRAMID of Learning:

   Level 1: Memorize. ______________________________

   ____

   Level 2: Translate. ______________________________

   ____

   Level 3: Interpret. ______________________________

   ____

   Level 4: Apply. ______________________________

   ____

   Level 5: Analyze. ______________________________

   ____

   Level 6: Synthesize. ______________________________

   ____

   Level 7: Evaluate. ______________________________

   ____

2. List one new idea you've gained about learning as a result of this chapter. ______________________________

   ____

3. Describe one change you plan to make in the way you study and learn as you apply the PYRAMID to the content of your courses. __________

   ____

Thinking It Through

Read the following passage and then answer the questions by applying what you've learned about fixed versus dynamic knowledge and the PYRAMID of Learning. As you read, identify the type of learning necessary (fixed or dynamic) for the two courses described.

Nancy, a Business Education and Technology major, is taking two courses this term. One course, called Introduction to Gregg Shorthand, presents the Gregg shorthand system and teaches basic dictation skills. The other course, Principles and Problems of Business Education, teaches the history, purpose, and development of curricula for teaching Business Education.

When studying for her Introduction to Gregg Shorthand, Nancy uses a lot of memorizing, practice, and repetition. She looks over her notes, repeats shorthand symbols from memory, and checks to see if she was correct. She also practices her shorthand skills from other sources such as tapes and lectures.

To study for Principles and Problems of Business Education, Nancy uses the same type of procedure. She looks over her notes daily and tries to memorize all of the information she receives on how to teach Business Education. As she reads her text, she highlights important information. After reading, she reviews her highlighting over and over again.

Although Nancy appears to be devoting enough time to both of her courses, she is doing much better in Shorthand than in Business Education.

1. Compare the fixed versus dynamic nature of Nancy's two courses.

   a. Introduction to Gregg Shorthand is ____________________

   because ______________________________

   ____

   b. Principles and Problems of Business Education is __________

   because ______________________________

   ____

2. Describe what Nancy is doing correctly. ____________________

   ____

   ____

3. Describe what Nancy is doing incorrectly. ___________________

   ____

   ____

4. How could Nancy translate, interpret, and apply the content from her Business Education course? ____________________

____

____

Applying Your Skills 1 *Fixed versus Dynamic: Charting Your Course*

Instructions: To analyze the level of learning required in each of your courses, create a chart like the one below for each of the courses you are taking. List the course, and give examples of material you must learn at various levels. A short sample is provided below.

Course: *Health*

Level of PYRAMID	*Material to Be Learned*
Memorize:	Anatomy terms; lists of steps
Translate:	Definitions (must be understood)

Course: ____________________

Level of PYRAMID	*Material to Be Learned*
Memorize:	____________________ ____________________
Translate:	____________________ ____________________
Interpret:	____________________ ____________________
Apply:	____________________ ____________________
Analyze:	____________________ ____________________
Synthesize:	____________________ ____________________
Evaluate:	____________________

Applying Your Skills 2 *Climbing the PYRAMID: Getting to the Point*

Instructions: Most of the information that you must learn does not have to be taken through all the levels of the PYRAMID of Learning. However, in order to practice and apply the information presented in this chapter, do the following: Select from another course something from your text or notes that you must learn. Give examples of how you would learn this material at each level of the PYRAMID.

Memorize (Learn the material just as it's stated. You can use mnemonics.)

____

____

____

Translate (Put the material into your own words.) ________________

____

____

____

Interpret (Illustrate, diagram, or chart the material.) ________________

____

____

Apply (Give an example of how you could use the material.) ____________

____

____

____

Analyze (Look at each part of the material, and figure out why it is so.)

____

____

____

Synthesize (Use what you know about the material to invent something new.) ________________________________

____

____

Evaluate (Judge your invention. Look at its good and bad points.)

____

____

____

Applying Your Skills 3 *Analyzing Levels of Test Questions*

Instructions: Have you ever taken an exam and felt that your instructor required you to know material that he or she never gave you? This can happen when you learn material at one level and are tested at another. To analyze the level of learning required in each of your courses, do the following:

1. Get an exam you've taken this term in each of your courses.
2. For each exam, read each test question and decide whether it is asking you to memorize, translate, interpret, apply, analyze, synthesize, or evaluate.
3. For each exam, tally each of these levels.
4. For each course, add up the number of test questions you have for each level of the PYRAMID and complete the chart below. The first column has been done for you as an example.

Level of question / Course	History								
Memory	25								
Translation	5								
Interpretation	10								
Application	25								
Analysis	2								
Synthesis	–								
Evaluation	1								

↑ Example

SOURCE: From Bernice Jensen Bragstad and Sharyn Mueller Stumpf, *A Guidebook for Teaching Study Skills and Motivation.*

Based on your findings, what level(s) was used the most in each course?

____

____

What changes do you need to make in the way (level) that you study for each course?

Course	*Change*

Applying Your Skills 4 *Using Your Resources*

Instructions: To know where to "radio for help," you will be asked to visit various school resources throughout this text. Keep this information so that you can refer to it when you are in need of help outside the classroom.

Complete the information below after touring your school's Office of Financial Aid.

Location: ____

Hours of operation: ____

Contact person: ____

Phone: ____

Services offered: ____

____

____

Personal comments:

Briefly discuss how you could use this resource.

____

____

____

____

C H A P T E R

6 Critical Thinking and Problem Solving

Use organized, thoughtful behaviors as you think and learn.

Chapter Goals

After you read this chapter, you will be able to:

- Assess your current views about effective thinking.
- Compare effective and less effective thinking behaviors.
- Recognize problems that interfere with your ability to look clearly at all sides of an issue.
- Practice seeing things from different viewpoints in order to develop a creative attitude.
- Assess your current problem-solving methods.
- Apply a system for solving problems that uses your ability to think creatively and critically.

To be effective in your chosen field and to remain that way through life, thinking must become a part of the way you learn. During your education, much information may be given to you at what may appear to be a surface or fixed level. It may even be possible to memorize your way through school and to get good grades simply by storing information exactly as it is stated in a text or in your notes. Ultimately, however, you will be expected to use or apply this information in your career. There will not be a fill-in-the-blank selection or a multiple-choice response when you have to make decisions on the job. Even if you graduate with the skills necessary to do your job well, much of what you learn in school will no longer be current a few years from now. Therefore, along with higher levels of learning must come techniques for learning new information and solving problems.

This chapter will assist you in determining what effective thinking involves and how you can begin to incorporate it into your life. Defining good thinking is essential in order to determine what changes you need to make in a process you already perform daily. Just as most of us are able to run, most of us are able to think. There is a difference, however, between knowing how to do something and knowing how to do it well.

Concept of a Good Thinker

Have you ever thought about how to think effectively? Sit back for a moment and reflect on your ideas about what makes someone good at thinking. Has anyone directly instructed you on how to think? Chances are, you have been told many times in school *to* think but have never been told exactly how. Where, then, did your ideas about good thinking begin? Perhaps by observing students who were often rewarded for the end result of their thinking—*the* right answer.

Let's start at the beginning of your education and look closely at your experiences to determine how your ideas about good thinking were formed. Visualize Jason Carter, the smartest kid in your elementary school. The teacher asks a question. What is Jason's response? His hand shoots up like a cruise missile in search of the teacher's approval. Everyone else is still trying to figure out what she asked. "Oh," you think, "a good thinker must be able to think fast." You try to imitate Jason's behavior, and you rate your own thinking ability on how well or how poorly you are able to do this.

And so it goes. Your ideas are formed in this manner throughout your education. By the time you get to high school, you have observed many students who either performed like Jason Carter and won the teacher's approval or performed like the class troublemaker and did nothing but try the teacher's patience. Thus, your ideas of effective thinking may be a combination of information you have gained indirectly through observations. Your actual thinking behaviors may have been formed on the basis of these observations.

Concept Inventory

To help you determine what ideas about good thinking you have compiled up to this point, complete the inventory below as honestly as you can. Circle the one letter for each item that *best* describes your concept of a good thinker.

1. A good thinker:
   a. Tries to block out emotional responses to a problem.
   b. Analyzes emotional responses to a problem.
   c. Uses emotion to respond to a problem.

2. A good thinker:
   a. Excludes creative thinking from critical thinking.
   b. Reserves creative thinking for the arts.
   c. Combines creative and critical thinking.

3. A good thinker:
   a. Can be developed through practice with specific critical thinking exercises.
   b. Needs to develop a critical spirit as a way of life.
   c. Integrates critical principles and critical spirit when thinking.

4. A good thinker:
   a. Knows the answers to the instructor's questions.
   b. Knows how to find the answers to the instructor's questions.
   c. Questions the answers to the instructor's questions.

5. A good thinker:
   a. Needs to make mistakes and recognize errors.
   b. Does not make mistakes.
   c. Makes few mistakes.

6. A good thinker:
   a. Carries on mental or out-loud conversations as he or she thinks.
   b. Recalls information quickly without having to think about it.
   c. Knows that sane people do not talk to themselves.

7. A good thinker:
   a. Should not let his values interfere with his reasoning.
   b. Should be aware of her own values and those of others when reasoning.
   c. Should not let others' values affect his reasoning.

8. A good thinker:
   a. Is receptive to change.
   b. Is wary of change.
   c. Changes only when proved wrong.

9. A good thinker:
   a. Knows all the answers.
   b. Is always learning.
   c. Knows all the questions.

10. A good thinker:
    a. Takes little time to respond to questions.
    b. Is reflective.
    c. Completes his or her work first.

11. A good thinker:
    a. Revises work often.
    b. Gets it right the first time.
    c. Revises work on rare occasions.

12. A good thinker:
    a. Knows the answer is the most important part of a test item.
    b. Knows the questions are the most important aspect of a test.
    c. Knows the process for obtaining the answer is as important as the answer.

13. A good thinker:
    a. Uses hunches, intuition.
    b. Doesn't jump to conclusions.
    c. Makes prompt decisions.

14. A good thinker:
    a. Pays attention to detail.
    b. Should not be bothered with detail.
    c. Gets right to the point.

15. A good thinker:
    a. Does not need to make visual aids to thinking.
    b. Is able to think without visualization.
    c. Makes visuals such as diagrams to aid the thinking process.

16. A good thinker:
    a. Knows that learning means being able to recite information presented.
    b. Knows that learning is a process of understanding and analyzing information.
    c. Knows that learning has taken place when his or her grades are high.

17. A good thinker:
    a. Knows that knowledge requires a mind slow to believe.
    b. Knows that knowledge requires a mind quick to believe.
    c. Knows that knowledge requires both of the above.

18. A good thinker:
    a. Solves problems in a new manner each time.
    b. Has a consistent system for solving problems.
    c. Does not need a system for solving problems.

19. A good thinker:
    a. Is usually valued in the traditional classroom.
    b. Is often the teacher in the traditional classroom.
    c. Is often irritating in the traditional classroom.

20. A good thinker:
    a. Accepts information given by a reputable source.
    b. Rejects information regardless of the source.
    c. Analyzes all information.

As your instructor reads the best responses for these items, mark those that differ from yours. Keep in mind that answers different from those given may be acceptable if you can justify them with reasons that relate to being orderly and thoughtful.

The answers you have now marked as correct may cause you to realize that the ideas about good thinking presented in this survey differ somewhat from the ones you've compiled throughout your education. To analyze where and why your ideas about good thinking were formed, share that information with others, and to describe the new ideas you've received, complete the following activity.

Sharing Your Ideas

1. Choose a partner, and discuss with your partner the events or observations that caused you to select each answer that differed from the one given by your instructor.
2. List the different concepts that you had.

    ____

    ____

    ____

    ____

3. With your partner, discuss new ideas about good thinking that the concept inventory presented to you. ■

Obstacles to Critical Thinking

What is critical thinking? How can you identify obstacles to critical thinking if you're not even sure what it is? Many involved definitions are given for this aspect of thinking. Richard Paul, author of *Critical Thinking: What Every Person Needs to Survive in a Rapidly Changing World,* finds it so complicated a process that he compares trying to define it to trying to define ourselves. When asked to reduce critical thinking to words, Paul described it as "the art of thinking about your thinking, while you're thinking, in order to make your thinking better." Now that requires thinking!

In his article "Educational Virtue: Becoming a Critical Thinker," Gerald Nosich provides us with a framework for Paul's ideas by describing what a critical thinker does. A critical thinker "is someone who is able to think well and fair-mindedly not just about her own beliefs and viewpoints, but about beliefs and viewpoints that are diametrically opposed to her own. . . [Critical thinking] involves attitudes and passions as well. It is not just something you do in school and then go home and get on with your life. To the extent that a person acquires the skills, attitudes, and passions of a critical thinker, it will permeate her life." A good critical thinker, then, will exhibit the characteristics of good thinking that we identified in the preceding concept inventory while looking at issues and problems from all sides, at all times.

Therefore, understanding what behaviors constitute good thinking is a beginning in this process. However, even if we were able to program these good thinking behaviors into our daily existence, there is a slight problem—*we are human!* As humans, we not only think—we also react. Our natural tendency is to react in an unthinking manner because our feelings get in the way.

Vincent Ruggiero, in his book *Beyond Feelings: A Guide to Critical Thinking,* addresses this difficulty by identifying nine problems to critical thinking:[1]

1. Mine is better.
2. Resistance to change.
3. The urge to conform.
4. The need to save face.
5. Stereotypes.
6. Faulty common sense.
7. Oversimplification.

[1]Reprinted from *Beyond Feelings: A Guide to Critical Thinking,* by Vincent Ruggiero, by permission of Mayfield Publishing Company. Copyright © 1975 by Mayfield Publishing Company.

8. Hasty conclusions.
9. Unwarranted assumptions.

As you read about these problems, you will begin to realize that many of them occur in combinations. Being able to identify them in yourself and in others is a requirement for clearly seeing all sides of an issue. This is the next step in thinking critically.

Mine Is Better

From the time we are small, we learn to have special feelings about ourselves and our things. It's a natural tendency to believe that "my dad can beat yours any day." This continues somewhat into adulthood as we find ourselves thinking, "My major is better than yours. My car is faster than yours. My crowd has more fun than yours." This tendency is usually accepted by most of us because most of us realize that others feel the same way about themselves as we do about ourselves.

A "mine is better" attitude becomes a genuine problem, however, with "know-it-alls." Such people believe that everything about them is superior to everything about all others. Nothing they say or do can ever be questioned because what they say or do is always right. If you do not share the values, culture, religion, or ideas of the know-it-all, there is something wrong with you.

To relate to the problem of mine is better and to identify how it applies to your life, think of some experiences you've had with people who exhibit a mine is better attitude. Although you probably were unable to change their minds, were you able to reason with them? Perhaps the best way to accomplish this is to acknowledge what a mine is better person is saying and to attempt to understand why he or she feels this way. For instance, you might say, "Grandma, I understand that you can't stand men who wear an earring. Tell me about experiences you've had that make you feel that way." You could then go on to explain your experiences and feelings in the same way. In this manner each party is listening to the viewpoints of the other party. If you are unable to do this, you may want to examine your own mine is better attitude.

Resistance to Change

Resistance to change occurs when our sense of security is threatened or when we fear the unknown. When asked to develop a time management schedule, some students respond, "Why should I have to do that? I never had to do that in high school, and my grades were just fine." Many people refuse to wear a seat belt because "they never wore them in my day, and I'm still here to tell it." The list goes on and on: granting women equal rights, admitting gays into the military, providing condoms in schools. In order to critically see all sides of any issue, we must analyze why we feel a resistance to doing so.

To identify this problem within yourself, think of some issues on which you currently feel a resistance to change and write them in the spaces provided below. Try to examine your reasons for feeling the way you do. Did a specific experience cause your resistance, or are you reacting with an emotional response? Write the reasons for your beliefs beside each issue. Are you able to look at all sides of the issue by citing the pros and cons of your viewpoint?

Issue on Which Change Is Resisted	*Reasons for Beliefs*
______________________	______________________
______________________	______________________
______________________	______________________
______________________	______________________

The Urge to Conform

Conformity is a necessary part of life. We have to obey rules for our own safety. Our society would be chaotic if everyone did whatever he or she wanted to do. To feel a sense of belonging, we tend to desire the acceptance of others and we conform to avoid rejection. Conformity becomes a problem when we are faced with situations that require us to make our own decisions and we knowingly or unknowingly end up relying on the judgments of others. When "out with the guys," you may find yourself doing and saying things in order to fit in with the group.

Yale psychologist Irving L. Janis coined the word *groupthink* to describe decisions made by groups that, because of the desire to conform, made decisions without taking into account other points of view. Be aware that you belong to many "groups" that can affect your thinking. Your gender, clubs, family, friends, and church are all examples of groups that can affect the way you view various issues.

To determine the effect of groupthink on your views, consider your feelings about an issue such as abortion. How do you feel about the issue? Is this really your viewpoint, or do you feel this way because your friends and family have this viewpoint? To be sure that your feelings are your own, ask yourself to cite specific reasons why you feel strongly one way or the other about the issue.

The Need to Save Face

How do you view yourself as a person? Do you see yourself as a decent, law-abiding, honest individual? Most of us have a pretty positive view of ourselves and would like others to have the same view of us. Because of this, it's a natural reaction to try to protect that view. Thus, when something happens to threaten it, we tend to blame others rather than accept the fact that we may not be quite as faultless as we would like to believe. By doing this, we become limited to conclusions that support our self-image. For instance, Joe views himself as a good student. Upon receiving a failing grade on his accounting exam, he immediately blames the instructor, who is "a disorganized, senile jerk." Instead of correcting his problem through tutoring or another means of self-improvement, Joe sees the problem as his teacher's. The situation does not disappear, but Joe's chances of dealing with it do.

Before you attempt to save face by deciding that you don't have this problem, think of any difficulties you have experienced recently at home, school, or work. Ask yourself what caused these difficulties. As you respond, how many times do you find yourself trying to save face by faulting others?

Stereotypes

Stereotypes are fixed beliefs about people, places, or things. When you stereotype, you group people, places, or things together and say they are all the same. By doing this, you can get to a point at which you accept only those facts that fit into your stereotype and reject all others. For instance, you may feel that football players are big and dumb. You use the team's offensive tackle I. R. Dense as an example. As a student in your computer class, Dense has had difficulty in remembering important dates, times, and places, such as when and where the class meets. Also in this class are five other members of the football team who are average and above-average students. In forming your opinion, you overlook these individuals and focus only on the student who confirms it. Although this is an extreme example, you need to be aware that everyone tends to stereotype somewhat in his or her daily life.

Think of some common and not so common stereotypes that you and others accept. Try to analyze the source of these generalizations. Are you able to think of examples that run counter to opinions you currently hold?

Faulty Common Sense

How can common sense be faulty? Everyone knows that common sense is good and wise and wonderful. For that very reason, it may go unquestioned even when it's wrong. It used to be "common sense" to bleed evil spirits from the ill. "Common sense" told us that women could not be intelligent enough to vote. Is it "common sense" that good thinking means fast thinking and the ability to always find *the* one right answer? In all cases, we need to have a questioning attitude instead of an accepting attitude. We should examine evidence for all sides of an issue before claiming that something is common sense.

Many beliefs about school and learning that were once thought to be common sense have since been proven to be otherwise. Think about some current rules at your institution that you feel need to be changed. Cite specific reasons why they could have been established. For each of these reasons, list as many pros and cons as possible. Be sure to attempt to think like those who made the rules when reasoning from a viewpoint other than your own.

Oversimplification

"Ignorance is bliss." "The early bird catches the worm." Words to live by, yes? Remembering that there are at least two sides to everything, let's look at another side of these one-liners. Sure, being ignorant of the fact that you're going to have a major exam tomorrow may indeed make tonight's socializing a blissful event, but tomorrow you will most likely have to pay for it. Getting an early start on things may help you succeed, but it may also make you tired if you were up late the night before. Oversimplifications contain an element of truth that often blinds us to their weaknesses. Although partially true, oversimplifications are also partially false.

To avoid oversimplification, we need to be aware that most issues cannot be viewed as either/or. It is possible to agree in part and disagree in part without being wishy-washy. To practice doing this, find something that could be true and something that could be false in each of the following statements.

1. If the student hasn't learned, the teacher hasn't taught. ________

   ____

   ____

   ____

2. Spare the rod and spoil the child. ________________

   ____

   ____

   ____

3. The best things in life are free. ________________

   ____

   ____

   ____

4. Honesty is the best policy. ____

    ____

    ____

    ____

Hasty Conclusions

A hasty conclusion is a judgment drawn without enough evidence. Such judgments may be drawn because of convenience. It's easier and often more fun to believe that Elvis was recently seen at the neighborhood supermarket than to believe otherwise. Another reason hasty conclusions are drawn is that we have a tendency to use them to support our own desires and beliefs. Let's suppose you and a friend see your father leaving a music store with a large bag. Since it is close to your birthday and you gave your parents a list of several CDs that you would like, you conclude that your father has just purchased them for you. Your friend, on the other hand, has parents who enjoy music. He therefore concludes that your father was probably buying some CDs for himself. Who is right? Neither of you. You both have insufficient evidence at the moment, and you have both drawn a hasty conclusion. From this example, you can see that when drawing conclusions, it is important not only to collect enough evidence but to be aware of personal bias.

Can you think of an instance in which you were unjustly accused? What hasty conclusions were drawn? What evidence was ignored? Did your accuser's personal feelings toward you come into play when he or she judged your guilt or innocence? Have you ever unjustly accused someone? Did you fail to collect enough evidence? Did personal bias influence your accusation?

Unwarranted Assumptions

An assumption is a "given"—an idea you come to have without really giving it any thought. After all, you can't think about *everything*. You get up in the morning and assume your room is still there. You take for granted that your car will be there when you go to the parking lot after class—well, maybe not! By being able to take some things for granted, you avoid having to think about every single move you make. This, of course, is necessary.

Unwarranted assumptions occur, however, when you treat situations that require thought as ones that you can take for granted. In the above example, the car may not be in the parking lot. Perhaps you should have invested in an antitheft device. Suppose your doctor tells you that you need immediate facial surgery to correct the unusual way you smirk when you sleep. Only when you are in the operating room counting backward from 100 do you stop to think that maybe the doctor made a mistake.

To avoid similar turns of events, you must evaluate situations that go beyond the routine. It's OK to question information that does not seem accurate, no matter whose information it is. Think of some instances in which you should have questioned what you assumed about college, teachers, and learning in general. What difficulties did your unwarranted assumptions cause?

Sharing Your Ideas

Select any of the activities below to practice identifying problems in critical thinking in yourself and others.

1. Discuss formerly held beliefs about the effects of alcohol, tobacco, and drugs. Then discuss currently held beliefs about their effects. As a class, discuss the possibility that the currently held beliefs may be examples of faulty common sense. Remember to examine evidence on all sides of the issue.
2. As a class, discuss the following statement. Eliminate oversimplifications by looking at all sides of the issue. "Alcohol consumption should be legal for those who are 18 years old. If they are old enough to vote and fight for our country, they are old enough to drink."
3. Discuss the following issue as a group. While analyzing the responses, be aware of hasty conclusions and other problems in critical thinking. "A mandatory test for AIDS should be administered to every man, woman, and child in the United States." ■

The Need for Creative Thinking

Albert Einstein said, "Imagination is more important than knowledge." Now that you've become more aware of some of the obstacles to critical thinking, you may be able to identify that statement as a possible oversimplification with some truth and some untruth. Whether imagination is more important than knowledge may be up for debate. The important point to note is that imagination is an often overlooked factor in thinking. When we overlook imagination, we tend to look at problems in the same way and find ourselves unable to arrive at new solutions. The following poem, written by Sam Walter Foss, demonstrates the need for creative thinking:

> One day through the primeval wood
> A calf walked home as good calves should;
> But made a trail all bent askew,
> A crooked trail as all calves do.
> Since then three hundred years have fled,
> And I infer the calf is dead.

But still he left behind his trail,
And thereby hangs my moral tale.
The trail was taken up next day
By a lone dog that passed that way;
And then a wise bellwether sheep
Pursued the trail o'er hill and glade
Through those old woods a path was made.
And many men wound in and out
And dodged and turned and bent about
And uttered words of righteous wrath
Because 'twas such a crooked path;
But still they followed—do not laugh—
The first migrations of that calf,
And through this winding wood-way stalked
Because he wobbled when he walked.
This forest path became a lane
That bent and turned and turned again;
This crooked lane became a road,
Where many a poor horse with his load
Toiled on beneath the burning sun,
And traveled some three miles in one.
And thus a century and a half
They trod the footsteps of that calf.
The years passed on in swiftness fleet,
The road became a village street;
And thus, before men were aware,
A city's crowded thoroughfare.
And soon the central street was this
Of a renowned metropolis;
And men two centuries and a half
Trod in the footsteps of that calf.
Each day a hundred thousand rout
Followed this zigzag calf about
And o'er his crooked journey went
the traffic of a continent.
A hundred thousand men were led
By one calf near three centuries dead.
They followed still his crooked way,
And lost one hundred years a day;
For thus such reverence is lent
To well-established precedent.[2]

Instead of viewing creativity as an *aptitude* that only a few artistic people possess, try seeing it as an *attitude* that we all had at one time. What attitude? Think back to the beginning of your education, and see for

---

[2]Excerpt from *The Art of Thinking: A Guide to Critical Thought,* by Vincent Ruggiero. Copyright © 1984 by Harper & Row, Publishers, Inc. Reprinted by permission of HarperCollins Publishers, Inc.

yourself. When you were in preschool and the teacher asked if you could sing, dance, or draw, you probably had little difficulty in coming up with your own version of a song, some dance moves, or a picture of the first thing that popped into your head. Now, when asked if you can sing, dance, or draw, how do you answer? What happened to that attitude you used to have? Do the activity below for a brief demonstration of what happens to our thought processes as we get older.

In the examples below, circle the thing that goes with the name of the picture.

1. Clothing

2. Body

3. Toy

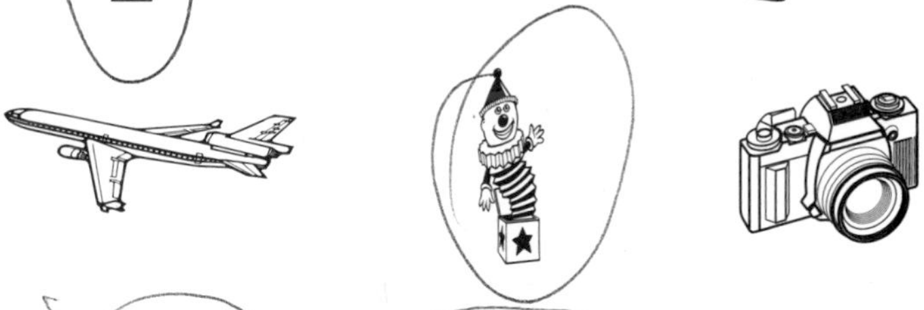

4. Word

Any problems? Perhaps you have become so ordered in your thinking that item 4 was a puzzle to you. Vincent Ruggiero, in *The Art of Thinking,* states, "Many problems are not solved because people see them in one way only." Through your many years of schooling you may have come to believe that there is one right answer and one right way of doing things. This hinders the *attitude* so necessary to creative thinking: the willingness to see things from an alternative perspective. Instead of seeking a different way of doing item 4, you probably tried to analyze which of the three pictures could possibly be correct. Actually, the word *word* could have been circled as a response. Your past experience kept you from even considering it as an answer. It was on the *wrong* side. How many other choices do you eliminate daily because you see your options in one way only?

Methods of Good Problem Solvers

Solving problems requires the ability to think both creatively and critically in an organized manner. In the preceding sections you were presented with a general idea about the need to see things from a different perspective in order to think creatively. You also read about the nine problems in critical thinking that make it difficult to see all sides of an issue. Now, let's put these ideas together to develop a formula that uses creativity and critical thinking in problem solving. Gardner Lindzey, Calvin Hall, and Richard Thompson illustrate the need for such a formula in their article "Creative Thinking and Critical Thinking." They define creative thinking as "thinking that results in the discovery of a new or improved solution to a problem." They define critical thinking as "the examination and testing of suggested solutions to see whether they will work." Even though these two processes are different, Lindzey, Hall, and Thompson believe that they can work together in solving problems. Creative thinking can lead to new ideas, and critical thinking can check those ideas for errors.

To improve your ability to solve problems in this manner, you need to identify the method or methods you currently use. Do you have specific techniques that work for you? Are those techniques organized so that you go through the same procedure each time you solve a problem? Most of us are unaware of how we problem-solve. Thinking out loud while another person listens can help you identify the thought processes you use. Determine how you go about solving problems by working with another person to complete the activity below.

Sharing Your Ideas

As you work in pairs, take turns solving a problem aloud. One person will read problem 1 below. As that person solves the problem, she must vocalize her thoughts every step of the way to let her partner know exactly what she's thinking. The other person's role is to listen and ask guiding questions but not to solve the problem. Exchange roles for problem 2.

Problem 1

Circle the word to the left of the word that has the fewest consonants and the fewest long vowels.

college study think brain pain

Problem 2

If the phrase "my dog has frenetic fleas" has more than seven vowels, four words, and 21 letters, circle the first word. If not, circle the word that has more consonants to the left of the first vowel and more letters to the right of the second to the last consonant.

What did you discover about your method for solving problems? ________

____ ■

Good Problem Solvers versus Poor Problem Solvers

In the book *Problem Solving and Comprehension,* Arthur Whimby and Jack Lochhead discuss five areas in which good academic problem solvers differ from poor academic problem solvers:[3]

1. Attitude toward problem solving.
2. Concern for accuracy.
3. Breaking the problem into parts.
4. Guessing.
5. Activeness in problem solving.

As you read about each area, ask yourself which characteristics you displayed in solving the preceding problems.

Attitude toward Problem Solving

Good problem solvers believe that a problem can be solved if they take their time and carefully look at all parts of it. Poor problem solvers, on the other hand, often lack the confidence to stick with a problem until it has been solved. If they don't know the answer and are confused by a problem, a poor problem solver might give up or guess. Poor problem solvers usually don't break a problem into parts to be analyzed. They read through a problem once and try to solve it.

Concern for Accuracy

Good problem solvers are very careful when solving problems. They check and recheck their understanding of the facts as they solve a problem. This often means reading it several times. Poor problem solvers are usually less

[3]Arthur Whimby and Jack Lochhead, *Problem Solving and Comprehension,* 3rd ed. (Philadelphia, Pa: Franklin Institute Press, 1982), pp. 26–27. Copyright 1982 by Lawrence Erlbaum Associates, Inc. Reprinted by permission.

concerned about their understanding of a problem. They may make mistakes because they do not know exactly what a problem is stating. They do not reread the problem until they understand it.

Breaking the Problem into Parts

Good problem solvers break difficult problems into parts. They start a problem at a point where they can make some sense of it and then go on from there. Poor problem solvers do not break a difficult problem into parts in order to solve it one step at a time.

Guessing

Good problem solvers do not guess at an answer to a problem. They know that if they work carefully in steps and check their work throughout a problem, they can solve it. Because poor problem solvers lack confidence in their ability to solve problems, they tend to give up, to use little or no reasoning, and to give a quick answer.

Activeness in Problem Solving

Good problem solvers do things to help them understand a problem. If a problem is hard for them to follow, they may visualize the problem in their mind's eye, think about their own experiences, draw pictures or diagrams, talk about the problem, or move objects to represent parts of the problem. They do whatever it takes to get a clearer understanding of the problem. Poor problem solvers try to solve a problem simply by reading through it. They lack other methods to aid them in their thinking process.

Steps in Good Problem Solving

Identify the Problem

You now have all the information you need to begin using both creative and critical thinking in problem solving. The first step in solving problems in this manner is to identify the problem. It is tempting, when solving problems, to try to jump into a solution without identifying the actual problem or problems. Let's look at an example to see how identifying the problem is correctly done.

Mary is a student having difficulty in her psychology course. She says she can't read the text because it's boring. When she goes to class, she has trouble understanding the lecture because much of it is based on information in the reading. What would you identify as the problem or problems in this instance?

You might say that one problem is that Mary isn't taking good notes. However, no evidence was given that Mary's notes were poor. You might feel that another problem is that Mary needs to read the text. This is an example of jumping to a solution without identifying the problem. A better statement of the problem or problems would be that, first, Mary is unable to read the text because she finds it boring. Another problem is that lectures are difficult for Mary because the instructor's lectures come from the text. Notice that these problems were clearly identified in the example.

If you would like to comment on problems that are not clearly stated but could possibly be contributing to the difficulty, be sure to use such verbs as *may, might,* and *could,* which express a possibility but not a certainty. When doing this, always be sure to give a reason for your ideas. You could say, for example, that Mary *could* be finding the text boring because it *may* be too difficult for her to read. In this instance, you could describe your own experience as a reason for believing this could be a problem.

Creative Thinking

Once you have identified the problem or problems, the second step in good problem solving is to use your creativity. Think of the knowledge you already possess, ask others, and do a bit of research if necessary. Then brainstorm or list as many solutions as you can think of. Don't be afraid to suggest something unusual. Be as silly or as serious as you care to be. The only limitation is that you cannot think about or judge any of your responses at this point.

Several possible solutions to Mary's problems could be charted in the following manner:

Problems / Solutions

Problem 1: *Text is boring*
Solutions:
- Drop the class.
- Break up reading into chunks.
- Use rewards for reading.
- Take notes when reading to be more active.
- Get more background before reading.

Problem 2: *Lecture is difficult*
Solutions:
- Tape lecture.
- Read before class.
- Compare notes with classmate.
- Take study skills course.

Problem 3: *Reading may be difficult*
Solutions:
- Go to reading skills center.
- Get a tutor.
- Take a reading class.

Critical Thinking

The next step is to choose and evaluate possible solutions from the above list. To do this, look at the pros and cons of each solution. Since the problem is not your own, try to reason as Mary might. Again, a charting-type format is useful.

Problems / Solutions	*Pros and Cons*
Problem 1 Text is boring	
Drop the class.	*Pro:* No more boring reading! *Con:* I need this class to graduate.
Break up reading.	*Pro:* I can focus better if I read in small chunks. *Con:* Man, this is too much work. It will take forever!
Use rewards.	*Pro:* I can work if I know I get a break every half hour. *Con:* I give myself a reward, then I hate to get started again.
Take notes when reading.	*Pro:* If I put things in my own words, I understand and remember better. *Con:* This is too much trouble. I don't have time for this.
Get more background.	*Pro:* I can tie the reading into what I already know. *Con:* This is too time consuming. I have better things to do with my time.
Problem 2: Lecture is difficult	
Tape lecture.	*Pro:* I can listen to the lecture again to understand it better. *Con:* I spend another entire hour listening to something I already heard. I need my time to read.
Read before class.	*Pro:* I take much better notes when I know about the subject beforehand. *Con:* I have difficulty forcing myself to read.
Compare notes.	*Pro:* I can get information that I missed or did not understand. *Con:* Everyone has to leave after class for their next class or their job.
Take study skills course.	*Pro:* I've heard those courses really help. *Con:* I don't want to take more time or spend more money in order to graduate.
Problem 3: Reading may be difficult	
Go to reading skills center.	*Pro:* I know I can get help there, and it's free. *Con:* I'll feel stupid asking for help.
Get a tutor.	*Pro:* I think it would really help if someone could show me a better way to read. *Con:* It's expensive and I don't need it. That jerk of an instructor isn't doing his job. If he'd give better lectures, I wouldn't have to read the stupid book.
Take a reading class.	*Pro:* This is something that could help me in every class I take. *Con:* No time, no money, no fun!

Devise and Implement a Plan

After your analysis is complete, weigh the pros and cons. Select the solutions that appear to be the best in terms of your ability to put them into action. Then decide on and list the exact steps necessary to accomplish the solutions. Be very specific, citing who, what, when, where, and how your solutions can be achieved.

For the example above, the best solutions seem to be going to the reading skills center and either getting a tutor or taking a reading class. This would probably help Mary with both her reading and her notetaking. These services are often free. In order to do this, Mary will have to look in her student handbook or ask an instructor, an adviser, or a friend where the center is located. She could then call the phone number given in her handbook or visit the center. She may have to reschedule her date for graduation and spend more money, but unless she does this, she may never be able to complete her program.

Evaluate the Plan

While the plan is being carried out, you may have to make adjustments. No plan is perfect. This is why it is necessary to monitor or evaluate your progress toward a solution. If you feel the solution you chose is not working, ask yourself how it should be revised. For example, perhaps Mary is not experiencing the progress she needs in her ability to read her text. In thinking about it, she realizes that her tutor is using workbooks instead of her actual text in their tutoring sessions. She must now think of a way to fix this, such as a discussion with the tutor or his supervisor. After this occurs, Mary should again evaluate her progress and make further changes if necessary.

Problem-Solving Flowchart

You have now worked through a process for solving problems in an organized, thoughtful way using both creative and critical thinking. This process can be used to remedy both personal and school-related difficulties. The process is illustrated in the problem-solving flowchart shown in Figure 6–1. As you study the parts of the flowchart, see how the problem you just solved fits into them.

FIGURE 6–1
Problem-solving flowchart

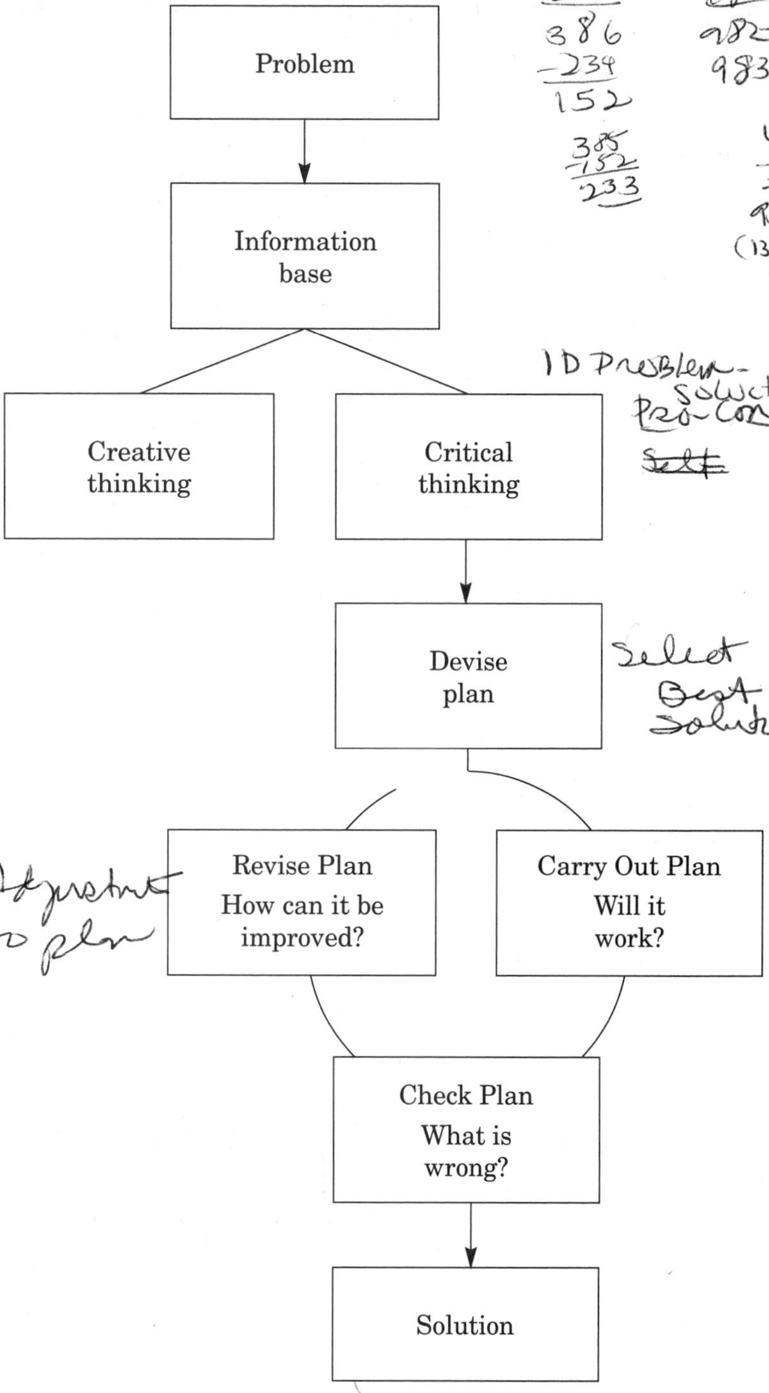

Putting It All Together

A good critical thinker uses organized, thoughtful behaviors while looking at issues and problems from all sides. The first step in becoming a good thinker is to gain an understanding of the specific behaviors that can be classified as organized and thoughtful.

Difficulties occur in our attempts to incorporate these behaviors because we often react with emotional responses rather than with reason. These responses can be categorized as nine problems to critical thinking: mine is better, resistance to change, the urge to conform, the need to save face, stereotypes, faulty common sense, oversimplification, hasty conclusions, and unwarranted assumptions. Identifying such responses in ourselves and others is necessary in order to begin the second step in critical thinking: looking at issues and problems from all sides.

Whimby and Lochhead have identified five areas in which the methods of good academic problem solvers differ from those of poor academic problem solvers: attitude toward problem solving, concern for accuracy, breaking the problem into parts, guessing, and activeness in problem solving.

Both academic and personal problems can be solved in an organized, thoughtful manner by utilizing the following framework: identifying the problem, using creative thinking to discover new solutions, using critical thinking to refine those solutions, devising a specific plan of action, and evaluating the results.

Making the Connection

Check your understanding of the concepts presented in this chapter by completing the following activity. If you are unable to recall information in a particular area, go back and review that material before completing the rest of this section.

1. Write one or two sentences to summarize what you recall about each of the following topics:

   Concept of a good thinker ______________________________

   ____

   ____

   Obstacles to critical thinking ___________________________

   ____

   ____

   The need for creative thinking __________________________

   ____

   ____

   Methods of good problem solvers ________________________

   ____

   ____

   The problem-solving flowchart __________________________

   ____

   ____

2. List one new idea you've gained about effective thinking and problem solving as a result of reading this chapter. ____________________

   ____

   ____

3. Describe one change you plan to make in the way you go about thinking or problem solving. ______________________________

   ____

   ____

Thinking It Through

Read the following passage. Answer the questions following the passage by applying what you've learned about problem solving.

Ned's quarter was off to a great start. He was taking several business classes and maintaining an organized study schedule. To do all he required of himself, it was necessary for him to stay up each evening until 1 A.M. Unfortunately, he had an 8 A.M. class each day.

As the term progressed, Ned began to have to force himself to stay up late and to get up in time for class. When he complained of his exhaustion to a friend, the friend suggested using pills to help him stay alert. Ned put off the idea until midterm, when he felt so overwhelmed that he considered it his only alternative.

The good grades on Ned's exams were enough to make him realize that the pills he took could give him the energy he needed to continue to do well in school. It became a habit to take a pill to stay awake each evening and a pill to wake up each morning.

By finals week, Ned realized he had a problem. He was always tired unless he took pills. He had to continue taking pills to get through finals week. He told himself that afterward he would stop.

1. State what you see as Ned's specific problem(s).

____

____

____

2. Withhold judgment. Use both brainstorming of current information and research of other sources if necessary to list possible solutions for his problem(s). ______________________________

____

____

____

____

3. List each solution's advantages and disadvantages from Ned's point of view. ______________________________

____

____

____

4. Select a solution, and describe how Ned could carry it out.

5. How could Ned evaluate this solution?

Applying Your Skills 1 *Effective Thinking versus Less Effective Thinking*

Instructions: To interpret your understanding of effective thinking behaviors, review the correct responses to the Concept Inventory found on pages 116–119. Read the comparisons of effective versus less effective thinking on the table below. Add comparisons of your own that you would like to make.

Effective Thinking versus Less Effective Thinking

The Effective Thinker	*The Less Effective Thinker*
• Thinks about feelings before reacting.	• Uses feelings to react.
• Is flexible, looking at all sides of an issue.	• Focuses on one point of view.
• Realizes that no one knows all the answers	• Views the teacher as the source of all knowledge.
•	•
•	•
•	•
•	•

Applying Your Skills 2 *Creative Thinking with a Tangram*

Instructions: The shapes below are pieces of an ancient Chinese puzzle called a tangram. They can be used to form many figures and are helpful in practicing the ability to see things in different ways. Cut them out or trace them onto a piece of sturdy cardboard to complete the activity below.

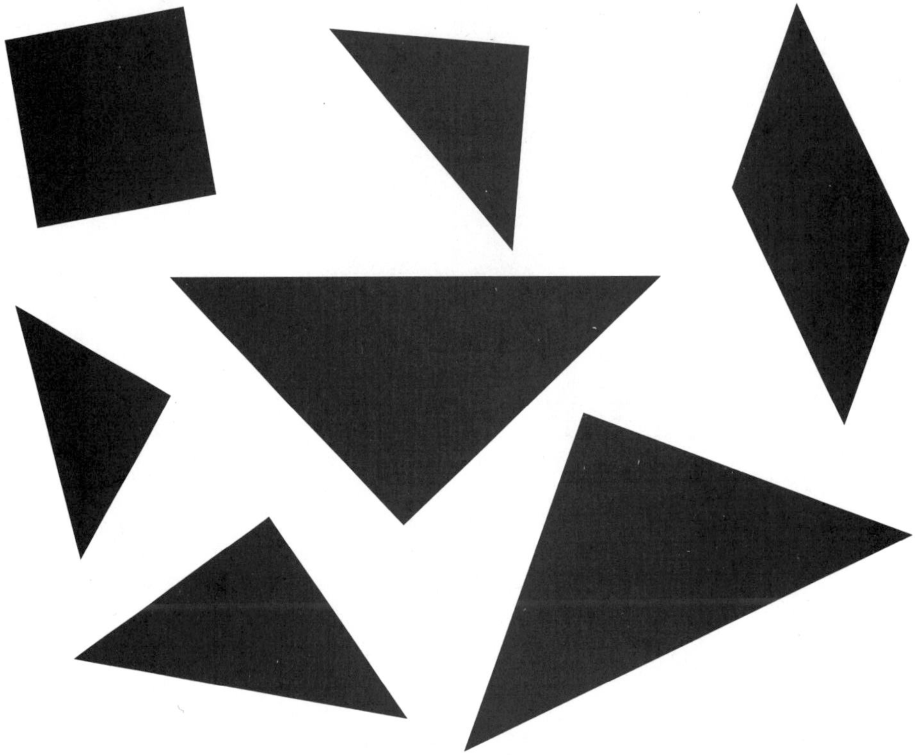

Directions: Arrange the seven shapes shown above to create the figure that follows. Notice how many times you find it necessary to look at the figure in another way. Your instructor will give you the solution to this puzzle.

Applying Your Skills 3 *Good Problem Solvers versus Poor Problem Solvers*

Directions: Review the information found under the heading "Good Problem Solvers versus Poor Problem Solvers." Create a table to compare effective problem solvers with ineffective problem solvers. An example has been done for you.

Effective Problem Solvers	*Ineffective Problem Solvers*
• Don't give up.	• May give up and guess.
•	•
•	•
•	•
•	•
•	•
•	•

Applying Your Skills 4 *Solve Your Problems*

Directions: To use the problem-solving process with a problem you are currently experiencing, complete the activity below.

1. Think of a problem you have. Write it here.

2. Use what you already know, ask others, and perhaps do a bit of research to brainstorm and list as many ideas as you can to solve the problem.

3. Give the pros and cons for *each* of the solutions you listed above. You may need to use another piece of paper.

4. Select the solution that appears to be the best in terms of pros and cons and your ability to carry it out. List the steps necessary to carry out the solution. Be sure to describe the details, such as who, what, when, where, and how.

5. How could you evaluate this solution?

Applying Your Skills 5 *Using Your Resources*

Instructions: To know where to "radio for help," you will be asked to visit various school resources throughout this text. Keep this information so that you can refer to it when you are in need of help outside the classroom.

Complete the information below after touring your school's Health Services and/or Drug Information Center.

Location: ______________________________

Hours of operation: ______________________________

Contact person: ______________________________

Phone: ______________________________

Services offered:

____

____

____

____

Personal comments:

Briefly discuss how you could use this resource.

____

____

____

____

PART III LEARNING SYSTEMS

C H A P T E R

7 The PPR Notetaking System

Apply the principles of thinking and learning to take notes effectively.

Chapter Goals

After you read this chapter, you will be able to:

- Describe the physical and mental processes that occur before, during, and after performing a task.
- Use mental and physical strategies for focusing your attention in order to prepare to take notes.
- Use mental and physical strategies for processing information as you take notes.
- Use mental and physical strategies for recalling information after you take notes.
- Apply notetaking methods that require the use of higher levels on the PYRAMID of Learning.
- Select notetaking methods that are appropriate to your learning style.

Now that you have a thorough knowledge of the principles of memory, the levels of learning, and the elements of effective thinking, you are ready to use that knowledge as you learn. The next four chapters of this text will show you how. You will learn strategies for notetaking, reading, test taking, and writing that use the three stages of memory—prepare, process, recall—and so are called the PPR Systems. At each stage of the PPR Systems you will learn techniques that will help you translate, interpret, apply, analyze, synthesize, and evaluate information as you learn. Not only will you learn new techniques for notetaking, reading, test taking, and writing, but you will also learn new ways of thinking as you go about these tasks.

The PPR Concept: A Systematic Approach to Learning

Imagine that tomorrow you are going to get out of bed and run your first marathon. When your alarm clock rings, what will you need to do physically in order to prepare to run? First, of course, you had better get dressed. Next, you may either wash your face or look in the mirror and say, "Forget it." You may want something light to eat and something to drink. You'll probably want to do some stretching and some warm-up exercises.

What do you need to do mentally in order to prepare to run? Although you may never have thought about it, things are going on inside your head as you go about your daily activities. If you could step inside your brain at the moment your alarm clock rang in the above example, you might hear something like this: "Oh no! I've got to shut that #!?# thing off. It's the big day! I don't know if I can do this. *Why* am I doing this? I'd better calm myself down before I have a heart attack. Let's see, how do I feel? Actually, I feel pretty good. I should be able to run a decent race today. Gee. I'm hungry. I think I'll grab a glass of OJ and a doughnut before I get dressed. Maybe I'd better wash my face before I run. Ugh! Why bother—I'll just get sweaty anyway. It looks nice today. I don't think I'll need my warm-up clothes. Guess I'll get dressed and do a little jogging. I'm going to take it a mile at a time."

As you can see, there is plenty going on both mentally and physically as you prepare for the race. Notice how the in-the-head talk was constantly checking out and evaluating the situation? There was some questioning of the task and some setting of the purpose in order to prepare to run. The same physical and mental activities continue as you are running and after you run.

While you run, not only must you physically move your body, but you must also check out or monitor the situation mentally. You might do this by asking such questions as these: "How do I feel? Should I speed up or slow down? Do I need to grab a drink when water is offered? Where is the next hill? How much farther do I have to go? How do I want to pace myself at this point? Why am I doing this?"

After the race you need to continue moving around in order to cool down. Your in-the-head talk will probably involve some evaluation or judgment of your performance. You might make such mental comments as these: "I really ran well today! What did I do to have such a good race? I'd like to be able to do the same things again so I can repeat this performance. Boy, am I hot! I'd better keep walking. I can't believe I just ran 26 miles! I feel tired but great!"

You may be asking yourself, "Wait—this isn't a book on running. How does all of this tie into the PPR concept? Isn't that the title of this section?" The next two paragraphs answer these questions.

The PPR concept has been illustrated in the running example. This example contains all the elements of the PPR Systems: a preparation stage before the activity begins, a processing stage while the activity takes place, and a recall stage after the activity has been completed. You will remember that these are the three stages necessary for memory to take place: prepare, process, recall. These three stages should be present in every learning activity you perform.

In addition, like the running example, the PPR Systems contain a way of being more aware of both the mental activities and the physical activities you must do before, during, and after each learning task you perform. Becoming more aware of what is going on inside your head can help you better your performance. By checking or monitoring the mental activity you use to learn and study, you will be more aware of what you're doing, how you're doing it, why you're doing it, and whether you're doing it well.

Sharing Your Ideas

To help you become more aware of your mental processes, complete the following activity as a class:

1. Select a partner to work with.
2. Take turns reading one of the paragraphs below out loud.
3. As each person takes a turn, he must try to think out loud by saying everything he is thinking.
4. Each time you come to the symbol *, you must stop reading and tell your partner what you're thinking, even if it's not related to the topic.

Paragraph 1: Gun Control*
Although I have felt the terror of helplessness, owning a handgun is something I cannot do.* And the shoot first, ask questions later approach is an attitude I don't want to teach my children.* Guns are like cars. We are so inured* to their power, we tend to treat them irresponsibly. We see them as commodities that we have a right to own and use as we please.* Instead, we should limit the right to bear arms so that only trained, responsible citizens can buy guns for sport, recreation and protection.*

Barbara L. Keller, "Frontiersmen Are History,"
Newsweek, August 16, 1993

Paragraph 2: Athletes, Sex, and AIDS*
So when will athletes wise up? The consensus seems to be never, even after what has happened to Magic Johnson.* "The biggest problem in our universe for men is our weakness for ladies," says Tampa Bay linebacker Jesse Solomon.* "They know if they have a knockout body, they can get what they want by giving us what we want."* "It really has nothing to do with the women or the travel," says Hale.* "Athletes, married or not, are very promiscuous."*

E. M. Swift, "Dangerous Games,"
Sports Illustrated, November 18, 1991

Were you surprised at the number of thoughts going through your head as you read your paragraph? Are you usually this aware of what you're thinking as you perform a task? Did you notice how being aware of your thoughts caused you to be actively involved in the passage? By using the mental strategies of the PPR Systems, you will become more actively involved in notetaking, reading, test taking, and writing. ■

PPR Notetaking

What do you *do* before class in order to prepare to take notes? What do you *think* before class in order to prepare to take notes? What do you *do* as you take notes? What do you *think* as you take notes? What do you *do* after taking notes? What do you *think*? Most students would probably answer, "I don't know" or "Nothing." Of course, when asked what they learned in class, the same students would also answer, "I don't know" or "Nothing."

To get the most out of each class you attend, you must prepare to learn, process as you are learning, and recall what you learned. Table 7–1 illustrates the PPR System for notetaking. Notice that it contains three stages: before notetaking: *prepare,* while notetaking: *process,* and after notetaking: *recall.* It also provides for both the mental and physical aspects of notetaking, with *mental* and *physical strategies* at each stage. Each part of the PPR System will be explained individually in this chapter.

Prepare: Mental and Physical Strategies

Think back to the information about memory and learning in Chapter 4 of this text. You learned to apply three general principles in order to prepare to learn: (1) eliminate distractors, (2) establish a purpose, and (3) activate prior knowledge. By preparing to learn in this manner, you are able to (1) properly focus your attention, (2) figure out what you need to know and why you need to know it, and (3) get those memory strands ready to tie in new information.

You can use specific strategies to prepare to take notes that will help you apply the three general principles. Both mental and physical strategies will be presented so that you can be aware of what you're doing, how you're doing it, why you're doing it, and whether you're doing it well.

Prepare: Mental Strategies

Before taking notes, select a seat that will help you limit distractors. If you are an auditory learner, sit close to the lecturer and away from friends so that you won't be tempted to socialize. If you are a visual learner, choose a

TABLE 7–1 PPR Notetaking System

Stages	*Mental Strategies*	*Physical Strategies*
Before notetaking: *Prepare*	*Ask yourself:* • What do I already know? • What will the lecture cover? • What new concepts and terms will be presented? • At what rate will information be given? • How full of facts is this information? • What type of exam does this professor give?	• Survey or read assignment. • Prepare questions to ask in class. • Review previous notes. • Have materials: three-ring binder, text, handouts.
While notetaking: *Process*	*Ask yourself:* • What is the topic? • What are the subtopics? • What organizational pattern is being used? • How are points related? • Is this material in the text? • Do I understand this? • How is the speaker's language affecting my understanding?	• Write on right side only. • Leave 2″ margin. • Use lecturer's words if necessary. • Use key words and abbreviations. • Work toward indented format. • Indicate relationships with arrows. • Identify unclear areas with question marks—leave space. • Circle unknown words. • Explain diagrams in notes. Copy diagrams in text later.
After notetaking: *Recall*	*Ask yourself:* • What was covered today? • What was it all supposed to mean? • What were the topics? • What did I not understand? • How does this relate to previous material? • Do I agree/disagree with information given? Why/Why not?	• Review ASAP/edit. • Look up, learn new words. • Add recall topics in margin. • Label with organizational pattern. • Write additional information on left side of notebook. • Briefly study current and past notes using recall cues in margin.

seat where you have a good view of the board, the overhead projector screen, or any other visual that may be used. Sit away from windows to eliminate distractions outside. Kinesthetic learners should prepare to stay physically involved in the lecture by writing or drawing lecture content. Adjusting your environment to your learning style before taking notes can help you use the following mental strategies to your advantage.

Focus on the Topic, and Activate Prior Knowledge. Before you begin to take notes in any class, you need to focus on the topic and activate your memory strands. In order to do this, you must ask, "What will the lecture cover?" and "What do I already know about this topic?" You must also be aware of any new words or ideas that will be presented so that you can make completely new memory traces. Asking the question "What new concepts and terms will be presented?" will help you do this.

Think about a class you will be attending tomorrow. Find out what topic will be discussed. Do you know anything about this topic? Read through tomorrow's reading assignment, and find new terms and ideas that may be used in class. Use this information to complete the information below:

Class: ______________________________

Topic: ______________________________

What I already know: ______________________________

____

____

____

New terms and ideas: ______________________________

____

____

____

____

Set Purpose. Before notetaking, determine whether you will need to take down details or ideas, or both. Think about how difficult the material will be for you and how quickly or slowly the instructor speaks. This will help you prepare for the amount of information you may need to write and the rate at which it will be given. Questions that will help you do this are: What type of exam does this instructor give? How full of facts is this information? At what rate will this information be given?

Use the same class that you used in the above example to answer the following questions:

What type of exam will I be taking in this class? ______________________________

____

How full of facts are the lectures? ______________________________

____

At what rate does my instructor talk? ______________________________

____

Prepare: Physical Strategies

The actual physical things you can do to answer your mental questions make up the observable part of the PPR System. Before going to class and taking notes, you must know what subject the lecture will be about and have memory traces in that subject ready to catch what is thrown their way.

Survey or Read before Class. The best way to have a good background on the subject of the lecture is to read your assignments before coming to class. If, for some reason, you are not able to read an entire assignment before coming to class, reading and thinking about the following parts of a chapter will help you focus on the important parts of the subject:

- The chapter title.
- The chapter objectives or outline.
- The chapter introduction.
- The chapter headings and subheadings.
- Boldfaced or italicized vocabulary words in the chapter.
- Illustrations.
- The chapter summary.
- End-of-chapter exercises or questions.

Review Previous Notes. When you're sitting in class waiting for the lecture to begin, ask yourself questions about the notes you took during the last class session. You will learn an easy way to do this in the "Recall" section of this chapter.

Have Materials Needed. You should also be physically ready with the materials you need to take notes. A three-ring binder permits you to easily insert handouts and organize your notes. Bring at least one pen or pencil (a pen is preferable because ink doesn't smear and it won't fade). Bring your textbook if it is needed, and bring any handouts that will be useful during the lecture.

Process: Mental and Physical Strategies

Once you've focused your attention, know your purpose, and have the proper memory strands ready to receive information, you can begin to take notes. Remember, the process stage of memory is when information is held in the mind long enough to store it. The problem with notetaking is that your instructors will never talk slowly enough for you to store information completely during a lecture. Your job, then, is to organize the information in such a manner that you can easily store it as soon as possible after the lecture.

Some of the general storage principles you studied in Chapter 4 that you can use during a lecture are:

- Associate and label.
- Learn actively.
- Select and organize.
- Chunk it.
- Get the big picture.

Specific ways of applying these principles during notetaking will be explained next.

Process: Mental Strategies

Often, while taking notes, you may find yourself not focused on anything, but just trying to get it all down on paper. As a result, you end up writing complete sentences and paragraphs. Because this doesn't allow you to select what is important from the lecture and to organize it, the information is difficult to store. Try using the following techniques to help you stay focused and organized as you take notes.

Listen for Topics and Subtopics. A way to take notes that makes storage easier is to listen for main points and subpoints. Ask these questions: "What topic is the instructor talking about?" and "What is she saying about it?" By asking these questions constantly as you listen to a lecture, you will be able to stay focused, to listen actively, and to select and organize what is being said.

Look at a set of notes that you took yesterday. Can you find topics and subtopics? Are you writing in complete sentences? What words could you omit from your sentences that would help you select what is important and put it in a shorter form for easier storage?

Identify How the Topic Is Organized. Sometimes, even if you are very focused and know the topic, you can get completely lost. For example, perhaps you know that your instructor is talking about flat-footed flamingos, but you have no idea what else he is talking about. Your mental question at this point should be: "How is he trying to organize the information on this topic?" Table 7–2 illustrates that all information can be placed into one of six patterns of organization:

1. Definition/example.
2. Chronological (time) order.
3. Simple list.
4. Cause/effect.
5. Comparison/contrast.
6. Problem/solution.

TABLE 7–2 Patterns of Organization

Pattern	*Description*	*Example*
Definition (description, example)	A topic is explained by means of examples, a definition, or a description.	Sociology is the study of. . . A good thinker is one who. . . An example of good thinking is. . .
Chronological (time) order	Information about a topic is listed in a specific sequence or order.	To run this computer program, you must first . . ., next. . ., then. . .
Simple list	Information about a topic is listed and can be in any order.	A successful job search should include regular time devoted to your search, a well-prepared résumé, references, . . .
Cause/effect	Information about a topic shows what happened and why.	Filing a late tax return could result in the following penalties:. . .
Comparison/contrast	Similarities and differences of topics are identified.	While an annuity is usually purchased for retirement benefits, life insurance is purchased to protect dependents.
Problem/solution	Problem-solving procedures and solutions are described.	If you can't find a file on your computer, you can do the following: . . .

By identifying how the information is being organized or categorized, you can often zero in on what is being said. In the flamingo example, you might ask, "Is he (1) defining something about flamingos, (2) putting the flamingo information in a specific order, (3) simply listing things about flamingos, (4) showing a cause or effect of flamingos, (5) comparing flamingos with something else, or (6) describing a problem and solution about flamingos?"

Check Your Understanding. You should ask other questions as you take notes to help you check your understanding of the material and tie topics together for the big picture. Some examples are: "How does this fit in with what I learned before?" "Is this material in the text?" and "Do I understand this?"

Evaluate How Language Is Affecting Your Understanding. A speaker's use of words has an effect on your understanding of a lecture. If many new words are used in a lecture, you will have a hard time understanding what is being said. Because each area of study uses its own special vocabulary on a regular basis, be sure to note new terms that you hear in a lecture and make it a point to learn them. Suggestions on how to learn new words will be made in the "Recall" section of this chapter.

Words can also be used to persuade you to feel a certain way about a subject. For example, instead of saying how she feels about a subject, a lecturer may slip in emotional words or examples to try to make you feel as she does about it. This use of words to bring about strong feelings is called connotative language.

Suppose the example below came from a lecture on television violence. Read it, and circle words that may have been used to make you feel a certain way about the issue of regulating television violence.

TV Violence: A Senseless Crime

Each day thousands of crimes are committed in plain view of innocent children. From the ghettos to the suburbs, mere babies are exposed to bloody acts of death and destruction simply by turning on the television. What can you do to stop this insane outrage against our children? Write your state representatives and your local TV stations before it's too late.

How did this paragraph try to make you feel about violence on TV? What words did it use to make you feel that way? As you can see, it is important to be aware not only of what a lecturer says but also of how she says it. Asking the question "How is the speaker's language affecting my understanding?" during a lecture can help you identify a speaker's attempt to persuade you.

Process: Physical Strategies

The answers to all of the above mental questions can be found in the actual physical things you should do as you take notes. Figure 7–1 illustrates the observable strategies for taking notes. As you read through each explanation, refer to Figure 7–1 to find it illustrated.

Prepare Your Paper. Before you begin to take notes, write the class and instructor's name at the top of the page. Include the date and page number.

Make Notes on One Side of the Paper Only. If you take notes on the right half of your notebook, you can use the left half to add material from other sources to aid your understanding. Material that you missed during the lecture or information from the text that further explains something in the notes can be added across from its topic. Diagrams or copies of illustrations can be pasted across from related information in the notes.

Leave a 1″–2″ Margin. Draw a line down the left side of your paper in order to leave a 1″–2″ margin. This is your recall column, and you will use it to translate and store information after taking notes.

TABLE 7–3 Common Abbreviations for Lecture Notes

&, +	and	intro	introduction	amt	amount
=	equals	@	at	vs	versus, against
ex, eg	for example	wd	word	def	definition
#	number	co	company	Am	American
i.e.	that is	w/o	without	sp	spelling
p, pp	page, pages	>	greater than	subj	subject
contd	continued	<	less than	pt	point
impt	important	yr	year	concl	conclusion

Use the Lecturer's Words. In lecture-style classes, you will want to use the lecturer's words instead of trying to translate information into your words. Although this means taking notes at the memory level of the PYRAMID of learning, you usually do not have time to do much else. As soon as possible after the lecture, you will translate the information in the left-hand recall column.

If you are taking a discussion-style class, you may have time to think about what is being said before writing things down. In this type of class, you will want to record general topics of discussion and translate the points made about them into your own words.

Use Key Words. In order to be selective and organize as you take notes—and to save yourself from severe writer's cramp—do not try to write in complete sentences. Remember, you can neither learn it all nor write it all. By taking down only key words in the form of topics and subtopics, you can chunk information for easier storage. This takes practice. You will want to be sure that you take down enough to maintain the meaning of what was said.

Abbreviate. As you take more and more notes, you can develop your own system of abbreviations. Be sure that you use the same abbreviations each time you take notes. Examples of abbreviations that you might want to use are found in Table 7–3.

Indent Topics and Subtopics. If you tune into your mental strategies as you notetake, you will find yourself focusing on what the lecturer is talking about (the topic) and what he or she is saying about it (the subtopics and examples). To write this down in a selective and organized way, the following outline-style format could be used:

Major heading
—Topic
  —Subtopic
  —Subtopic
    —Example

Figure 7–1A
Left side of notebook

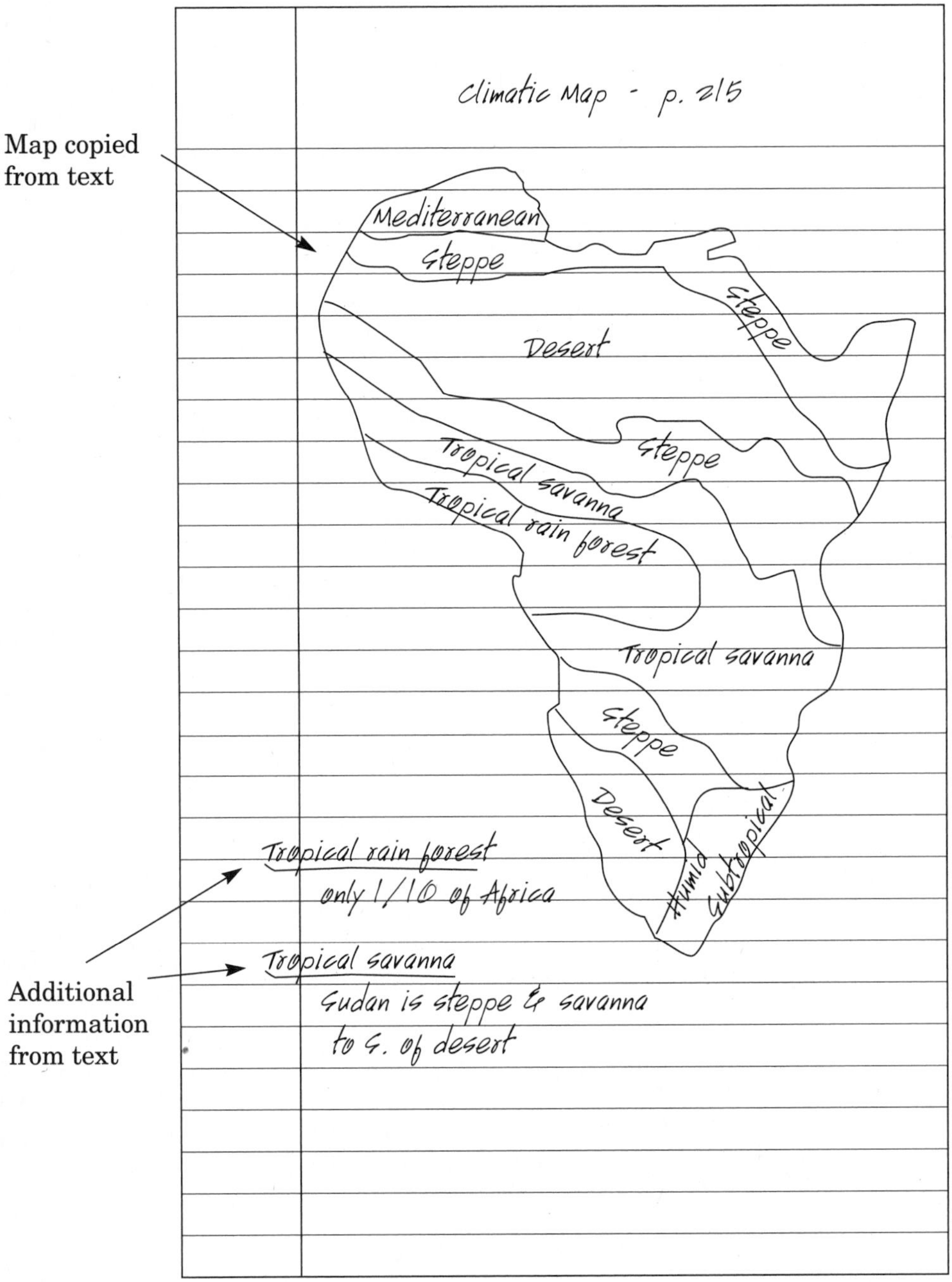
Climatic Map - p. 215
Map copied from text
Mediterranean
Steppe
Steppe
Desert
Tropical savanna
Steppe
Tropical rain forest
Tropical savanna
Steppe
Desert
Humid Subtropical
Tropical rain forest
only 1/10 of Africa
Tropical savanna
Sudan is steppe & savanna
to S. of desert
Additional information from text

FIGURE 7-1B
Right side of notebook

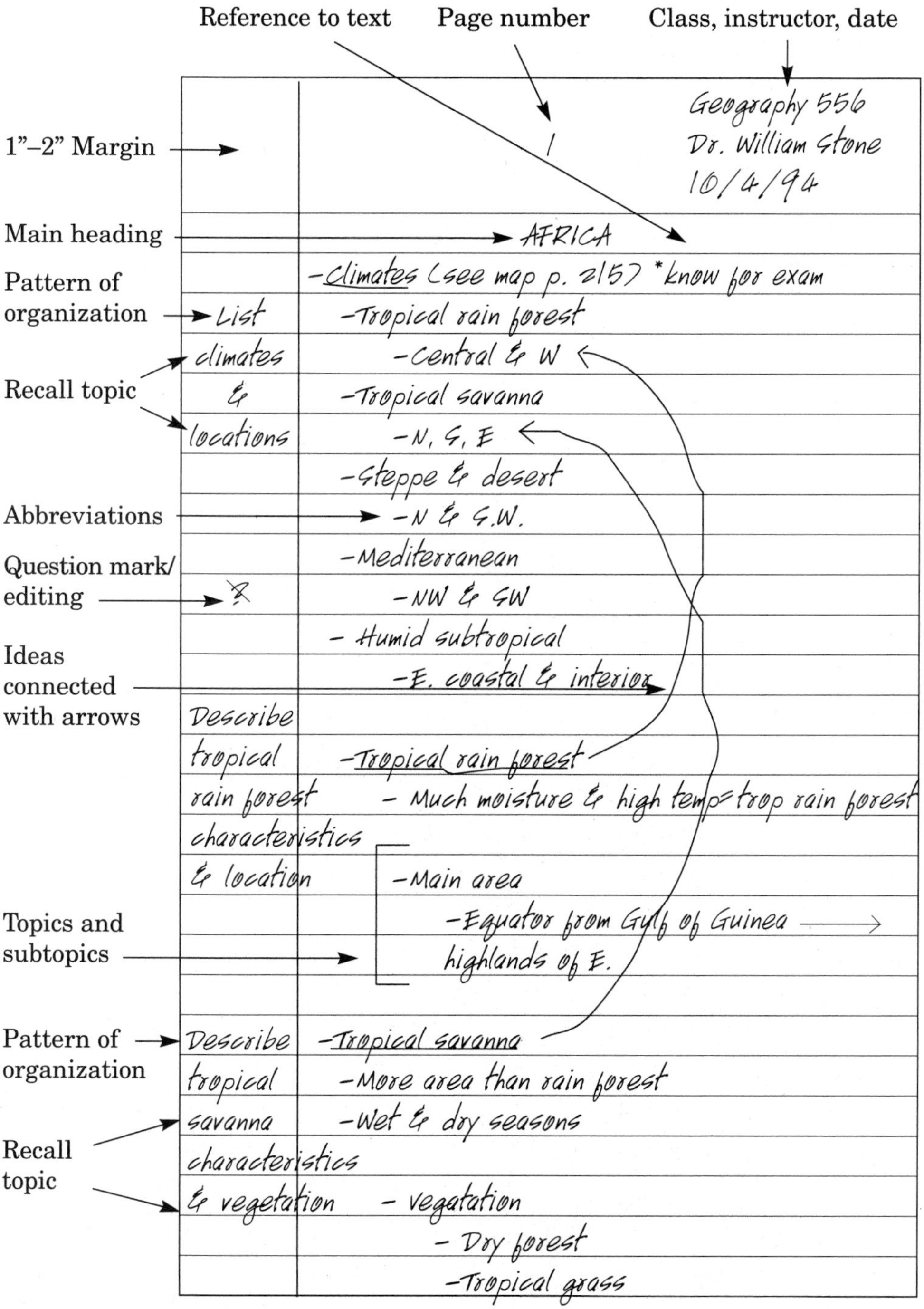

Reference to text
Page number
Class, instructor, date
Geography 556
Dr. William Stone
10/4/94
1
1"–2" Margin
Main heading
AFRICA
Pattern of organization
-Climates (see map p. 215) *know for exam
List
-Tropical rain forest
climates
-Central & W
Recall topic
&
-Tropical savanna
locations
-N, S, E
-Steppe & desert
Abbreviations
-N & S.W.
-Mediterranean
Question mark/ editing
?
-NW & SW
- Humid subtropical
Ideas connected with arrows
-E. coastal & interior
Describe tropical rain forest characteristics & location
-Tropical rain forest
- Much moisture & high temp = trop rain forest
-Main area
Topics and subtopics
-Equator from Gulf of Guinea
highlands of E.
Pattern of organization
Describe tropical savanna characteristics & vegetation
-Tropical savanna
-More area than rain forest
Recall topic
-Wet & dry seasons
- vegatation
- Dry forest
-Tropical grass

Major heading
—Topic
—Subtopic
—Subtopic
—Topic
—Subtopic
—Example

Notice that major headings are selected and labeled, giving the material a file name so that you can later recall how and where you stored it. Information is chunked and organized on the basis of important ideas and less important ideas. This enables you to see, at a glance, how ideas tie together and relate to one another. If information is stored in this way, remembering one part or subtopic could trigger recall of the whole.

Use the major heading, topics, subtopics, and example listed below to practice the outline-style or indented format. Write each item on the proper line.

Places to work	Factories	Insurance office
Steel mill	Law office	Auto plant
Offices	Auto body assembly	Textile plant

Major heading: ____________________
Topic: Factories
Subtopic: ____________________
Subtopic: ____________________
Subtopic: Auto plant
Example: ____________________
Topic: ____________________
Subtopic: ____________________
Subtopic: ____________________

Use Coping Strategies when Lost. Sometimes you may find yourself lost and unable to immediately figure out a major heading or subheading. Don't panic! There are several strategies you can use to help you keep focused when this happens. If you can't figure out the major heading, one way to cope is to skip a space and fill it in later. After taking down several subtopics, you can sometimes figure out what the major heading should be.

If you get lost and can't figure out topics and subtopics, take down the information in any form and leave space for later corrections. Anytime you have difficulty with your notes, place a question mark in the recall column where you'll be sure to see it after class. Then, before you leave the room, ask your instructor or a classmate for the information.

If your instructor uses words that are new to you, take a guess about how to spell them. Circle new terms, and put question marks in the margin beside them. You can ask your instructor or a classmate about the words or look them up in your text or dictionary later. After correcting any areas of difficulty, cross out the question marks in the margin.

If you have an instructor who leaps from one topic to another and then goes back to the first one, use arrows to connect ideas instead of trying to recopy former information. If she uses a diagram that you know is in your text, instead of taking the time to draw it, take notes on what is being said. Then copy the diagram on the page opposite your notes after class.

Sharing Your Ideas

To practice selecting information and organizing it into the outline-style form that you will use for notetaking, read the paragraph below as a class and discuss how to fill in the blank lines with the proper information. Remember to abbreviate and to use key words instead of complete sentences.

Who Is the Real Teacher?

The real teacher of life is not experience. It's not overheard conversations or lines from songs or what you read in books (or the people who wrote the books).

The real teacher is you. You're the one who must decide, of all that comes your way, what is true and what is not, what applies to you and what does not, what you learn now and what you promise yourself you'll learn later.

John-Roger and Peter McWilliams
Life 101

Who Is the Real Teacher?

____

not experience

____

____

____

____

real teacher = you

____

what's not

____

____

____

______________________ ■

Recall: Mental and Physical Strategies

Many students end the notetaking process when class is over. Actually, most learning or storage must take place after class. Making the physical change in the brain that is necessary to store information takes time—time that you don't have during a lecture. After class is the time to take to a higher level of understanding the material you copied at the memory level and to learn in a manner that fits your learning style. Read through the Learning Suggestions in Chapter 4 to help you recall methods appropriate to your style of learning.

All the general principles of memory can be applied at this stage. When you sit down to go over your notes, you must:

1. Establish a purpose.
2. Eliminate distractors.
3. Activate prior knowledge.

As you store the information in your notes, you may:

1. Immediately review.
2. Associate and label.
3. Learn actively.
4. Select and organize.
5. Chunk it.
6. Use mnemonics when appropriate.
7. Get the big picture.
8. Distribute practice.

If you apply all of these principles effectively, in order to recall the material from your notes you will be able to:

1. Visualize.
2. Use high-level retrieval cues.
3. Retrace your steps.

Recall: Mental Strategies

After notetaking is the time to mentally reflect on the entire lecture. You now have the chance to look at and make sense of all that was presented. Use the following suggestions to help you.

Get the Big Picture. Suppose you are in your study area, ready to go over your notes. You have determined the purpose for learning the material, and you are away from things that distract you. To get the big picture and to activate memory traces, you should ask yourself, "What was covered today?" "What was it all supposed to mean?" and "What were the topics?" If you can recall the general topic of the lecture and think about how the subtopics were used to explain it, you can begin to see how the entire lecture fitted together.

Locate Areas of Difficulty. By asking yourself "What did I not understand?" you will be identifying areas in your notes on which question marks appear so that you can give those areas further attention.

Connect to What You Know. The question "How does this relate to previous material?" will cause you to associate or tie new information into already established memory strands, thus making the new information easier to store and recall.

Form an Opinion. By asking "Do I agree or disagree with the material?" and "Why?" you will be using evaluation, the highest level of the PYRAMID. To do this, you will have to analyze the material and to compare it with what you already know. You will also have to think in an organized, effective way, looking at the material from all sides as you form your opinion.

Recall: Physical Strategies

After taking notes, you must store the information they contain. The suggestions below will help you to further organize your notes and to store their content so that it can be remembered for future use.

Use Immediate Review. In Chapter 4, memory was compared to a path across a field that begins to fade when it is not used. By the time you finish class and go home, the memory traces you made during a lecture have already faded dramatically. As a matter of fact, your level of recall may drop below 50 percent in that short period. Therefore, you must edit and study your notes as soon as possible after each lecture.

Edit Problem Areas. Editing your notes means going through them and fixing places where there were problems. You already have these places labeled with question marks in the margin, so you shouldn't have to reread every page to find them. You will also correct spelling errors; fill in headings, topics, or subtopics that you missed; and perhaps check out text information that was referred to during the lecture.

As you edit, look up new words and make an effort to learn them. Figure 7–2 illustrates a vocabulary list and a vocabulary study card. You may want to keep a special vocabulary list or a special stack of vocabulary cards for each of your classes. Notice that both the list and the card in Figure 7–2 contain the word being defined, a sentence demonstrating itsuse, a definition, and a cue for remembering the word through association. Visual learners should use illustrations as memory cues whenever possible.

Add Recall Topics and High-Level Retrieval Cues. After all of your corrections have been made, it's time to understand exactly what your notes are saying. This is the thinking part of the notetaking process because it takes the information in your notes from the memory stage to higher levels of the PYRAMID. To do this, read through the topics and subtopics under each heading and choose a word or short phrase that describes the information. Write this recall topic in the margin you drew on the left-hand side of your page. It will serve as a label that you can use to file the information in your brain.

Remember that if your label is too general, you may have difficulty in finding the information later. You need a way of telling your brain exactly what you have to know about the recall topic. The best way to do this is to analyze the topics and subtopics and decide which pattern of organization they incorporate: (1) definition, (2) chronological order, (3) simple list, (4) cause/effect, (5) comparison/contrast, or (6) problem/solution. You must analyze what your notes are saying before you can add a pattern of organization to the recall topics in the margin. By doing this, you will be able to better understand and store your notes and you will know exactly what you must recall about them.

Tie Together Text and Notes. If any topic in your notes can be further explained by information in the text, provide that information in the left-hand side of your notebook. Write additional notes and copy maps, diagrams, or charts beside the material they describe.

Use Recalls for Distributed Practice. Because strong memory traces are built through repeated practice, you should review your recall topics daily. Cover your notes, and use your recall topics and retrieval cues to question yourself. Be sure to translate the information from your notes into your own words. As they recall, auditory learners may want to recite out

FIGURE 7–2

Vocabulary list and vocabulary card

Word	Sentence	Meaning	Memory Cue
Trademark	A trademark is often used when marketing a product.	A word, letter or symbol to show ownership of a product.	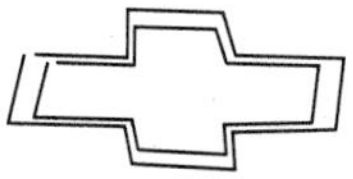 Trademark
Tariff	The product from Japan had a tariff levied on it.	A tax on imported goods.	 Tariff
Gift tax	When Fred was given Grandpa's house, a gift tax was paid.	A tax on large amounts of property given away.	 Gift tax

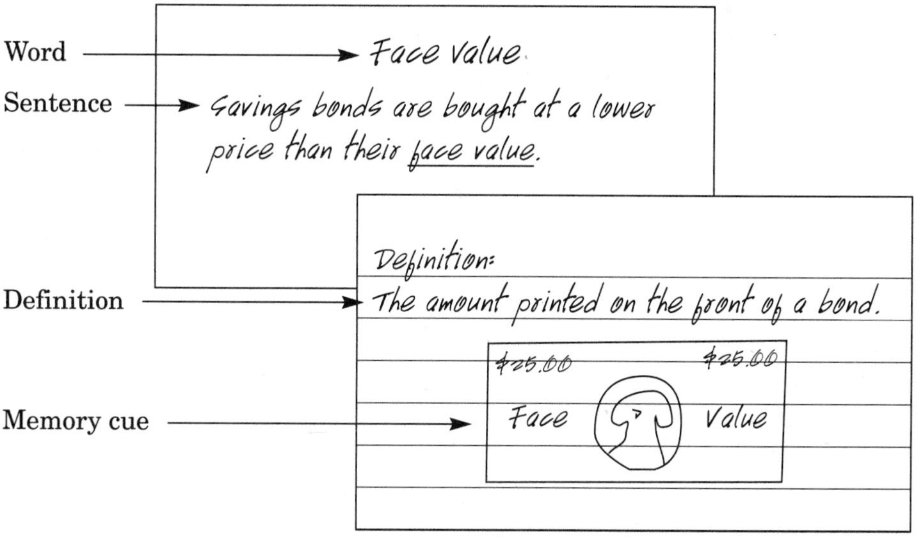

FIGURE 7–3
Study card

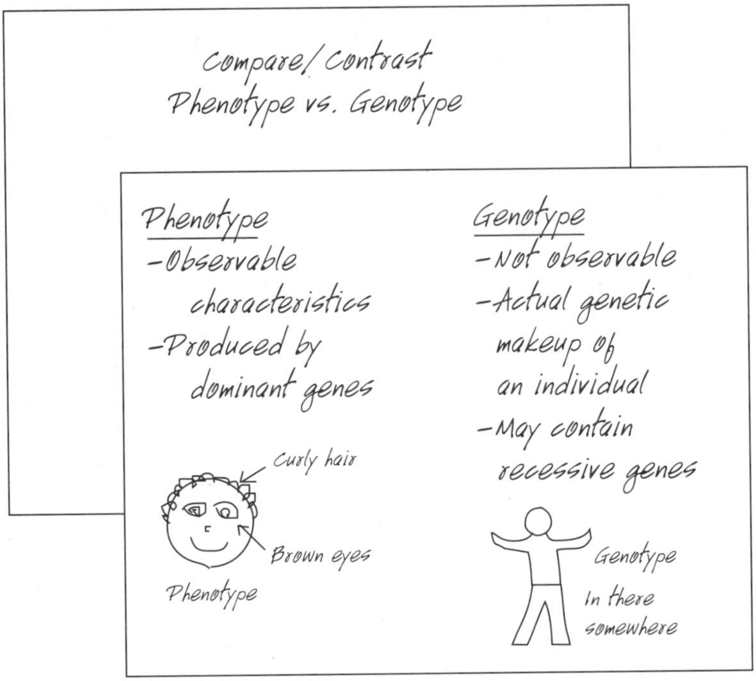

loud, visual learners may want to write or draw, and kinesthetic learners may want to move about.

Any topic that you have difficulty in recalling after several attempts should be put on a study card that can be carried around for additional practice. Figure 7–3 illustrates a study card with a recall topic and a retrieval cue on the front and material from notes on the back. Again, be sure to translate the material into your own words or to interpret it by making diagrams or pictures.

Sharing Your Ideas

Selecting effective recall topics and retrieval cues takes practice but is well worth the effort. To gain experience in using this skill, work together to complete the following activity:

1. Select a partner who is in one of your other classes and has a set of class notes similar to yours. If this is not possible, use notes from two different classes.
2. Use a recent set of notes, and draw a 1″–2″ line down the left side of your paper.

3. Together with your partner, try to label each topic in your notes with a recall topic and a retrieval cue.
4. Use Table 7–2 to help you with your retrieval cues. ■

Putting It All Together

To get the most out of each class you attend, you must prepare to learn, process as you are learning, and recall what you learned. During each of these three stages, you should monitor both the physical activities and the mental activities you perform so that you can be aware of what you're doing, how you're doing it, why you're doing it, and whether you're doing it correctly. The PPR Notetaking System contains both mental and physical strategies that you can use at each stage of the notetaking process.

As you mentally prepare to take notes, you must focus on the topic, activate what you already know, and determine your purpose for learning. You must physically prepare for a lecture by surveying or reading before class, reviewing previous notes, and having all the necessary materials ready.

As a lecture is being given, you should listen for topics and subtopics, identify the organizational pattern of the topic, and monitor your understanding throughout the lecture. Physically, during a lecture you should prepare your paper, write on the right-hand side only, leave a 1″–2″ margin, use the lecturer's key words, abbreviate, indent topics and subtopics, and use coping strategies if you get lost.

After a lecture you should think about how the topics and subtopics fitted together, locate areas of difficulty, relate the new information to what you already know, and form an opinion. Physically, you should edit your notes as soon as possible, write recall topics and retrieval cues in the margin, and recite and review these recalls on a regular basis.

Making the Connection

Check your understanding of the concepts presented in this chapter by completing the following activity. If you are unable to recall information in a particular area, go back and review that material before completing the rest of the exercises in this section.

1. Write one or two sentences to summarize what you recall about each of the following topics:

   The stages of the PPR System ______________________________

   ____

   ____

   Mental strategies for preparing to take notes ________________

   ____

   ____

   Physical strategies for preparing to take notes _______________

   ____

   ____

   Mental strategies while taking notes _______________________

   ____

   ____

   Physical strategies while taking notes ______________________

   ____

   ____

   Mental strategies after notetaking _________________________

   ____

   ____

   Physical strategies after notetaking ________________________

   ____

   ____

2. List one new idea you've gained about notetaking as a result of this chapter. ____

   ____

3. Describe one change you plan to make before notetaking, one change you plan to make during notetaking, and one change you plan to make after notetaking. ______________________________

Thinking It Through

Read the following passage, and then answer the questions by applying what you've learned about notetaking.

> Janice is a college student who is having difficulty in taking notes. She sits with her friends during class and tries to take down every word her instructor says. Sometimes her instructor goes too fast and she gets lost. When this happens, she panics, remains lost until the instructor pauses, or asks a friend. When she looks at a friend's notes, she tends to fall even further behind.
>
> Sometimes Janice reads her notes after class. Often she does not read them until the night before a test, and then she reads them several times. She has not been happy with her test results, and she feels that her problem is with notetaking.

1. Based on information in the passage, what do you see as Janice's specific problem(s)? ______________________________

2. By using knowledge you already have, asking others, and possibly doing a bit of research, list as many solutions to Janice's problems as you can. ______________________________

3. List the pros and cons for *each* of these solutions from Janice's point of view. ____

4. Select the solution that appears to be the best in terms of pros and cons. List the steps necessary to carry out this solution. Be sure to describe the details, such as who, what, when, where, and how.

Applying Your Skills 1 *Notetaking Questionnaire*

Instructions: Use the following questionnaire to evaluate your current notetaking strategies. Circle the letter that best answers the corresponding question.

A = Always S = Sometimes N = Never

Before Notetaking:

1. I focus on the topic of the lecture by reading assignments before class. A S N

2. I think about the topic before class and ask myself what I already know. A S N
3. I set my purpose for learning before the lecture by thinking about the instructor's rate, the type of exam she gives, and whether I need to recall facts or ideas. A S N
4. As I wait for class to begin, I review my recall topics and retrieval cues from previous classes. A S N
5. I organize my notes in a three-ring binder. A S N
6. I prepare my paper with the date, instructor, class, and page number. A S N

While Notetaking:

1. I use only the right side of my paper for notetaking. A S N
2. I draw a 1″–2″ margin down the left side of my paper. A S N
3. I listen for topics and subtopics and try to indent as I record my notes. A S N
4. For most classes, I use the lecturer's words rather than my own. A S N
5. I abbreviate and use only key words as much as possible. A S N
6. When I get lost or have difficulty in taking notes, I skip spaces and put a question mark in the margin. A S N
7. I use arrows to connect ideas. A S N
8. Rather than trying to draw charts or diagrams that my instructor uses from our text, I refer to the page number in my notes. A S N
9. As I am taking notes, I try to think about how all the topics tie together. A S N
10. If I am having difficulty in understanding what is being said about the topic, I try to determine its organizational pattern. A S N

After Notetaking:

1. I try to clear up notetaking problems with my instructor or classmates before I leave the room.	A	S	N
2. I try to put the entire lecture together in my mind as I leave the room.	A	S	N
3. As I think about the lecture, I tie new information into what I already know.	A	S	N
4. I ask myself whether I agree or disagree with the information given in the lecture and determine why.	A	S	N
5. I edit or fix areas with question marks as soon as possible after class.	A	S	N
6. I add recall topics and retrieval cues as soon as possible after class.	A	S	N
7. I tie my text and notes together by using the left-hand side of my notebook for additional notes or charts from my text.	A	S	N
8. I study my recalls on a daily basis.	A	S	N
9. As I study my recalls, I recite information in my own words.	A	S	N
10. I use study cards for material that needs extra practice.	A	S	N

Look over the results of your notetaking questionnaire. Count the A, S, and N responses for each section, and enter those totals below.

Before Notetaking	*While Notetaking*	*After Notetaking*
A = ________	A = ________	A = ________
S = ________	S = ________	S = ________
N = ________	N = ________	N = ________

More than four S or N responses may indicate an area of weakness in your notetaking. Highlight the items in the questionnaire receiving S or N. Plan to include those items as a regular part of your notetaking system.

Applying Your Skills 2 *Notetaking Evaluation*

Instructions: Use the chart below to monitor your progress as you improve your notetaking skills. Exchange your chart and a set of your notes with those of another class member. Evaluate each other's notes, and give them a total score. Mark that score on the progress chart at the end of this activity. Try to exchange and evaluate notes with a different classmate on a weekly basis.

Rating Scale

1 = Improvement needed
2 = Fair
3 = Average
4 = Good
5 = Outstanding

Notetaking Evaluation Record

Three-ring binder				
Page heading (number, dates, etc.)				
Use of right side only				
1″–2″ margin				
Use of key words				
Use of abbreviations				
Use of main headings				
Use of topics				
Use of subtopics				
Indenting topics and subtopics				
Use of question marks in margin				
Use of arrows				
Space for editing				
References to text				
Recall topics				
Retrieval cues				
Total				
Evaluator/Date				

After your notes have been evaluated, mark your total score on the following chart by filling in the bars up to the score you received. To chart your progress, use a different column each time you have your notes evaluated.

Progress Chart

80				
75				
70				
65				
60				
55				
50				
45				
40				
35				
30				
25				
20				
15				
10				
5				
0				
Date				

Applying Your Skills 3 *Lecture Goal-Setting Sheet*

Instructions: Select a lecture that you would like to use in order to practice your best notetaking behaviors. Use the steps below before, while, and after notetaking.

Class: ____

Step 1: Before Notetaking

Establish your purpose. Answer the following questions as a way of using mental strategies before notetaking.

1. What will the lecture cover? ______________________________
   ____
   ____
2. What do I already know? ______________________________
   ____
   ____
   ____
3. What new terms may be presented? ______________________________
   ____
   ____
   ____
4. What new ideas may be presented? ______________________________
   ____
   ____
   ____

Step 2: While Notetaking

Set goals for improving your notes. Circle the number of each goal that you would like to accomplish while taking notes. Attend the lecture, and take notes according to your goals.

1. I plan to head my paper with page numbers, dates, and the class name.
2. I plan to draw a 1″–2″ margin on the left of my paper.
3. I plan to indent topics and subtopics.

4. I plan to use the lecturer's key words.
5. I plan to abbreviate.
6. I plan to use arrows when necessary.
7. I plan to use question marks in the margin to identify unclear areas.
8. I plan to edit my notes as soon as possible.
9. I plan to use recall organizers and retrieval cues.
10. Other (describe goal).

Step 3: After Notetaking

Complete the chart below by listing each goal that you set above and evaluating how well you think you met that goal.

Number	*Goal*	*Evaluation*

Applying Your Skills 4 *Using Your Resources*

Instructions: To know where to "radio for help," you will be asked to visit various school resources throughout this text. Keep this information so that you can refer to it when you are in need of help outside the classroom.

Complete the information below after touring your school's Student Services Office.

Location: ______________________________

Hours of operation: ______________________________

Contact person: ______________________________

Phone: ______________________________

Services offered:

____

____

____

____

Personal comments:

Briefly discuss how you could use this resource.

____

____

____

____

C H A P T E R

8 The PPR Reading System

Apply the principles of thinking and learning to read effectively.

Chapter Goals

After you read this chapter, you will be able to:

- Compare and contrast college reading, high school reading, and pleasure reading.
- Use mental and physical strategies for preparing to read.
- Use mental and physical strategies for processing information as you read.
- Use mental and physical strategies for recalling information after you read.
- Apply reading strategies that require the use of higher levels on the PYRAMID of Learning.
- Select methods for reading that are appropriate to your learning style.

Can you remember, as a child, devising a painless way to eat your peas? The best way to eat peas without tasting them was to swallow them whole and quickly forget about the entire process, lest you gag.

In the same way, many students have devised a painless way to read college texts. They mindlessly open a text, read its words without thinking about them, then close the text and quickly forget about the entire process, lest they gag.

The problem is that the content of texts, unlike that of peas, must be "savored" to be digested. This "savoring" of text content is the thinking part of text reading. If you often find yourself looking at words but not really understanding them, you need to apply your knowledge of thinking, memory, and learning to the reading process. Through the PPR Reading System, this chapter will give you strategies to help you focus your attention before you read, organize and store information as you read, and recall what you read. Mental strategies will increase your awareness of what you're reading, how you're reading it, why you're reading it, and what you think about it. Physical strategies will suggest ways of physically preparing for, organizing, and storing information as you read. By applying the three stages of memory to the reading process, not only will you be able to painlessly digest what you read, but you will perhaps even begin to enjoy the reading process.

Textbook Reading

Why does textbook reading seem so difficult, boring, and time consuming? Because it is. College reading, unlike reading in high school or reading for pleasure, is difficult because it is full of facts. It is boring if you do not have a background or an interest in the subject. And it is definitely time consuming because there is a lot of it to do.

Table 8–1 compares college textbook reading with high school reading and reading for pleasure. Notice the differences in content, purpose, rate, interest, and background. As you read through Table 8–1, think about the changes you should make in your present reading techniques to account for these differences.

TABLE 8–1 College Reading versus High School Reading and Pleasure Reading

	College Reading	*High School Reading*	*Pleasure Reading*
Content	Many new words, ideas, and facts to select and remember on your own.	Several new words, ideas, and facts that will be reviewed and learned in class.	Few new words, ideas, or facts. No learning required.
Purpose	To organize and store information at high levels for recall on tests and use on the job.	To gain general knowledge of facts presented in class.	To enjoy the content.
Rate	Determined by your ability to organize and store information: slow for difficult ideas, moderate for other content.	Moderate. Ideas will be organized by teacher.	Fast. No need to organize and store facts.
Interest	Often very little. You are responsible for creating your own interest.	Teacher will discuss reading and attempt to create interest.	High. Material selected on the basis of interest.
Background	Often very little. You are responsible for creating your own background.	Teacher will attempt to create background before you read.	High. Material selected in areas of experience.

Content

Textbook reading differs from other types of reading because it is fact filled. Each paragraph of a textbook may contain many new and important facts and ideas. Your job is not only to read these facts and ideas but also to select those you feel you need to organize and store for later recall.

Textbook reading also differs from other types of reading in the amount and type of new vocabulary words presented. You must learn to speak the language of each course that you take. There will be a special, technical vocabulary in each textbook that you read. Your instructors may not take the time to drill you on this vocabulary, but they will use it in class and they will expect you to understand it.

Purpose

In high school, you could always count on your teacher to go over the reading material assigned and tell you which facts needed to be learned. Now, your instructors may not want to take the time to go over something that you can get on your own. Your reading, then, is an addition to the content of lectures rather than a restatement of that content. It is your job to select what's important and decide how to organize and store it for later use.

Textbook reading requires you to have higher levels of understanding than you may have had in high school. You must not only select and store facts from your reading—you must also translate, interpret, apply, analyze, synthesize, and evaluate ideas.

Rate

How quickly or slowly you read a college text will be determined by your ability to organize and store the material it contains. If the ideas in the text are new, it will take more time to file them in your memory because you will be making completely new memory traces. If you have already established memory traces and you have activated them, then it will take less time to tie new material into the old.

Interest

Lack of interest is a major problem when you are trying to read a textbook. Unless there is interest, it is difficult to focus your attention. If your attention is not focused, you cannot organize and store content. And if you do not organize and store as you read, you'll have nothing to show for your efforts when you're done. It is therefore important to find ways of developing an active mind before you read a textbook. This chapter will provide methods for preparing to read that will help you establish an interest before you read.

Background

Think about the last time you tried to read about a new topic. Did the material seem to be written in another language? This was because you had nothing with which to relate. Since there were no memory traces to tie into, you had to either make new ones or not store the material at all.

Much of what you learn in college will be new to you. You must, then, take the time to build new memory traces or background. You can do this by reading your textbooks at a slower pace, getting additional information from other books, talking about the material with your instructor or classmates, or even obtaining a tutor.

PPR Reading

Now that you know how college reading differs from other types of reading, you can see why your approach to it needs to differ as well. College reading contains many facts and ideas that you must select, organize, and store at higher levels. As a result, you must vary your reading rate, create an interest, and overcome a lack of background. You cannot read a college text as you would read a high school text or as you would read a book for pleasure. The system you use must give you the proper tools for the job.

The PPR Reading System, illustrated in Table 8–2, contains mental and physical methods for preparing to read, processing as you read, and recalling what you have read. Within the system are the tools you need to help you deal with the task of textbook reading. While reading the descriptions of the various parts of the PPR Reading System, refer to Table 8–2.

Prepare: Mental and Physical Strategies

When you sit down to read a text, your first order of business is to get focused on the task. Remember that to do that you must:

- Eliminate distractors by reading in your study area.
- Establish your purpose by thinking about the type of exam you will be taking.
- Activate what you already know about the topic.
- Determine whether you have enough background in the topic.
- Create an interest in the topic.
- Determine how difficult the material will be.
- Set the reading rate necessary for good storage.

Table 8–2 PPR Reading System

Stages	*Mental Strategies*	*Physical Strategies*
Before reading: *Prepare*	*Ask yourself:* • What do I already know? • Do I need more information? • What is my purpose? • What strategies will best help me remember? • How full of facts is the material? • What rate will I use? • How is the material organized?	• Survey text. • Survey chapter. • Make mini outline.

While reading:
Process
	Ask yourself:
	• What is the author saying?
	• What do I think about this information?
	• How is the author influencing my thinking?
	  • Credentials
	  • Language
	  • Evidence
	  • Reasoning
	• How can I organize this material in order to store it?
		Read paragraph or section:
		• Write topic.
		• Write topic/organizational pattern.
		• Write topic/organizational pattern and underline.
		• Write topic/organizational pattern, underline, and:
		  • Summarize.
		  • Map.
		  • Chart.
		Mark each passage according to your ability to organize and store the material.

After reading:
Recall
	Ask yourself:
	• What was this chapter about?
	• What were the headings and subheadings?
	• How does this material relate to what I already know?
	• What did I not understand?
	• What do I need to learn?
		• Review/recite from mini outline.
		• Review/recite topics and organizational patterns in text margins.
		• Create study aids:
		  • Maps
		  • Charts
		  • Study cards

By preparing to read in this manner, you will be able to:

- Focus your attention on the material in your text.
- Figure out what you need to know and how you're going to learn it.
- Get the proper memory strands ready to tie in new information.

The PPR Reading System presented below will help you prepare both mentally and physically for the task of college reading.

Prepare: Mental Strategies

As you prepare to read a text you must think about using your learning style to help you stay focused. If you are an auditory learner, you should have a relatively quiet place where you can feel free to read and recite out loud if necessary. As a visual learner you should be in an area away from anything that you might be interested in watching such as people, television, or the view from your window. If you learn best visually, prepare to think in pictures as you read, focus on the visuals in your text, and draw your own pictures to help you stay focused. If you are kinesthetic you need to set a specific goal for how much you want to cover in a specific time period. Think about how long you can concentrate and set a timer for that time period or decide upon a certain number of pages to read. As a kinesthetic learner you need to be active as you read. You may want to gesture with your hands, talk out loud, act out parts of your text, or read and then walk about and recite what you remember.

Thinking about your learning style before you read can help you use the following mental strategies to your advantage.

Focus on the Topic, and Activate Prior Knowledge. Before you begin to read, you must focus on the topic. This will activate your memory strands for easier learning and help you create an interest in the topic. By asking the question "What do I already know about the topic of this chapter?" you can begin thinking about how this topic can relate to you now and in the future.

Turn to a reading assignment in one of your textbooks. Use this assignment for the short activities throughout this chapter. Write the chapter title below. List what you already know about this topic.

Chapter title: ____

What I know about this topic: ______________________________

____

____

Examine Your Background. Once you've determined the subject of the material you are about to read, you must ask yourself, "Do I need more information on this subject in order to understand it?" If the subject is completely new to you, you must begin to build a background and construct some memory traces on the subject. Otherwise, what you read will have nothing to tie into and you will not be able to store it in your memory.

Methods you can use to build background on the subject are: reading other sources such as an easier, more basic book on the subject or an encyclopedia; talking to classmates about their knowledge of the subject; asking the instructor for ways to better your understanding of the subject; and getting a tutor. A more basic course may be offered on the same subject that can help you establish a better foundation for learning.

Set Your Purpose. You need to determine your purpose for reading before you begin to read so that you know exactly how you want to approach the material. By asking "What is my purpose?" you're making yourself think about the type of learning necessary. You will be asking yourself whether you need to select and learn facts or select and understand ideas. Once you've answered this question, you will need to ask yourself, "What strategy or method can I use as I read to help me learn in this way?"

Continue to use your textbook reading assignment to answer these questions:

What must I learn from this assignment? ______________________________

____

How will I be tested? ____

____

Determine the Difficulty of the Material. Before you begin reading, you should check the material to see if it contains many facts. By asking the question "How full of facts is this material?" you can decide how quickly or slowly you'll be able to read and still use proper methods for organizing and storing the content.

Choose Your Reading Rate. The rate you use to read will change according to your purpose, your interest, your background, and the difficulty of the material. If the material is fact filled, you will need to use a slower reading rate so that you can select, organize, and store important information as you read. If you lack interest or background in the subject, you will need to take more time and use more active storage techniques as you read. If your instructor tells you to read in order to gain a general background knowledge of the subject, you will not have to select and learn minor details, but will only have to focus on major ideas.

Look through your textbook reading assignment, and answer the following questions:

How difficult will this material be for me? Why? ____________________

____

At what rate will I read this material? Why? ________________________

____

Get the Big Picture. Some textbook chapters are so long that you may get lost along the way and have no idea where you are. To give yourself direction, you should ask, "How is this chapter organized?" Getting an overview of all the main headings and subheadings of a chapter before you begin to read is like seeing your entire journey mapped out in front of you. You will be able to see where you're going, what you're going to be reading about, and how it all fits together.

Prepare: Physical Strategies

Suppose you were in a plane that crashed in the middle of a desert in a foreign country. If you had no idea where you were, you really couldn't make good decisions about which way to go to find help. When you buy a textbook and begin to use it without knowing how it is set up, you're putting yourself in a similar situation. You can't make informed decisions about how to use a book until you know what's in it.

Survey the Textbook before Reading. Table 8–3 lists the parts of a textbook that you should examine before reading the first chapter. By doing this, you will be able to effectively use all of the information that the textbook has to offer.

Survey the Chapter before Reading. If you try to dive right into a book and begin reading without any preparation, you will probably have difficulty in remembering what you read. This happens because, for memory to occur, you must first focus your attention on the topic, then activate what you already know about it so that you can store new

TABLE 8-3 How to Survey a Textbook

Read	*Ask*
Title page	What is the title of this book? How might the book cover this subject? Who is the author? Is she an expert in this field? Have I read any other books by her? When was this book written? Is the information up-to-date?
Table of contents	How many chapters are there? What topics will be covered? How are the chapters related? How is each chapter organized?
Preface	Why was this book written? What can I expect to learn from it? What is the best way to use this book?
Appendix	Does this book have an appendix? What kind of information does the appendix contain?
Glossary and index	Does this book have a glossary and index? Where is each located?

TABLE 8–4 How to Survey a Chapter

Read	*Ask*
Title	What do I already know about this topic?
Introduction	Are there chapter objectives or goals? What am I supposed to learn? What will this chapter cover? How is it organized? What is its purpose?
Summary (and review questions)	What are the key ideas in this chapter? What do I need to learn?
Headings	What are the main headings/subheadings? What do I already know about them? What might I expect to learn from them?
Words (boldface and italics)	What do I already know about this word? Do I need to learn this word?
Visuals	What can I learn from this table, graph, diagram, or picture?

information on the activated memory strands. The best way to prepare your mind to receive new information before you read is to do a chapter survey. Table 8–4 lists the parts of a chapter survey. The mnemonic TISH WV can help you remember *T*itle, *I*ntro, *S*ummary, *H*eadings, *W*ords, and *V*isuals.

Make a Mini Outline. One final observable strategy that may help you get the big picture before you read a chapter is to make an outline consisting of the chapter's boldfaced topic and subtopic headings. Use an indented format to copy the headings provided in your text. Below is an example of a mini outline from a Business Communication chapter. Notice that this outline could be used as a guide while you read to let you know where you are and how all of the information fits together. It could also be used after reading to help you recite what you learned about each heading.

Developing Visual Aids

Planning visual Aids
  —Why business professionals use visual aids
  —The process of "visualizing" your text
Designing visual aids
  —Understanding the art of graphic design
  —Selecting the right visual aid for the job
Producing visual aids
  —Using a computer graphics system
  —Fitting visual aids into the text
  —Checking over the visual aids

Sharing Your Ideas

In pairs, make a mini outline of this chapter. Remember to use the main topic and subtopic headings and to indent. When all of the pairs have completed their outlines, compare outlines as a class. Discuss how you could use your outline to help you store and recall the content of this chapter. ■

Process: Mental and Physical Strategies

Once you've focused your attention, determined your purpose for reading, obtained information about the difficulty level and organization of the reading material, and activated what you already know, you're ready to begin the reading process.

The process of reading a textbook needs to be more than just organizing and storing facts. Because what you read is a combination of the author's information, thoughts, and beliefs and your own information, thoughts, and beliefs, reading requires proper thinking. Proper thinking means that you use good thinking behaviors to look at what you read from all sides. To do this, you must translate, interpret, apply, analyze, synthesize, and evaluate what you read.

Process: Mental Strategies

As you read, you must question both the author's point of view and your own. Errors in thinking may be made on both sides. Use the following suggestions to help you think clearly about what you read.

Analyze Point of View. To give words meaning when you read, you tie them into what you already know. This provides you with your own understanding of the material. But there is much more to understanding than looking at things from your point of view. Remember, reading is a combination of the author's information, thoughts, and beliefs and your own information, thoughts, and beliefs. To understand information from all sides, you must think about what you already know, how you feel about it, and why you feel that way. Then you need to consider what the author knows, thinks, and feels. First ask yourself, "What do I think about this information?" Then ask, "How is the author influencing my thinking?"

Question the Author's Credentials. One way an author can influence your thinking is to refer to his experience, ability, or background as reason for you to accept what he is saying. When you read, you must ask yourself whether the author's background or experience is reason enough to believe what he has to say. Read the following statements. Decide whether the persons making the statements have proper experience, ability, or background in the areas that they are addressing. Write why they are or are not qualified to make their statements.

1. "Having been a grandmother for 20 years, I feel qualified to say that letting gays in the military is wrong." ____________________

   ____

2. "After studying this matter extensively, I have come to the conclusion that men are smarter than women."

   ____

   ____

3. "As president of this university, I can honestly say that we are in good financial standing." ____________________

   ____

Question the Author's Use of Language. The way an author feels about a topic may not always be clearly stated. Sometimes an author may be trying to persuade you to share her views about a topic without your even knowing that this is being done. Instead of coming right out and stating her views on a topic, an author may use examples or words meant to make you react with emotion rather than reason.

Detailed examples or emotional scenes can be used to persuade you to feel a certain way. A mother who writes the following is using an emotional scene to win your strong support for her stand on drunken driving: "I remember my beautiful daughter when she was full of love and joy and life. I carry those memories in my heart and relive them daily. Those brief moments of pleasure also bring me much pain. I will never again see the beautiful child that I lost at the hands of a drunken driver." When you read about controversial subjects such as abortion, AIDS, homosexuality, and gun control, be aware of vivid descriptions that may be using emotion to make you feel strongly one way or another. Decide whether emotion is being used to further a good cause or a bad one; then use facts to help you decide on a position.

Sometimes authors use emotionally loaded words to try to make you feel as they do about an issue. Notice the strong words in the following example: "The use of poor, helpless little animals in inhumane laboratory experiments must be stopped." The words *poor, helpless, little,* and *inhumane* may have made you feel strongly opposed to the use of animals in lab experiments. A very different effect on your feelings is produced by reading this example: "The use of animals in lab experiments must be stopped." Emotionally loaded language that brings out strong feelings is called *connotative language.* Because such language can influence your ability to clearly see all sides of an issue, you must be able to recognize when it is being used.

An author can also use language to persuade you by comparing the qualities of two very different items to try to make you feel the same way about both. This is called *figurative analogy.* Suppose a politician is trying to persuade you to support his health care plan. To make you feel good about the security and individual concern of his plan, he may compare it to a symbol of security and individual concern—your mother. "My health care plan will make you feel as if you're in your mother's loving arms." His hopes are that you will shift the same feelings you have for your mother to his health care plan.

Sharing Your Ideas

Read the following passage as a class. As you read, circle and label examples of emotional scenes, connotative language, or figurative analogies. Discuss how the author is trying to make you feel about the teaching techniques of her daughter's coach.

> His narrowed eyes burn like hot little coals, and he screams through clenched teeth, his face thrust into hers. She's young and scared and stands with head hung, eyebrows raised in an expression that, while failing to acknowledge his accusations, is careful not to challenge them. Even in her obvious distress she's practiced and automatically leans back a bit from time to time to avoid the spray of spit he spews as he spells it out for her: she's stupid, lazy and worthless, and if she doesn't shape up someone else will soon be doing her job. ■

Rosemary Parker, "Learning by Intimidation," *Newsweek,* November 8, 1993

Question the Author's Evidence. An author can influence your thinking by the way she gives evidence to back up what she is saying. When evidence is used, decide whether it is fact or opinion. Remember that a fact is something that can be proved, whereas an opinion is a judgment. When analyzing statements that appear to be factual, be aware that some statements are presented as true when they really are not. Always try to check the facts with another source. In many instances, this could be your instructor. Authors sometimes try to stack the facts, that is, to give you many facts on one side of an argument and few on the other. Remember that, as a critical thinker, you must look at issues from all sides.

Two kinds of opinion are often used to try to persuade: expert opinion and uniform opinion. When an author gives an expert opinion, she is claiming that she is an expert and that she should therefore be believed. Check it out. If she is an expert in her field, her opinion has value;

otherwise, it does not. A uniform opinion, on the other hand, should never be believed. When an author says things like "*they* say" or "*everyone* agrees," he is using a uniform opinion. In this instance, there really is no expert.

When examples are given as evidence, be sure (1) that they are true, (2) that enough examples are given to prove the point, (3) that the examples given are up-to-date, and (4) that they present all sides. To prove his point that most violent crimes are committed by repeat offenders, James Wootton, founder and president of Safe Streets Alliance in Washington, D.C., begins an article with these examples: "Criminologist Marvin Wolfgang compiled arrest records for every male born—raised in Philadelphia—in 1945 and in 1958. Just 7 percent of each age group committed two-thirds of all violent crime." At this point in the article, can you be sure that these examples are true? Are enough examples given to prove Wootton's point? Are the examples given up-to-date? Do they present all sides? You would have to continue to read the article and look for more and up-to-date examples on both sides before coming to your own conclusion about violent crimes and repeat offenders.

Question the Author's Reasoning and Your Own. When an author is trying to make a point, he will sometimes make errors in critical thinking. The same thing can happen when you err in your thinking about material. It is difficult to look at all sides of an issue when the following obstacles to critical thinking exist: mine is better, resistance to change, the urge to conform, the need to save face, stereotyping, faulty common sense, oversimplification, hasty conclusions, or unwarranted assumptions. Be aware that these obstacles can occur both on your part and on the part of an author and that they can interfere with your ability to clearly see all sides of an issue.

Decide How to Organize and Store. In addition to critically thinking about the ideas presented in material as you read, you must also be able to recall information at higher levels for use on exams and on the job. Asking the question "Is this material organized enough for me to store?" will help you determine textbook-marking strategies. The methods you use to mark material will depend on your purpose and background and on the difficulty of the material. Various marking methods will be presented next as physical strategies.

Process: Physical Strategies

What method do you use to select important information in your textbooks as you read? Do you often find that even after rereading you have no idea what you read? The method you use to mark your text should help you organize and understand the material as you read so that it can be easily stored. The suggestions below will show you how this can be done.

Use the PYRAMID to Mark the Text. If you use a highlighter as your only source of organizing reading material, you are storing at the lowest level of the PYRAMID. By learning material at the memory level, you will be recalling information exactly as it is stated in your text. This involves no thinking and no understanding.

To translate, interpret, and analyze as you read, use the following method. Refer to Figure 8–1 to see the method illustrated.

How to mark a text:

1. Read a paragraph or short passage, but don't mark it.
2. Ask: "What is this material about?"
3. Write the topic in the margin of your text.
4. Ask: "Is this material organized enough for me to store?"
5. If you could learn the information in the paragraph by studying what you've written in the margin, go on to the next paragraph. If the information is not organized well enough to store at this point, take the following steps:

Step 1: Determine the pattern of organization being used in the paragraph (definition, time order, simple list, cause/effect, comparison/contrast, or problem/solution), and write it under the topic in the margin.

Ask: "Is this material organized enough for me to store?"

If yes: Stop.
If no: Proceed.

Step 2: Select key points about the topic and the organizational pattern by underlining them.

Ask: "Is this material organized enough for me to store?"

A way to test this is to look at the information you've underlined. If the underlined information has a lot of important facts to remember and you have underlined a lot, you probably need to organize the information further in another way.

If yes: Stop.
If no: Proceed.

Step 3: To help you better organize and store the information that you labeled and underlined, write a summary phrase in the margin or make a diagram, chart, or picture.

Marking the text in the above manner ensures that you will understand the material at higher levels and that you will label and mark it in a way that will help you organize and store it for future use. Figure 8–1

FIGURE 8–1

A Marked Text Passage

Database Searching

Databases in business:
- Define function
- List 2 ways to access

Computers offer the most advanced method of conducting secondary research. As you know, the capacity of computers to collect and retrieve information has expanded phenomenally over the past decade. Business research has been a primary beneficiary of these advances. Much information routinely recorded in printed form and accessed through directories, encyclopedias, bibliographies, indexes, and the like is now collected and stored in computer files as well. When these files, known collectively as databases, are in turn accessed by computer, the result is research that can be more extensive and complete than any conducted through traditional means. You may access databases in two ways: (1) through *online* information retrieval systems that use a terminal connected to a large mainframe computer usually through telephone lines, and (2) through CD-ROMs (compact disk—read only memory) that use microcomputers.

Online databases:
- Define
- List types

Online databases (those accessed through online searches) are usually produced by private information services and offer a variety of materials essential to business. For example, Dialog Information Systems (DIALOG) includes in its selection of more than 350 bases the *American Statistics Index*, the *Encyclopedia of Associations*, a number of Predicasts services *(PTS F&S Indexes, International Forecasts,* and *Prompt),* and *Standard & Poor's News*. Two other producers, Bibliographic Retrieval System (BRS) and System Development Corporation (SDC), offer many of the same information files. In addition, prominent business resources, including Dow Jones & Company, *Harvard Business Review, The New York Times,* and Standard & Poor's, now offer computer access to their data and files. You can find 3,000 online databases listed and briefly described in *Directory of Online Databases*.

Online database searching service:
- Explain where & how to use

Most public, college, and university libraries offer online database searching service for a fee that reflects the computer time employed and the number of items identified. Before you begin the search, you will need to work closely with trained staff to design a strategy that will use computer time effectively and retrieve only relevant information. However, considering the potential advantages of computer-assisted research, the cost of the service is a small price to pay. For an excellent discussion of the online search process, you can read Part III of *Introduction to Reference Sources* by William A. Katz.

CD-ROM databases:
- Define
- List types

CD-ROM databases use microcomputers with special features such as compact disk drives, coin box connections, and laser printers to access stored information on compact disks. For example, *ABI/Inform* offers abstracts on compact disks of 800 business and management periodicals that have been published since 1985. In addition, *Business Periodicals Ondisc* focuses on 300 of the most frequently used journals indexed by *ABI/Inform* and covers articles that have been published since 1987. Also, *Business Periodicals Ondisc* will provide you with a complete copy of the article using laser printing. Many of the indexes and reference sources mentioned in this chapter are currently offered or soon will be available through this laser optics technology. You may consult *CD-ROMs in Print: An International Guide* for a listing of compact disk database services.

Online & CD-ROM databases:
- Compare/contrast

Most authorities believe that these two database forms will complement rather than compete with one another. Online systems provide more capacity and faster processing of information. CD-ROM, however, is less expensive. Thus, CD-ROM disk systems will likely be provided to users on a monthly, quarterly, or semiannual basis. If researchers need more current information they can use an online database that is updated daily or weekly.

Growth in computer tech:
- Effects

As you can see, computer technology in information storage and retrieval continues to expand. Because of this growth, computer-assisted research is unquestionably becoming a routine step in the research process of preparing business reports.

SOURCE: Raymond V. Lesikar and John D. Pettit, Jr., *Report Writing for Business,* 8th ed. (Burr Ridge, Ill. Richard D. Irwin, 1990), chap. 4, pp. 43–44.

illustrates a passage marked with this method. Note that each paragraph may be labeled differently, depending on your purpose, your background, and the difficulty of the material. If your purpose is to read for background and you already know quite a bit, you may find yourself using step 1 strategies throughout a passage. On the other hand, if your purpose is to know details of material that is new to you and full of facts, you may find yourself using step 3 strategies for many sections.

This process will take more time than reading and underlining. If you use it however, you will have to read a chapter only once and you will know what you've read. When studying this material, instead of rereading page after page of highlighting, you will simply use your topics and organizational patterns to ask yourself questions and recite the content of the paragraphs in your own words.

Sharing Your Ideas

Work with a partner to mark the text passage below. Read a section silently. Together, decide on the topic and write it in the margin. Then determine what other steps are necessary to help you organize and store the material. Discuss your markings with other members of the class. Explain how and why you marked your passage as you did.

Using Periodical Indexes[1]

The card catalog helps you identify books for your bibliography. To identify articles published in newspapers, magazines, or journals, you will need to consult an index, either a general one or one that specializes in the field you are researching. Indexes are available in the reference section of most libraries and are regularly updated.

If you are like most business researchers, you will start your search for periodical literature with the *Business Periodicals Index.* Issued monthly and cumulated yearly, this guide covers 345 major business periodicals and indexes by subject headings and company references. It also lists articles on a wide variety of business areas, industries, and trades. A partial list of the business areas includes accounting, advertising, banking, communications, computer technology and applications, economics, finance, industrial relations, insurance, international business, management, marketing, and public relations.

Another guide you will find useful is the *Predicasts F&S Index United States,* which covers over 745 business-oriented periodicals, newspapers, and special reports. It includes company, product, and industry information as well as information on corporate activities, new products and technologies, and on social and political developments with business implications. Each entry contains a brief abstract of the article as well as bibliographical notations.

[1]Raymond V. Lesikar and John D. Pettit, Jr., *Report Writing for Business,* 8th ed. (Burr Ridge, Ill.: Richard D. Irwin, 1990), chap. 4, pp. 48–49.

A third index that may be helpful to you is the *Public Affairs Information Service Bulletin,* which lists by subject information relating to economics and public affairs. Its sources are extensive. They include, in addition to books and periodicals, pamphlets and reports published by associations and businesses as well as materials issued by the government.

There are a number of useful specialized indexes as well. Guides covering just pamphlets and reports are the *Vertical File Index.* For the best known business-oriented newspaper, there is the *Wall Street Journal Index;* and for the acknowledged newspaper of record, the *New York Times Index.* For research in marketing there are two useful listings: *Findex: The Directory of Market Research Reports, Studies, and Surveys* and the *Marketing Information Guide.* If you are doing accounting research, you are well advised to consult *The Accountants' Index.* And if you are interested in economics, you will find relevant listings in *The Social Sciences Index.*

Rounding out this selection of readily accessible printed indexes is the familiar *Reader's Guide to Periodical Literature,* which is useful in very general research, and a loose-leaf Information Access Corporation publication called *Hot Topics,* which lists articles published on 20 to 30 timely issues.

An increasing number of libraries offer additional listings identified by computer and recorded on microfilm. Chief among these guides are *The Business Index, The Magazine Index,* and the *National Newspaper Index.* These listings include three or more times the items and sources as the indexes traditionally found in libraries and are updated and cumulated monthly. They are limited, though, to material published since the late 1970s, the time all three services were initiated. (Printed volumes are available for the *National Newspaper Index* and are planned for the other two.) ■

Recall: Mental and Physical Strategies

When you select and organize the information in a chapter while you are reading it, you make the job of storing and recalling that information much easier. Instead of rereading hundreds of highlighted pages in order to study, you need only recite and review the material you've already determined to be important.

During the last stage of the reading process, it is necessary to remember what you learned about distributed practice in Chapter 4. Learning is much easier if you use steady review than if you try to cram. Remember how much easier it is to digest a stick of beef jerky daily rather than trying to digest several weeks' worth in one sitting. In the same way, you must review what you read as soon as possible after reading and on a daily basis. Study aids should be used for material that you are finding difficult to learn. Maps and charts are examples of such aids. Study cards are also good aids to learning. Because they are small, study cards can be carried anywhere and can provide you with the extra practice you may need.

Recall: Mental Strategies

As soon as possible after you read, you should begin to study the material. Doing the following will help you to begin:

Get the Big Picture. After reading, in order to put what you've read together, you should ask the question, "What was this chapter about?" "What were the headings and subheadings?" "How does this relate to what I already know?"

Determine Areas of Difficulty. By asking yourself, "What did I read that was difficult for me to organize and store?" you will be identifying material that needs further attention. You may find that interpreting the material through a diagram, chart, or picture may help you to better store it for later recall.

Select Methods of Review. Some material can easily be stored because of background—the memory traces have already been established. Other material must be repeated over and over again in order to establish a new memory trace. The questions "What do I know?" and "What do I need to learn?" will help you to select material for distributed practice.

Recall: Physical Strategies

Once you have completed the reading process you must store the information that you selected and organized. The techniques listed below will help you store at high levels on the PYRAMID of Learning. Because the techniques are based on principles of memory, they will aid in your recall of information.

Review/Recite from Mini Outline. Once you have finished reading, an easy way to think about everything that you've read is to review the mini outline of headings and subheadings that you made before you started to read. As you read each heading, recite briefly what you learned about it from your reading.

Review/Recite Topics and Organizational Patterns. To determine what you were able to store as you read, and what content needs additional practice, use your topics and organizational patterns in the margin of your text to ask yourself questions about the material. If you are an auditory learner, try to recite what you remember in your own words. Visual or kinesthetic learners may want to write or draw information they recall. This will move your knowledge from the memory level to the translation or interpretation level.

Create Study Aids. If you are having difficulty in recalling information from your text or lecture notes, you need to store it in another way. Making a map or chart can help you understand and store difficult material.

Information can be put on study cards for distributed practice. These study aids are explained below. Be sure to label your study aid with a topic and an organizational pattern. This will help you properly file the information so you can recall it.

Study Aids

Diagrams or Maps

Description: Maps are visual organizers of topics and subtopics that show how ideas are related. They can be created in many forms.

Use: When information contains many related ideas that you have to learn, a map can help you see how the parts fit together. Because this method illustrates how ideas are organized, it is especially good for visual learners.

How to Make: Write the topic in the middle of a study card or a piece of paper. You can draw a box or circle around it to make it stand out. Identify the details or subtopics that describe the topic. Branch them off the main topic. Continue in this manner until you have included all of the information you need.

Example: Figure 8–2.

FIGURE 8–2
Examples of maps

A.

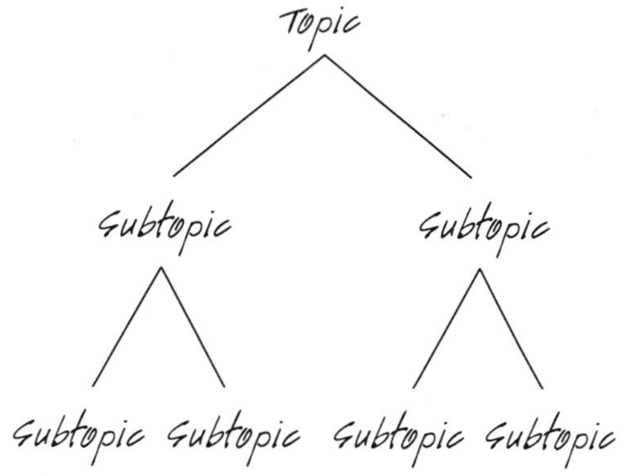

B.

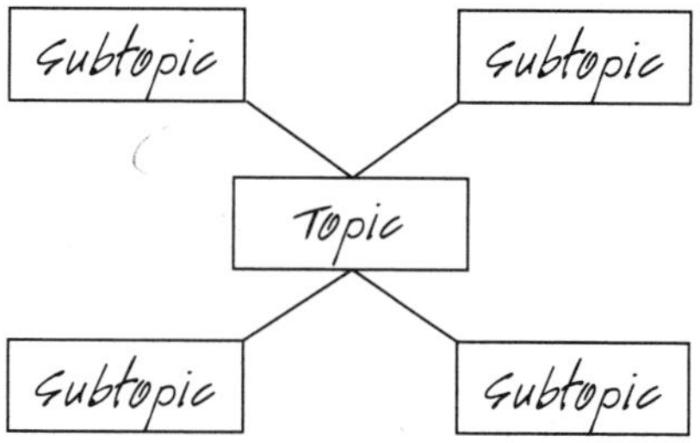

Figure 8–2
Continued

C.

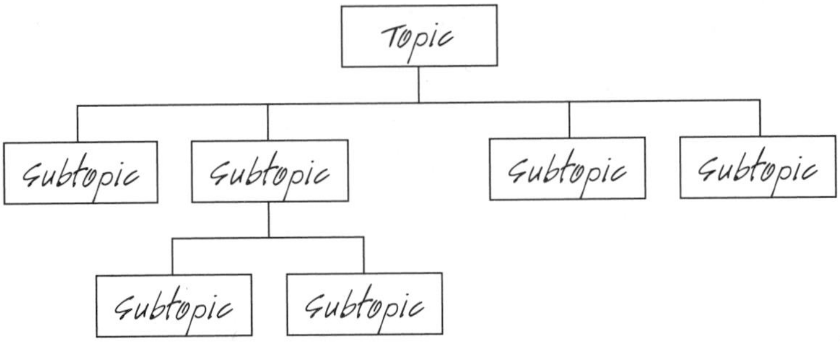

D.

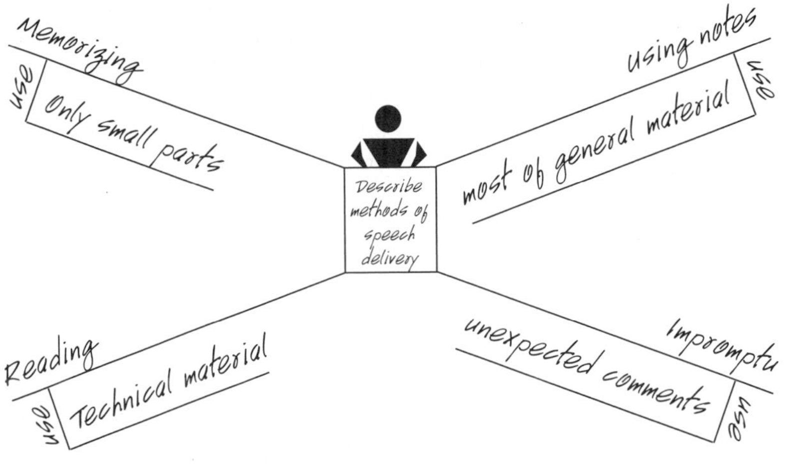

Charts

Description: A chart is a square diagram of repeating categories and details.

Use: When the same type of information needs to be learned for each topic you are studying, when you need to remember a large number of facts about repeating categories, or when you need to show how things are the same and how they are different, a chart can be used.

How to Make: Identify information that is repeated for several topics. Write the repeating categories as headings along the top of a square. Write the topics to be described down the left side. Fill in the facts or details about each topic.

Example: Figure 8–3.

Figure 8–3
Example of a chart

Compare Mapping to Outlining

	Description	use
Map	Major topics & details shown in visual relationship	Better for showing relationships of parts to whole
Outline	Major topics & details shown in order of importance	Better for showing the order of a process or events

Study Cards

Description: Index cards can be used as portable study devices for repeated practice.

Use: Vocabulary words or content that needs repeated practice can be placed on study cards. Information can be summarized, outlined, mapped, or charted in order to translate or interpret.

How to Make: Write the topic and organizational pattern of the information to be learned on the front of the card. In the case of a vocabulary card, write the word to be learned along with a sentence showing its use on the front. Map, chart, or outline content on the back of the card. Be sure to include a memory association to help you remember a vocabulary word.

Example: Figure 8–4.

FIGURE 8–4
Example of a study card

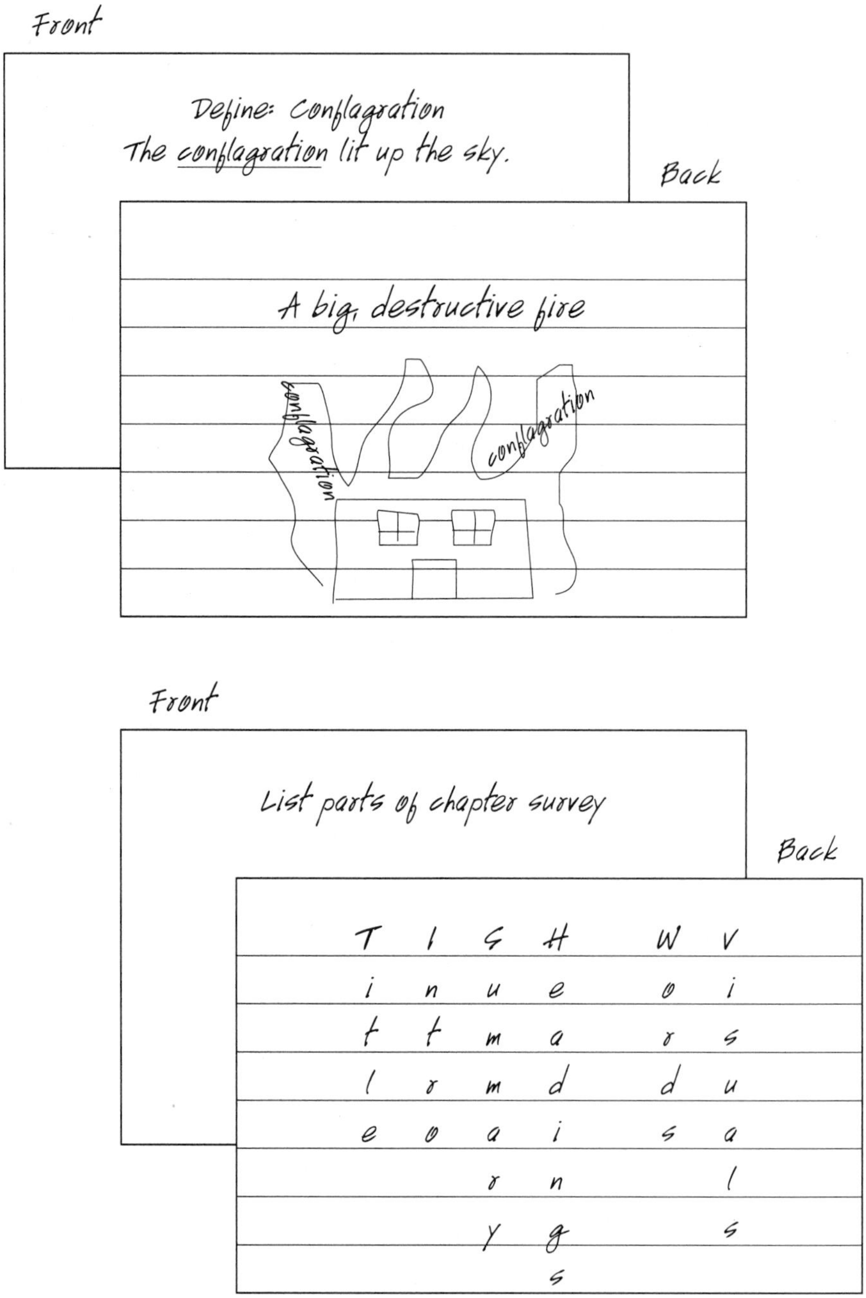

Putting It All Together

College textbook reading differs from high school and pleasure reading in content, purpose, rate, degree of interest, and amount of background knowledge needed. To read and understand material in your college texts, you must use techniques that provide for these differences. The methods you use must help you select and organize many new facts as well as think about ideas, store at high levels on the PYRAMID of Learning, adjust your reading rate, create an interest, and develop background knowledge. The PPR Reading System contains both mental and physical techniques that will help you prepare to read your textbooks, organize and store as you read them, and recall what you read in them.

Making the Connection

Check your understanding of the concepts presented in this chapter by completing the following activity. If you are unable to recall information in a particular area, go back and review that material before completing the rest of the exercises in this section.

1. Write one or two sentences to summarize what you recall about each of the following topics:

   The differences between college reading, high school reading, and pleasure reading ______________________________

   ____

   ____

   ____

   ____

   ____

   ____

   ____

   Mental strategies for preparing to read ______________________________

   ____

   ____

   Physical strategies for preparing to read ______________________________

   ____

   ____

   Mental strategies while reading ______________________________

   ____

   ____

   Physical strategies while reading ______________________________

   ____

   ____

   Mental strategies after reading ______________________________

   ____

   ____

Physical strategies after reading ______________________________

____

____

2. List one new idea you've gained about textbook reading as a result of this chapter. ______________________________

____

3. Describe one change you plan to make before reading, one change you plan to make during reading, and one change you plan to make after reading. ______________________________

____

____

____

____

____

____

____

Thinking It Through

Read the following passage, and then answer the questions by applying what you've learned about textbook reading.

> Jeff was never a great student. He was always told that he had ability, but he was not motivated to use it. Now that he is in technical school, Jeff has finally found something that interests him. However, since he never really studied in high school, he doesn't know where to begin.
>
> Jeff finds it hard to concentrate as he reads. Since he saw other students using yellow highlighting pens, he purchased one and uses it to mark many lines of information. Most of the material seems very difficult and new to him.
>
> After he reads, Jeff never looks at the material again until a few days before a test. Then he reviews his highlighting by rereading it.

1. Based on information from the passage, what do you see as Jeff's specific problem(s)? ______________________________

____

2. By using knowledge you already have, asking others, and possibly doing a bit of research, list as many solutions to Jeff's problem(s) as you can. ____

3. List the pros and cons for *each* of these solutions from Jeff's point of view. ____

4. Select the solution that appears to be the best in terms of pros and cons. List the steps necessary to carry out this solution. Be sure to describe the details, such as who, what, when, where, and how.

Applying Your Skills 1 *Preparing a Mini Outline*

Instructions: Use the text chapter found on pages 206–221. Construct a mini outline below, using the main headings and subheadings from this chapter.

Applying Your Skills 2 *Surveying a Text*

Instructions: Use the text chapter on pages 206–221 to practice doing a chapter survey. To show what you would survey, make a check mark beside everything you would read and think about before reading the entire chapter.

CHAPTER

3

Opportunities and Challenges in Small Business

A wise man will make more opportunities than he finds.—Francis Bacon

The role of small and midsized firms . . . has never been more important to America's future.—Tom Peters, co-author of *In Search of Excellence*

LEARNING OBJECTIVES

After studying the material in this chapter, you will be able to:

1. Discuss some of the currently promising opportunities for small business.
2. Present some practical ideas for small business opportunities.
3. Explain some of the growing opportunities in small business for women and minorities.
4. Discuss some areas of concern for small business owners, especially the problem of poorly planned growth, and the prospect for failure.

From William L. Megginson, Mary Jane Byrd, Charles R. Scott, and Leon C. Megginson, *Small Business Management: An Entrepreneur's Guide to Success* (Burr Ridge, Ill.: Richard D. Irwin, 1994), chap. 3, pp. 40–55.

PROFILE

SHERRI HILL: DRESSING THE WORLD'S MOST BEAUTIFUL WOMEN

Sherri Hill believes in taking advantage of opportunities when they knock! Opportunity knocked for her in 1985, when a contestant in the Miss Oklahoma pageant bought a dress from Sherri's family-run shop in Norman, Oklahoma.

Wanting to "watch our dress," she and her partners attended the pageant. She was disturbed during the show to see another contestant wearing the same design as theirs. While their client was understanding about the duplication, the partners were upset.

Seeing the problem caused by more than one contestant's wearing the same design, Sherri decided to capitalize on the situation by custom-designing and selling dresses on a registration basis. When a customer buys a "Temptations by Sherri Hill" dress costing anywhere from $1,500 to $6,000, the design is registered to that person on a computer system so that no other contestant can purchase the same dress.

Vonda Vass (left) and Sherri Hill show gowns worn by 1988 Miss USA contestants and a cocktail dress (held by Mrs. Hill) worn by 1989 contestants.

Source: Mobile (Alabama) *Press Register,* February 28, 1989, pp. 1B + 3B. Photograph by Jay Ferchaud, © 1989, *Mobile* (Alabama) *Press Register.*

Soon after her dresses were seen by the Miss Oklahoma and Miss USA pageant directors, she became the exclusive designer of gowns for the Miss Universe, Miss USA, and Miss Teen USA winners. At the 1988 Miss America contest, 48 women wore her gowns—which were all of different design! At the 1989 Miss USA pageant, seven finalists were gowned by Mrs. Hill, as was Courtney Gibbs, the 1988 Miss USA, who was also present.

As you can see, what was an embarrassing moment at the time proved to be the knock that opened the door to a successful enterprise.

Source: Cathy Jumper, "Oklahoma Woman Designer of Gowns for Beauty Pageants," *Mobile* (Alabama) *Register,* February 28, 1989, pp. 1-B and 3-B.

Figure 3–1 Where the New Jobs Will Be: These Industries Are Expected to Produce the Most New Jobs by the Year 2000

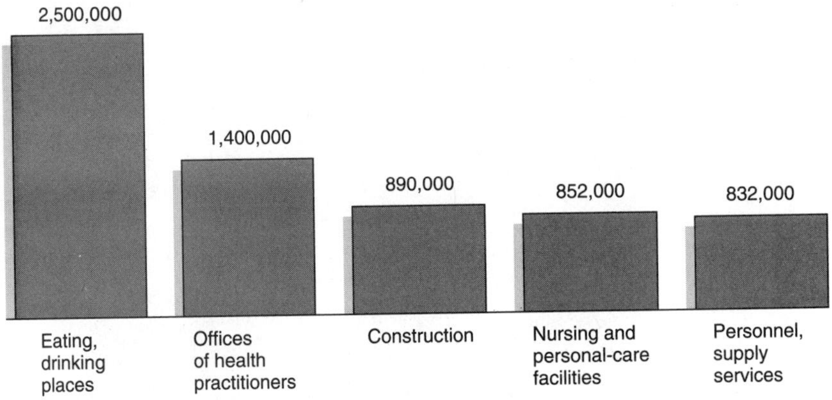

Source: U.S. Department of Labor, Bureau of Labor Statistics.

In Chapter 1, we described the dynamic role of small business, and in Chapter 2, we explained why you might want to own and manage such a business. In this chapter, as the Profile indicates, we discuss some of the opportunities available in small business, suggest areas for innovation by small business, explain some of the growing opportunities for women and minorities, and discuss some areas of concern for small business owners, especially the problem of poorly planned growth and the possibility of failure.

WHERE ARE THE OPPORTUNITIES?

You can explore the opportunities to become a small business owner in many ways. First, study industry groupings or categories to see what types of small businesses are growing. Second, study the factors affecting the future of industries and businesses. Third, study some innovative ideas that entrepreneurs are turning into successful businesses. From all this information, you can see where opportunities exist for a new business.

What Are the Fastest-Growing Industries?

According to the Bureau of Labor Statistics, no industry is growing faster than services, and this trend is expected to continue at least into the 21st century. This trend is evident in both the number of new businesses being created and, as Figure 3–1 shows, the number of new jobs being created. Most of the growing industries are dominated by small private companies. According to the SBA's Office of Advocacy, only construction and personnel/supply services tend to be dominated by larger businesses.

Figure 3–2 1990s Rage: Service

The hottest small businesses in the 1990s will be service firms such as accountants, lawyers, architects, and computer consultants. In this case, a small business is defined as having fewer than 100 employees.

Percentage change in number of firms, 1989-99

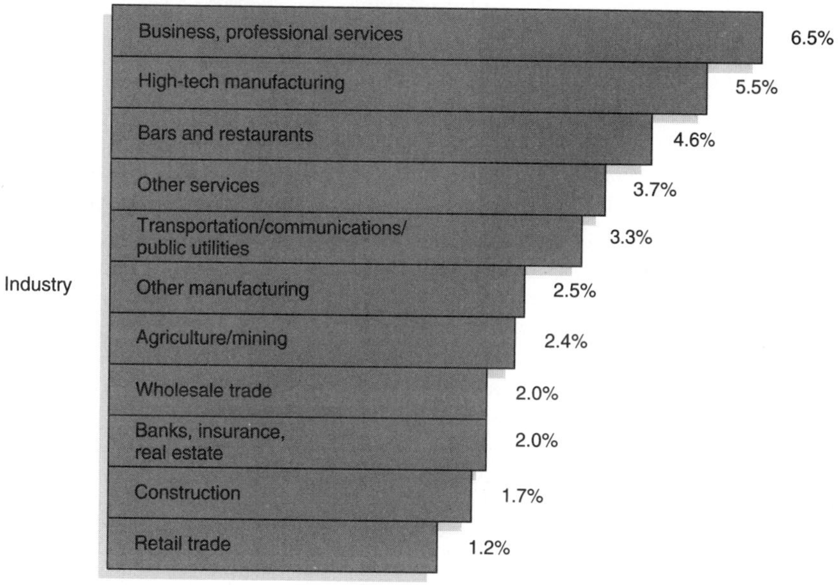

Source: Cognetics, Inc., as reported in *USA Today,* May 8, 1989, p. 1E. Copyright 1989, USA TODAY. Adapted with permission.

A similar picture emerges when we look at the number of *new firms expected to be established* during the 1990s. For example, as shown in Figure 3–2, services tend to dominate this group. Notice that 7 of the 11 industries shown are in the service-performing areas.

We may have led you to believe up to this point that small businesses are being formed primarily by daring young entrepreneurs who use their college degrees to turn brilliant ideas into glamorous high-tech firms. But these firms are only the most visible ones. Instead, most small firms are just that: small, limited in scope, and involving long hours of hard work to perform everyday activities needed by the general public. For example, the SBA has found from its data that the 10 small-business-dominated industries with the lowest failure rates have tended to be businesses of this kind.[1] These stable industries—such as funeral services; fuel and ice dealers; laundry, cleaning, and repair services; and drugstores—offer the public a service that is needed regularly by a large segment of the population.

USING TECHNOLOGY TO SUCCEED

TECHNOLOGY LETS TAXIS TRADE CASH FOR CREDIT

For years, taxicab companies have been trying to find a way to accept credit cards. The drawback has been to find a feasible way to check to see if cards have been stolen or if the owner has overused the credit limit. Also, cab drivers have been reluctant to fork over part of their fee to credit-card companies, instead of accepting the cash customers are in the habit of paying.

All that is now changing, as taxis are finally going plastic! In late 1992, over 600 of New York City's 12,000 cabs were equipped with machines connected to their meters that read the magnetic strip on American Express cards. The cab driver punches in tips and tolls, and a receipt, in duplicate, pops out. The driver still must check against a list of lost or stolen cards, but that is expected to change soon. By the end of 1993, cab companies will be able to obtain credit-card authorization by sending a signal to the dispatcher, who electronically checks the card number and then notifies the driver if everything is OK.

MasterCard International plans to test the system in Montreal and other major cities by 1994. It will also experiment with pizza deliverers, plumbers, and other workers on wheels to get them to use the system.

One drawback is that most of the 171,000 cabs in the United States are driven by independent contractors who are reluctant to pay the usual 3 to 5 percent of the amount charged as a discount fee to the credit-card companies. However, this is changing, as drivers say people who use cards generally leave fatter tips that more than offset the discount fee.

Source: Dell Jones, "Technology Lets Taxis Trade Cash for Credit," *USA Today*, November 1992, p. 6B. © 1992, USA TODAY. Adapted with permission.

Factors Affecting the Future of an Industry or a Business

Many changes are now occurring that will affect the future of an industry or business (see Using Technology to Succeed), and small business owners should study them intently in order to adjust to them. These changes can cause slow-growing industries to speed up or fast-growing ones to slow down. And a change that provides an opportunity for one industry or business may pose a threat to others. For example, aging of the population may increase the need for retirement facilities but hurt industries supplying baby needs.

Figure 3–3 shows some selected examples of factors that affect various industries and businesses. These factors will be discussed more fully in Chapters 5, 6, and 8.

Some Practical Ideas for Small Businesses

As shown in Chapter 1, entrepreneurs tend to be innovative and to develop new ideas. What are some of the innovative ideas currently being developed that should

Figure 3–3 Examples of Factors Affecting Industry and Business Trends

1. *Economics*—gross national product (GNP), interest rates, inflation rates, stages of the business cycle, employment levels, size and characteristics of business firms and not-for-profit organizations, and opportunities in foreign markets.
2. *Technology*—artificial intelligence, thinking machines, laser beams, new energy sources, amount of spending for research and development, and issuance of patents and their protection.
3. *Lifestyle*—career expectations, consumer activism, health concerns, desire to upgrade education and climb the socioeconomic ladder, and need for psychological services.
4. *Political-legal*—antitrust regulations, environmental protection laws, foreign trade regulations, tax changes, immigration laws, child-care legislation, and the attitude of governments and society toward the particular type of industry and business.
5. *Demographics*—population growth rate, age and regional shifts, ethnic moves and life expectancy, number and distribution of firms within the industry, and size and character of markets.

lead to the big businesses of tomorrow? These new types of business provide opportunities for those wanting to become small business owners.

One way to do this is to see which small businesses are growing most rapidly. *American Business Information* used a unique approach to determine the business categories that grew the most rapidly during a recent year. It surveyed Yellow Pages listings and found the following increases: (1) facsimile communication equipment, 119 percent; (2) money order services, 48 percent; (3) exercise and physical fitness, 43 percent; (4) bed and breakfast accommodations, 40 percent; and (5) collectibles, 37 percent.[2]

Some other innovative ideas for small businesses are specialized shopping, especially for dual-career families and shut-ins; desktop publishing; on-site auto tune-ups and cleaning at clients' homes; helping small businesses and other organizations computerize their activities; low-power TV stations for specially targeted audiences; presorting mail by ZIP codes for businesses sending out large mailings; at-home pet grooming; the use of fax machines for mass mailings and franchising fax vending machines; exotic family tours; utilization review firms to review hospital costs for employers, point out unnecessary treatments, and suggest cheaper alternatives; biotechnology; and specialized delivery services.

For example, Cuisine Express provides fast, effective delivery of meals from seven gourmet restaurants in Maryland to customers in the Bethesda, Chevy Chase, Glen Echo, and Somerset areas. Customers choose the restaurant and meal they desire and place an order with Cuisine Express's operator. The operator orders the meal from the restaurant, and a driver picks it up, delivers it, and collects payment by Visa, MasterCard, or personal check.

David Gumpert, author of *How to **Really** Create a Successful Business Plan*, looked at emerging trends and problems, talked to those in the know, and came up with the following ventures that seemed to be headed for success in the 1990s:[3]

1. Catering.
2. Computer and office machine repair.
3. Day care.
4. Educational services and products.
5. Career counseling.
6. Financial planning.
7. Home health care.
8. Printing, copying, and mailing.
9. Marketing, promotion, and public relations.
10. Senior fitness and recreation.

GROWING OPPORTUNITIES FOR WOMEN AND MINORITIES IN SMALL BUSINESS

Small firms provide excellent opportunities for women and minorities to gain economic independence. The opportunities for women, blacks, Hispanics, and Asians are increasing in number and frequency, as will be shown by several examples in this chapter.

For Women

The 1980s have been called the ''decade of women entrepreneurs.''[4] Women are now starting new businesses at twice the rate of men. In 1972, women owned only 5 percent of all businesses; in 1992, they owned one-third.[5] This is an increase of 184 percent from the 1.9 million owned in 1977. Moreover, women founded 70 percent of all new firms in 1991.[6] According to the SBA, women are expected to own half of the nation's small businesses by the year 2000.[7]

In 1992, women-owned firms employed 11 million people—and that number is increasing rapidly—while Fortune 500 firms, employing only 12 million, were regularly announcing reductions.[8] The change in women-owned businesses is occurring faster in the nontraditional industries such as transportation, construction, manufacturing, mining, and agriculture—as well as services, trade, and finance. However, 6 out of 10 women owners are still in public relations, marketing, data processing, business service/personnel, finance, and retailing.[9]

A poll of National Association of Women Business Owners members found that these owners are not the mythical women who inherited the family—or their spouse's—business. Instead, 90 percent of them either started the business for themselves, bought a business, or bought a franchise—primarily to prove that they could succeed, to earn more money, or to control their work schedule. The surveyed women entrepreneurs were highly educated—only 5 percent of those responding had a high school education or less—and over half (57 percent) worked over 50 hours per week.[10]

Opportunities for women entrepreneurs are growing all across the nation, as are the organizations to help women found their own businesses. These include the Women's Economic Development Corporation in Minneapolis, Minnesota; the Women's Business Development Center in Chicago; the Midwest Women's Business Owners Development Joint Ventures in Detroit; and the American Women's Economic Development Corporation (AWED) in New York. Also, Young Women's Christian Association groups around the country have been helping for years.

Yet there are many problems still facing women entrepreneurs, including getting a loan, dealing with male employees and clients, getting moral support in the industry, and dealing with female employees and clients.[11] In order to overcome some of these problems, the Women's Business Ownership Act, passed in late 1988, extended antidiscrimination laws to include commercial and personal credit for women.

For Minorities

Small business ownership also provides growing opportunities for minorities, that is, for blacks, Hispanics, and Asians. Small business has traditionally owed a great deal to immigrants, who have been responsible for much of the surge in new firms. A flood of immigrants poured into the United States around the turn of the century, and many of our great companies were started by the newcomers.

Now, the situation is quite similar, as 8.7 million people moved to the United States in the 1980s.[12] Nearly half of these were from Mexico, the Caribbean, and Central and South America; and over a third were from Asia. These promising entrepreneurs, with their bilingual skills, family ties, and knowledge of how things are done in other countries, can contribute—especially to the growing Asian and Latin American markets. But the influence of immigrants is also felt at home. For example, the computer industry today is highly dependent on microprocessor chips made by Intel, which was founded by Andrew Grove, a Hungarian immigrant.

Blacks

There are many good opportunities for blacks in small business. Small firms hire about 10.5 times as many blacks as do large firms. The number of black-owned businesses increased 38 percent, to 424,165, from 1982 to 1987,[13] as compared to 14 percent growth in the number of all U.S. companies.[14] Yet according to Barbara Lindsey, founder of the Los Angeles Black Enterprise Expo, while blacks make up 12 percent of the U.S. population, they account for only 3 percent of its business owners.[15] But some of those owners do quite well, according to *Black Enterprise* magazine, which found that its 100 largest black-owned companies grew 10.2 percent in revenues, as compared to 7.6 percent for the Fortune 500.[16]

Yet most black-owned businesses are small. While they account for 3 percent of all U.S. companies, they employ only 1.1 percent of U.S. workers. In fact, 87 percent of black-owned companies consist of only the owner.

The role of black entrepreneurs is rapidly changing. Once engaged primarily in mom-and-pop businesses such as barbershops, cleaners, and grocery stores, they are now moving into such fields as electronics, advertising, real estate development, insurance, health care, computers, and automobile dealerships. (See the case at the end of Chapter 21, and the Profiles for Chapter 7, ''Porterfield Wilson: From Shining Shoes to Importing Foreign Cars,'' and Chapter 11, ''Mel Farr: Sales Superstar,'' for outstanding examples.)

Big companies are also helping blacks start small businesses. They do it through creating joint ventures, lending their personnel to help start—or advise—the business, providing low-cost facilities, and providing an assured market, as the following example illustrates.

As part of its minority supplier program, McDonald's asked George Johnson and David Moore to start a business making croutons for the new line of salads it planned to introduce. Johnson and Moore, managers at a brewing company, had never run a business, knew nothing about baking, and had only one client—McDonald's. They invested $100,000 each and, with such an assured market, persuaded a Chicago bank to lend them $1.6 million. Also, a McDonald's bun and English muffin supplier bought a Chicago pork-processing plant and leased it back to their company, Quality Croutons, Inc. Sales for the first year exceeded $4 million, including sales to McDonald's, United Airlines, Kraft Foods, and Pizza Hut.[17]

Hispanics

According to the SBA's 1987 census of minority businesses, the number of businesses owned by Hispanics grew 80.5 percent between 1982 and 1987, to 422,373 firms (see Figure 3–4). This growth was nearly five times as great as that for all U.S. firms—including minority firms.

Hispanic businesses are particularly booming in the food area. This field was previously dominated by mom-and-pop grocers, but supermarkets are now invading the field because of the Hispanic view of shopping as an eagerly awaited social event.

The Hispanic market represents one of the fastest-growing groups of customers in the country. According to the U.S. Census Bureau, the Hispanic population

Figure 3–4 Hispanic-Owned Businesses Are Growing Rapidly

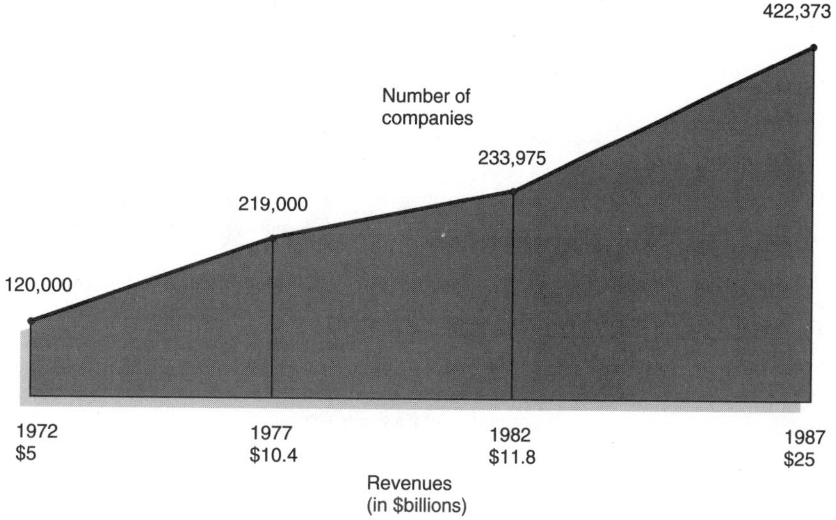

Source: U.S. Hispanic Chamber of Commerce, as reported in *USA Today,* November 2, 1984, p. 3B; and Dorothy J. Gaites, "Short-Term Despair, Long-Term Promise," *The Wall Street Journal,* April 3, 1992, p. R4.

grew 53 percent from 1980 to 1990, over five times the overall U.S. growth rate.[18] Entrepreneurs are trying to cash in on this market, as the following example illustrates.

After two years—and $2.5 million—spent researching the market, Vons Companies started Tianguis, a Southern California supermarket chain. The store's shelves are stocked with Spanish items, including handmade tortillas, and mariachi singers stroll the aisles. Hispanics are driving from as far as 65 miles away to shop in the stores because they like the products, the music, and the fact that "everyone speaks Spanish."[19]

Asians

The recent flood of Asian refugees entering the United States has resulted in a wave of small mom-and-pop businesses; according to the U.S. Census Bureau, there are now 57 Asian-owned firms in the United States per 1,000 Asians, compared to 21 Hispanic-owned firms and 15 black-owned ones.[20] This growth in business ownership partially results from the 105 percent increase in the U.S. Asian population during the 1980s. This increase was twice as high as that of Hispanics, almost 9 times as high as that of blacks, and 25 times as high as that of whites. Asians now account for 42 percent of U.S. immigrants.[21]

Figure 3–5 Asians Benefit from Networking

Recently arrived Asian immigrants establishing U.S. business enterprises gain support from cultural networks.

Source: U.S. Department of Commerce, as reported in Robert Lewis, "Asian Immigrants Find Large Profits in Small Stores," *Mobile* (Alabama) *Press Register,* March 5, 1989, p. G-1. Adapted with permission of Newhouse Graphics.

A key factor in Asians' success is their tradition of self-employment. Also, they are motivated to open their own businesses because language and cultural barriers prevent them from obtaining ordinary wage or salary jobs. Hence Asians—especially Koreans—go into business for themselves, even if it means setting up a street stand or opening a store in a poor, run-down neighborhood. Also, as shown in Figure 3–5 and in the following example, Asian immigrants receive considerable support from cultural networks when they try to set up a small business.

Dae Song, 36, arrived in Baltimore from Korea with $400, which he soon lost. Unable to speak or understand English, and not knowing what to do, he moved in with an aunt and started working in the family's drycleaning business in a Washington suburb. After learning the business, he opened his own shop with help from a Korean support group. Each of the 30 members of the group contributed $1,000 to Dae Song as a loan. Eventually, each of them will have access to the full $30,000 to finance his own business.[22]

Cultural factors alone do not explain the outstanding success of Asian entrepreneurs. Instead, a study of small businesses in California—the state with the highest concentration of Asian businesses—found several important differences between businesses owned by Asians and those owned by non-Asians. While only 69 percent of non-Asians had a business plan when they started their company, 84 percent of Asians did. Also, Asians were more prone to use outside attorneys and accountants to assist them, and to use personal computers. According to a spokesman for Pacific Bell Directory, which sponsored the study, Asian businesspeople are prospering not because they are Asians but because they understand the key ingredients of running a successful business.[23]

AREAS OF CONCERN FOR SMALL BUSINESS OWNERS

So far, we have indicated that opportunities abound for anyone with a good idea, the courage to take a chance and try something new, and some money to invest. That's what small business is all about. But, as shown in Chapter 1, the success of smaller firms tends to be limited by factors such as inadequate management, shortages of capital, government regulation and paperwork, and lack of proper record keeping. Two other concerns are (1) poorly planned growth that is too slow or too fast and (2) the danger of failure.

Poorly Planned Growth

Poorly planned growth appears to be a built-in obstacle facing many small businesses. For example, if the owners are incapable, inefficient, or lacking in initiative, their businesses may flounder and eventually fail. If the owners are only mediocre, their businesses remain small. However, if the owners are efficient and capable and their organizations succeed and grow, they risk losing the very things they seek from their companies.

Loss of Independence or Control

With growth, owners must please more people, including employees, customers, and the public. There are also new problems, such as hiring and rewarding managers and supervising other people—exercising the very authority they may resent in others.

Many otherwise creative entrepreneurs are poor managers. They are able to generate ideas and found the business but are unable to manage it on a day-to-day basis. If the firm becomes large enough to require outside capital for future success and growth, the owner may lose control over the company, as the following example shows.

Two design geniuses, Steven Jobs, 21, and Steve Wozniak, 19, founded Apple Computer in 1976 with capital obtained by selling Jobs's Volkswagen microbus and Wozniak's Hewlett-Packard scientific calculator. They managed its growth until 1980, when they sold stock in it to the public. Although Jobs and Wozniak were worth $165 million and $88 million, respectively, they could not manage the day-to-day operations, so they hired John Sculley away from PepsiCo in 1983 to manage the floundering firm.

But both men were unhappy when Apple grew so big that they lost control. In 1985, after a dispute with Sculley, Wozniak sold his Apple stock and founded another company, Cloud 9. And when Jobs was ousted as chairman by the directors representing the outside stockholders, he sold all but one share of his stock and also formed a new company, NeXT, Inc.

Figure 3–6 Stages in the Development of a Small Business

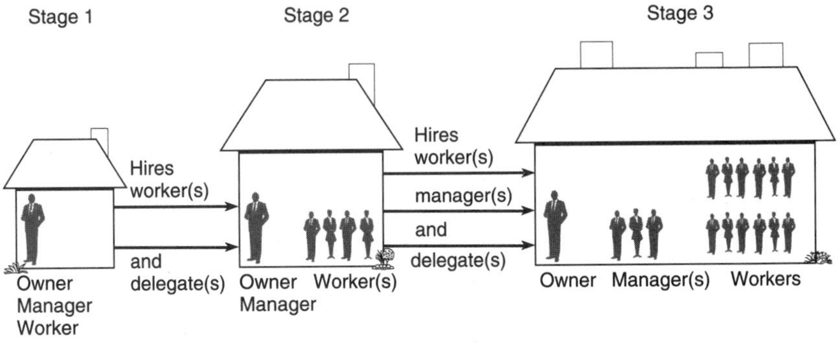

Typical Growth Pattern

Historically, the ownership and management of small businesses have tended to follow a growth pattern similar to that shown in Figure 3–6. During stage 1, owners manage the business and do all the work. In stage 2, the owners still manage their companies but hire employees to help with routine and/or management activities. In stage 3, the owners hire managers to run the firms. Thus, the business takes on the form, the characteristics, and many of the problems of a big business.

The length of service of professional managers (as opposed to owner-managers) in small businesses tends to be relatively short; they move from one company to another as they progress upward in rank and earnings. Often, owners must give managers a financial interest in the business in order to hold them.

Threat of Failure

A **discontinuance** is a voluntary decision to terminate a business.

A **failure** results from inability to succeed in running a business.

Formal failures are failures ending in court with loss to creditors.

In **personal (informal) failures**, the owner who cannot succeed voluntarily terminates the business.

As shown in Chapter 1, the threat of failure and discontinuance is a reality for many small businesses. A **discontinuance** is a voluntary decision to quit. A discontinuance may result from any of several factors, including health, changes in family situation, and the apparent advantages of working for someone else.

A **failure** results from inability to make a go of the business; things just don't work out as planned. There are two types of failure: (1) **formal failures**, which end up in court with some kind of loss to the creditors, and (2) **personal (informal) failures**, where the owner cannot make it financially and so voluntarily calls it quits. Personal failures are far more numerous than formal ones. People put their money, time, and effort into a business only to see losses wipe out the investment. Creditors usually do not suffer, as the owners tend to absorb the losses. The owners are the ones who pack up, close the door, and say, "That's it!"

WHAT YOU SHOULD HAVE LEARNED

1. There are many opportunities for prospective small business owners, especially in business and professional services, high-tech manufacturing, bars and restaurants, and other services. The best opportunities are in small firms, limited in scope, that involve long, hard hours working to satisfy basic human needs.
2. Some practical suggestions for future small firms are specialized shopping, desktop publishing, helping organizations computerize their activities, applications of fax machines, utilization review firms to help employers reduce their health-care costs, and specialized delivery services.
3. Opportunities in small business abound for women and minorities. Women are starting new businesses at a rapid rate. They now own one-third and are expected to own half of all small firms by the year 2000. Women owning small firms tend to be well educated, capable, and committed owners.

   While black entrepreneurs are progressing in small business, their firms tend to be smaller and less profitable than other firms. The Hispanic market is growing fast and expects to provide many opportunities in the future, especially in mom-and-pop food stores. Cultural networks, along with shrewd business practices—such as having a business plan, hiring professional consultants, and using computers—are aiding the flood of Asian entrepreneurs.
4. Unplanned growth and failure are of particular concern to small business owners. While poorly planned growth can be a real problem, failure to grow can mean the death of a business.

   Another problem is failure and/or discontinuance. Some businesses discontinue for health, family, or other personal reasons, while others fail. Although relatively few of these are formal failures, personal failures resulting from unprofitability or general discouragement can be just as devastating for small business owners.

QUESTIONS FOR DISCUSSION

1. Name the fastest-growing small businesses, as indicated by the number of jobs. Explain their growth.
2. As far as new firms are concerned, what are the fastest-growing industries during the 1990s?
3. Name some practical ideas for small businesses during the 1990s.
4. Evaluate the opportunities in small business for women, blacks, Hispanics, and Asians.
5. How does success cause problems for some small businesses? Can you give examples from your experience or suggest ways to avoid the problems of growth?

CASE

SHANGHAI RESTAURANT

Mai Gu (upper right) and one of her daughters greet two of their favorite customers.
Photo courtesy of Leon C. Megginson

Mai and Bob Gu are a perfect example of the adage, "Hard work pays off." Married for five years, the couple has gone from working in the kitchens of other people's restaurants to owning and operating a successful small restaurant, opened in Mobile, Alabama, in 1988. Their first establishment was a modestly sized operation, serving only takeout Chinese and South Vietnamese cuisine. Mai was the sole cook for the business, coming in at 9 A.M. and working hard until at least 10 at night, six days a week.

Business was very good, so the Gus decided to expand their operations. They moved to a larger building where they were able to include dining space and table service. Since their opening day, the Gus say, business has been steady.

The Gus also own a small Oriental market located adjacent to the restaurant. It offers everything from special Oriental teas and spices to hand-carved clocks. According to Mai, the market doesn't attract very much business on its own, but occasionally draws a curious restaurant customer.

The Gus used personal experience in the restaurant industry and a sharp business sense to successfully launch their own enterprise. Mai and Bob both held various jobs in restaurants long before they met in early 1988. Mai has always loved to cook, and she used her culinary skills to find work in Oriental restaurants, first in Los Angeles, California, then in Mobile.

In 1972, Mai divorced her South Vietnamese husband "to find my fortune in America." She knew that she wanted to cook, so she looked for work in the restaurant field. Not satisfied with the job prospects that Los Angeles offered, she moved to Mobile in 1975. For several years, she worked in the kitchen for the owner of a successful Hunan restaurant. Although working behind the scenes, she was learning all she could about the operations. Then Bob Gu, who had moved to Mobile from China, entered the picture. It wasn't long before the two were married—and starting their own business.

Bob is the planner; Mai is the implementer. Bob takes care of the "paper" end of the business, managing the books and ordering supplies and equipment, while Mai runs things in the kitchen and on the restaurant floor. Greeting customers with genuine graciousness when they enter the front door, cooking Oriental dishes with an expertise that comes only from years of hands-on culinary experience, and taking time out to chat with the regulars, Mai and Bob are the perfect hosts. It is quite obvious that they enjoy what they are doing.

Although they own a house in Mobile, Bob and Mai live in an apartment above the market in order to save money. They supplement their income by renting their house to carefully screened tenants. The Gus say the benefits of having additional funds for restaurant and market supplies outweigh any possible inconveniences of living above their business.

Employees of the restaurant, from the kitchen help to the waitresses, are family members lending a hand to make the operation a success. Mai seems especially proud of the fact that all of her children work for her in one way or another. This family involvement adds another dimension to the dining experience for the customer; customers see the same friendly faces each time they visit the restaurant, eventually making them feel almost as if they were eating a meal at home.

Hoping to attract new customers, Mai and Bob obtained a liquor license for the restaurant. They also advertised in the local newspaper in an effort to increase revenues. At present, the Gus say they have no plans to expand or move their operation.

QUESTIONS

1. What is your opinion of the Shanghai Restaurant? Would you choose to patronize the establishment? Why or why not?
2. Assume that the Gus have hired you as a consultant. Make at least three specific recommendations that would improve business and streamline operations.
3. What factors might affect the future of this small business? Discuss.
4. Speculate as to the future success or failure of this small business. Discuss.

Source: Prepared by Ragan Workman Megginson, with the Alabama Radio Network.

Applying Your Skills 3 *Marking a Text*

Instructions: Use the material found under the topic heading "For Women" found on pages 212–213. Read each passage and mark it using any of the following:

The topic.

The topic and organizational pattern.

The topic, organizational pattern, and underlining.

All of the above plus a map, chart, or summary.

Applying Your Skills 4 *Studying the Text*

Instructions: Describe below the methods you would use to study the material that you marked above. Include techniques for each stage of the memory process: prepare, process, recall.

Prepare

Describe how you will focus your attention to prepare to study your text markings.

____

____

____

____

____

Process:

Describe how you will actually study your text markings to store the information you marked.

____

____

____

____

____

____

____

Recall:

Use the space below to make one study device (map, chart, or study card) using material in the text that you found difficult.

Applying Your Skills 5 *Using Your Resources*

Instructions: To know where to "radio for help," you will be asked to visit various school resources throughout this text. Keep this information so that you can refer to it when you are in need of help outside the classroom.

Complete the information below after touring your school's Reading/Writing Center.

Location: ______________________________

Hours of operation: ______________________________

Contact person: ______________________________

Phone: ______________________________

Services offered:

____

____

____

____

Personal comments:

Briefly discuss how you could use this resource.

____

____

____

____

____

____

C H A P T E R

9 The PPR Test Taking System

Apply the principles of thinking and learning to take tests effectively.

Chapter Goals

After you read this chapter, you will be able to:

- Create a study plan to help you prepare for tests as part of your daily review.
- Use mental imagery or visualization to help you feel calm and confident before, during, and after taking tests.
- Use mental and physical strategies for preparing to take tests.
- Use mental and physical strategies for taking tests.
- Use mental and physical strategies for analyzing the results of tests.
- Select methods of test preparation and test taking that are appropriate to your learning style.

There once was a girl named Pam
Who went blank on a History exam.
When asked for her name,
From her brain nothing came.
That's what you get when you cram.

If you were to ask the other students in your classes, "What do you find most difficult about school?" many would probably answer, "Taking tests." Such responses as "I just go blank on tests" and "I study for hours and still don't do well" are common. What you don't hear is how those students prepared for their exams.

Even though most students think that tests give them the most difficulty, how well they do on tests is the end result of proper or improper preparation. This text has presented proper preparation procedures through the PPR Systems and their use of the principles of memory, learning, and thinking. If you employ these systems on a daily basis, you will be well prepared at test time, when you must demonstrate what you know. If you do not prepare properly for a test, no amount of instruction in test taking will help.

PPR Test Taking

Suppose that after a tennis tournament you talk to a player who was badly defeated. When you ask her about her performance, she says, "I don't play well in tournaments." Upon further investigation, you find out that she began preparing for the tournament the day before by hitting serves and thinking about how she would spend the prize money. How could this person expect to do well when she began to prepare so late and did not even practice playing an actual game?

The same idea can be applied to test taking. To take tests well, you must practice—study the content—on a regular basis. You must also practice the very process you are preparing for—taking tests. The methods you use in your practice sessions should include the three stages of memory to help you: (1) prepare properly *before* tests, (2) use what you know *while* taking tests, and (3) analyze difficulties that you had *after* taking tests.

The PPR Test Taking System incorporates the principles of memory, learning, thinking, and time management to help you prepare to take tests, to process information as you are taking tests, and to recall the material you stored. It is illustrated in Table 9–1. By using this system, you can make test taking what it is meant to be: a demonstration of what you have learned.

Prepare: Mental and Physical Strategies

Preparing to take tests requires mental conditioning as much as it requires physical studying. In test taking, as in any other kind of performance, you must have not only ability but also the belief that you can use that ability to succeed. Just as the athlete prepares for an event by both physical and mental conditioning, you, as a student, should mentally and physically prepare for the test taking process.

Prepare: Mental Strategies

Before taking a test, you must build up your confidence, think about how to prepare for the type of test you will be taking, and recall the types of mistakes you often make. The suggestions below will help you mentally prepare to take tests.

TABLE 9–1 PPR Test Taking System

Stages	*Mental Strategies*	*Physical Strategies*
Before test taking: *Prepare*	*Ask yourself:* • How can I gain confidence? • How should I schedule study time? • What levels of questioning will be used? • How should I go about learning? • What types of errors did I make on previous exams?	• List positive points. • Make daily study plan. • Analyze old tests. • Compose practice tests. • Review and recite maps, diagrams, charts, and vocabulary cards. • Review and recite note/text annotations. • Review error assessment of former exams.

While test taking:
Process
	Ask yourself:
	• How can I overcome negative thoughts?
	• How many items are on the test?
	• What are the point values?
	• How much time should I allow for each question?
	• What familiar material do I see?
	• What should I answer first/last?
	• What should I jot down immediately to aid recall?
	• How should I annotate questions?
	• What choices (multiple choice) can I eliminate?
	• What answers do I need to rethink?
	• Have I answered all the questions?
	• Are my spelling and punctuation correct?
		• Review positive point card.
		• Use the CALM test-taking approach:
		  • Calculate.
		  • Analyze questions.
		  • Logically answer.
		  • Make sure.

After test taking:
Recall
	Ask yourself:
	Were my errors the result of:
	  • Format?
	  • Anxiety?
	  • Fatigue/pacing?
	  • Reading errors?
	  • Anger?
	  • Studying in one direction?
	  • Second guessing?
	  • Knowledge gaps?
	  • Over- or underaccepting?
		• Create error assessment form.

Visualize Success. To gain confidence, you must first remember how it feels to be successful. Think back to a time in your life when you did something that made you feel proud. What words could you use to describe how you felt? Confident? High? Powerful? Recall how your entire being felt at that moment, and try to generate that feeling now.

The mind and body are so strongly connected that it is possible to program your body to behave any way you like. Unfortunately, many students program themselves for failure by saying things like "I can't" and "This is too hard for me." Henry Ford once said, "Whether you think you can or think you can't, you're right." He meant that if you think you will fail, you are programming your mind and body for failure, so, indeed, you will fail. But if you think strongly that you will succeed, you are programming yourself for success and you will, in fact, succeed. Through visualizing, you can tell your body exactly how you want it to feel and react in any situation.

To gain confidence when taking tests, you must visualize yourself successfully taking a test. A good time to do this is when you go to bed each evening. Instead of worrying about school or grades and creating negative thoughts, begin to see yourself studying and concentrating well. Picture yourself getting up the day of the test. Imagine yourself feeling calm and confident. Watch yourself prepare for class, knowing that you've studied and are ready for the test. See yourself walk into the room feeling ready to perform well. As the test is being distributed, recall those confident feelings. Program yourself to behave a certain way when you come to a question you are not sure you can answer. Perhaps you could imagine confidently circling the question and returning to it later.

Play this scene over and over in your mind each night—the more detailed, the better. When the actual day of the test arrives, your mind and body will feel as though you've taken the test many times and will react calmly and confidently. Remember, this is not a substitute for studying but a way of increasing the effects of study.

Set a Purpose. When you begin to study for a test, you need to think about how to study, what to study, and when to study according to the type of test you will be taking. Ask yourself the following questions to help you in this process: On what levels of the PYRAMID will I be questioned? Will this be an essay, multiple-choice, fill-in, or true-false test? What vocabulary, facts, and ideas do I need to know? According to my learning style, how should I go about learning them? How should I schedule my time?

Recall Past Mistakes. To avoid making the same mistake twice, think about the types of problems you have had on past tests. Many students continue to needlessly repeat mistakes because they never bother to analyze the results of former tests. For example, if you have missed more true-false questions than any other kind, you need to use that information to improve your performance. Asking the question "What types of errors have I made in the past?" will help you study with problem areas in mind. You will learn how to do an error assessment in the recall stage of test taking. Use the results of your assessment to help you prepare for future tests.

Prepare: Physical Strategies

Before taking a test, you must plan your study time and strategies on paper. The following techniques will aid you in your physical preparation for tests.

List Positive Points. One physical way to help you gain the confidence you need is to take an index card and write yourself a brief pep talk. Include comments about your best qualities and statements about what you are able to do well. For example, you could write:

> I am a kind and intelligent person. I have had the discipline to condition as an athlete. I have also had the discipline to keep up with my studies. I have done well on tests that I have prepared for in the past, and I can do well on this one.

Read this card frequently to yourself in preparation for the exam. When negative thoughts creep into your mind before and during a test, replace them with this positive self-talk. Remember, you must program your mind for success.

Use a Long-Range Study Plan. Test preparation should begin with your first week of class. From the time you begin to take notes or read your textbook, you should be selecting and organizing information to properly store it for later recall. Figure 9–1 illustrates a daily study plan that you could use to keep up with your work. By using this plan, you will be applying distributed practice. You will not have to try to cram four weeks' worth of material into your brain the day before a test. Studying for a test will mean nothing more than reviewing material you already know. The process of going over a little material each day will help you construct strong memory traces and give you confidence that you know the material. The combination of test taking confidence and strong memory traces ensures that you will not go blank when taking a test.

Analyze Old Tests. Do not ask your instructor what will be on the test. Instead, ask him about the kind of test he gives. Instructors are sometimes willing to go over previous tests or to make old tests available in the school library. Your purpose in reviewing former tests is not to memorize answers or avoid studying but to look at the way the test is constructed. What types of questions are included: multiple choice, true-false, fill-in, or essay? What is the level of questioning: memory, translation, interpretation, application, analysis, synthesis, or evaluation? How many questions are there? What is their point value? Read through the questions, and note the way they are worded. If possible, actually take the test and analyze your results.

Compose Practice Test Questions. The best way for an athlete to improve performance is to practice her actual sport. The same holds true for

FIGURE 9–1
A daily study plan

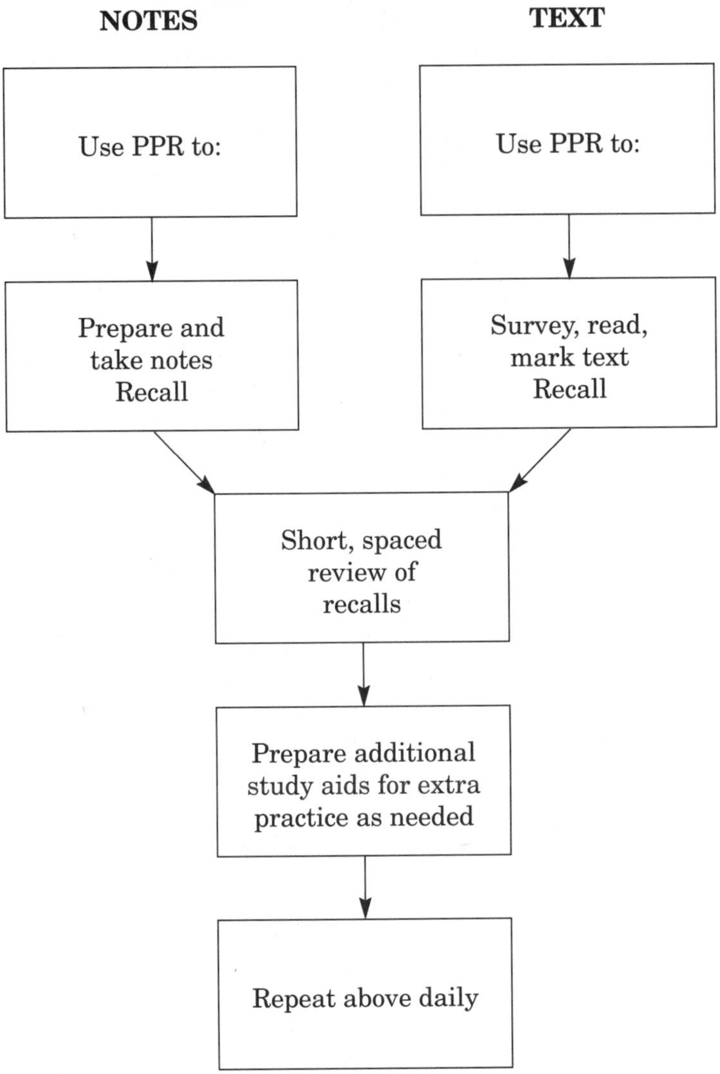

a student. Instead of reciting from your recalls and underlined material, use this information to make up test questions. For example, if you were studying the Business Communication notes illustrated in Figure 9–2, you could create the following test questions, depending on the type of test you will be taking:

FIGURE 9–2
Business Communication Notes

	Business Communication 1 Dr. Smith 12/3/93
	<u>Nonverbal Communication</u>
Define/Desc.	- Most basic form of commun.
Nonverbal	- Communicating by using body
Commun.	- 100,000 forms
List	<u>Types of Nonverbal Communication</u>
types of	1. Facial expression & eye behavior
Nonverbal	- face = primary site express emotion
Commun.	- eyes
Desc.	- indicate attention
effects of	- influence others
face & eye	- regulate interaction
behavior	- establish dominance
	2. Touching behavior
Desc.	- shows warmth & comfort
effects of	- accepted norms
touching	- business touching = dominance
	- sometimes can be interpreted as harassment
	3. Time & Space
Describe	- can show authority
effects of	- make people wait
time &	- show status
space	- take best space
	- determine comfort
	- too close/too far away

Essay test	List and describe the types of nonverbal communication.
True-false	Touching behavior is sexual harassment.
Multiple choice	Use of time and space can: *a.* Demonstrate authority. *b.* Show status. *c.* Determine comfort. *d.* All of the above.
Fill-in	There are over _______________ forms of nonverbal communication.
Vocabulary	Define nonverbal communication.

If you are in a study group, construct test questions for one another and evaluate the answers. Be sure to create study cards for the questions that were difficult for you. Put the question on the front, and outline, chart, summarize, or map the answer on the back. If you are a visual learner, make answers as visual as possible and study by writing or visualizing. An auditory learner should study by reciting or describing the answers to questions. A kinesthetic learner should move around or manipulate items to describe answers.

Review Past Mistakes on Tests. Instruction on how to construct an error assessment form can be found in the "Recall" section of this chapter on page 242–243. You will learn that test-taking errors usually result from the following:

1. *Format:* Certain types of questions, such as "All of the above," may be frequently missed.
2. *Anxiety:* Inability to concentrate due to nervousness may occur at the beginning of a test.
3. *Pacing or fatigue:* Inability to concentrate due to lack of time or fatigue may occur at the end of a test.
4. *Reading errors:* In haste, key words may be missed or directions misunderstood.
5. *Anger:* One test question may cause so much anger that the anger carries over to several of the following questions.
6. *Studying in one direction only:* Memorizing a list or chart in one way, such as cause to effect, may make recall difficult if a test asks for effect to cause.
7. *Second guessing when unsure:* Answers are sometimes changed when they should not be.
8. *Knowledge difficulties:* A question is missed because the information was not learned.
9. *Over- or underaccepting:* "All of the above" or "None of the above" questions may always seem correct.

Refer to pages 241–243 in this chapter to learn how to identify your test taking mistakes. When you know the kinds of mistakes you tend to make, reviewing them before each test can help you avoid making them again.

Sharing Your Ideas

Work in pairs with someone you know, and create a card listing your positive points to help you feel confident during test taking. On a 3″ × 5″ card, try to list your own best qualities. Share what you've written with your partner. Think of other strengths and abilities your partner may have that he can add to his list. ■

Process: Mental and Physical Strategies

If you have properly prepared to take a test, the actual test taking process can become a performance in which you demonstrate what you know. However, it may not become such a performance because even if you have all the knowledge necessary to take the test, there are things that can interfere with your ability to perform. Taking tests well requires good thinking and reasoning skills. These, in turn, require a calm and confident mind. The test taking strategy presented in this section is called the CALM approach. Each letter of CALM represents a stage of the test taking process:

C = *C*alculate the time needed.
A = *A*nalyze the test questions.
L = *L*ogically answer.
M = *M*ake sure you've checked your work.

By properly preparing and by applying the CALM approach as you take tests, you should be able to greatly improve your ability to perform.

Process: Mental Strategies

Taking tests is a thinking process. It requires proper recall of what you have stored. It also requires the ability to analyze what is being asked and to logically determine the best way to answer. The questions below list concerns that you should address as you take tests. Methods for dealing with these concerns will be presented in the CALM approach to test taking.

Calculate

How many items are on the test?
What are the point values?

How much time should I allow for each question?

What material should I answer first/last?

Analyze

What are the directions asking me to do?

What should I jot down immediately to aid recall?

What are the key words in this question?

How did I store this information?

How should I annotate or mark the question?

Logically Answer

Multiple choice

What are the key words in this answer?

Which answers are true, which are false, and which am I unsure of?

Are there any repeating words in the answers?

Are there any negative words in the answers?

Are there any qualifying words such as *always, never, all,* and *everything* in the answers?

Are there any totally unfamiliar answers?

Does this make sense?

Do I need to rethink this item later?

True-false

Are there any qualifying words that could change the meaning?

Are there any double negatives?

Are there two parts to this question? Are both parts true?

Is this statement totally unfamiliar?

Essay

What type of answer does this require?

How should I organize my answer?

What pattern of organization should I use?

What is my main point or thesis statement?

What topics and subtopics do I want to use to support my main point?

How many parts does this answer have?

Am I stating facts and explaining them or giving my opinion?

Fill-in-the-blank

What are the key words in this sentence?
Do I need to recall a name, date, place, or term?
What part of speech is the required word?

Make Sure

Have I answered all of the questions?
Have I reviewed all of the answers I wanted to check?
Have I marked my test booklet properly with my name, Social Security number, etc.?
Have I rechecked the types of items I usually miss?
How is my writing, spelling, punctuation, grammar (essays)?

Process: Physical Strategies

Use the CALM approach to take tests. The suggestions below will show you how.

Calculate. When you first receive your paper, look through the entire test. Determine how many items are on the test, how much each is worth, and how much time you should spend on each. If you have 60 minutes to do 60 multiple-choice items, each worth 1 point, you should do one test question per minute. However, if you have 60 minutes to do 30 multiple-choice items worth 2 points each and one essay question worth 40 points, how much time would you allow for the multiple-choice items, how much time would you allow for the essay question, and which would you answer first?

Generally, you should spend more time answering the questions with the highest point value. They should be answered first, especially if you tend to get tired toward the end of tests. However, you also need to consider that you should answer what you know first. If you read an essay question and do not feel confident about the content, sometimes working through some multiple-choice questions will help you recall more information.

Analyze. As soon as you receive your test paper, jot down any mnemonics, formulas, or facts that you need to remember. As you read each test question, underline words that seem important. Think about the topic and how you filed it in your memory. Try to recall your visual, auditory, or kinesthetic methods of storage. In your mind's eye, see your study aids, hear yourself reciting your study cards, or feel the movements you used as you learned kinesthetically.

Watch for qualifying words such as those listed in Table 9–2. Circle them, and be aware that they can change the meaning of a statement. For

TABLE 9–2 Qualifying Words

No Exceptions	*Some Exceptions*
best	sometimes
never	usually
always	often
all	some
no	may
none	few
entirely	frequently
completely	hardly ever
only	seldom
must	
everyone	

example, the true-false statement "*All* newer computers are user friendly" allows for no exceptions: It refers to *every* newer computer. Because information almost always has some exceptions, such words as *all, never, none, always,* and *best* usually make a statement false. The statement "*Some* newer computers are user friendly" means that some newer computers are user friendly and some are not. Because the statement allows for exceptions, it is true.

Negative statements and statements with double negatives cause difficulties because they require you to switch from positive to negative thinking. To avoid having to do this, use the following strategies: Double negatives, such as *not unusual,* cancel each other out. So *not unusual* should be read as *usual.* If the question reads *all of the above except,* cross out *except* and read it as *all of the above.* In this case, the one answer that does not fit will be the correct one.

When you read a question, translate it into your own words to be sure that you understand it. If important information comes to mind when you read the question, jot it down. On a multiple-choice exam, try to answer the question in your head before looking at any of the choices.

Logically Answer. As you read each answer, look for key words and underline them. Mark each answer T for true, F for false, and ? if you aren't sure. This makes it easy to logically eliminate answers and to focus on the answers you know. Write T, F, or ? for all of the answers. Even if one answer appears to be "true," another may be a better choice.

Circle any repeating words in the answers. If you have to make a guess, answers with repeating words are often good choices. Also circle any negative words in the answers. Remember that such words can change the meaning of the statement. If there are qualifying words in the answers, circle them too, and remember that when such words allow for no exceptions, they make an answer false. The test question and answers below illustrate some of these points.

1. All of the statements about intelligence below are true except:

    T a. Intelligence can be measured.

    T b. It is not unusual for environment to affect intelligence. *(usual)*

    F c. Intelligence is only gained through inheritance.

    T d. Intelligence is gained through environment and heredity.

If you have studied well and an answer is totally unfamiliar to you, it is probably false. Always ask yourself whether an answer makes sense. Completely recalling an answer happens less often than being able to use partial knowledge to reason out the right choice. Look at all of the information given and at the way an answer is worded, and then use your own general knowledge to figure out answers you are unsure of. Practice in this area will be given in the "Sharing Your Ideas" activity following this section.

Anytime you find that you have to make a complete guess, mark either A, B, or C consistently throughout the test. Doing this will statistically give you a better chance of hitting the correct answer. Be sure, however, to circle the number of any item you wish to come back to later if you have time.

When taking essay exams, read the directions carefully. Look for and underline the topic. Circle key words that tell you how to organize information about the topic and limiting words that tell you how much or what type of information to include. The example below illustrates marking in this manner.

Organizational pattern ↓ *Limiting word* ↓ *Topic* ↓

Compare and contrast three differences between a formal report and a proposal.

Before you begin to write your answer, make a brief outline on your paper of the points you want to cover and how you want to cover them. This will keep your answer organized, and if you run out of time, your instructor may give you credit for material that you were unable to expand on but had written in your outline.

Table 9–3 Key Words in Directions

Key Words	*Meaning*	*Level of PYRAMID*	*Pattern*
List, enumerate	List items briefly, one by one.	Memory	List
Trace	Put items in a specific order	Memory	Chronological order
State, summarize	Give an organized description in your words.	Translate	Description, example
Define	Give meaning, with details to show your understanding.	Translate	Definition
Explain, describe	Tell in detail who, what, where, when, why, and how.	Translate	Description, example
Diagram, illustrate	Explain, using concrete examples, maps, charts.	Interpret	Description, example
Use, apply	Use the information given in a new situation.	Apply	Example
Determine, deduce	Tell what happened and why.	Analyze	Cause/effect
Compare, contrast, relate, classify, categorize	Identify how topics are the same and how they are different.	Analyze	Compare/contrast
Devise, design, create, formulate	Use what you know to create something new	Synthesize	Description, example
Justify, prove, tell why	Give reasons in support of an action.	Evaluate	Cause/effect
Evaluate, judge	Come to a conclusion by looking at all sides of a topic.	Evaluate	Compare/contrast, cause/effect, problem/solution

Analyze the task required by your instructions. Table 9–3 shows examples of key words in directions, the PYRAMID level/organizational pattern they represent, and what they are asking you to do.

When you start to write your essay, be sure to begin with a general statement about the topic to explain what you will be discussing. This statement is your topic sentence. Follow the points in your outline, and use evidence to support or explain your topic sentence. Be sure to answer all parts of the question and to use facts rather than your own ideas or opinions unless the question calls for them.

Work for quality, not quantity. Your instructor is an expert in her field. Do not think that you can fool her by being wordy. Get to the point.

To logically answer fill-in-the-blank questions, underline key words in the sentence. Think about how you stored information about the topic. Decide whether your answer should be a name, date, place, or term.

Make Sure. After you have completed a test, go back and make sure you have answered all of the questions. Check the front and back sides of the test to be sure you have not skipped a page. Take another look at the questions you circled for later review. Do not change an answer unless you find that you misread the question, have a reasonable new thought, or recalled information in the process of taking the test that would change your answer.

If your instructor uses computerized scan sheets, check your test booklet for proper marking of your Social Security number, name, and answers. Look for blanks or double-marked spots.

Recheck the types of items that your error assessment showed you often miss. Perhaps, because of anxiety at the beginning of a test, it would be a good idea to review the first few items. If you were tired at the end of the test, review the last few items.

On essay exams, you may lose points for improper spelling or grammar or for writing that is difficult to read. Proofread for errors, and edit your work.

Sharing Your Ideas

Work in pairs to practice the test taking techniques presented above. Use the following procedure:

1. Take turns reading a test question out loud.
2. As you read each question, tell your partner what you are marking and why. If your partner has additions or corrections, she may give them.
3. As you read each answer, tell your partner what you are marking and why. Then answer T for true, F for false, or ? for unsure. Tell your partner why you chose each response. After your response, your partner may again give additions or corrections.
4. Read the correct answer and explanation below your question. Analyze your difficulties.

Directions: *Select the one best answer for each question below.*

1. On the average, white females born in 1960 could expect to live 73 years. This means that:
   a. The average age at death for white females was 73 in 1960.
   b. Everyone born in 1960 could expect to live to be 73.

c. Generally, women born in 1960 could expect to live to be 73.
d. Generally, white women born in 1960 could expect to live to be 73.

Item 1: The question calls for an average or general rule about women born in 1960. Rule out (*a*) because it refers to age at death instead of birth. Answer (*b*) uses the qualifying word *everyone* and so should be eliminated. Answer (*c*) refers to women instead of only to white women. Answer (*d*) is correct because it includes all of the information in the original statement.

2. All of the statements below about learning are true except:
   a. Learning takes place in three stages.
   b. Problems with recall can always be traced to difficulty in the storage stage.
   c. A student who does not focus his attention finds it difficult to store information.
   d. Because everyone learns differently, methods for storage can differ according to learning style.

Item 2: The question contains the negative word *except.* In order to read the answers as positives, cross out the word *except.* The one false answer will be the correct response. Answer (*a*) is true. Answer (*b*) contains the qualifying words *always,* making it false. Answers (*c*) and (*d*) are true.

3. An infant with AIDS:
   a. Most likely acquired the AIDS virus through his or her parents.
   b. Could have acquired the AIDS virus through a blood transfusion.
   c. Probably acquired the AIDS virus through contact with another infected child.
   d. Cannot transmit the AIDS virus to anyone else because of his or her age.

Item 3: The question requires only a general knowledge of how the AIDS virus is transmitted. Answer (*a*) contains the qualifying words *most likely* and so is false, given that the other answers are also general possibilities. Answer (*b*) contains the words *could have,* which seems likely and so should be marked true. Answer (*c*) sounds unreasonable because of the word *probably* and the fact that an infant would be unlikely to have the type of contact necessary to transmit the virus. Answer (*d*) contains the qualifying word *cannot* and so is false.

4. A student who has studied properly is least likely to:
   a. Be able to take a test with little anxiety.
   b. Recall what she learned.
   c. Have her test grade reflect what she knows.
   d. Go blank.

Item 4: The question contains the negative *least likely,* making it difficult to read positively stated answers. Cross out the words *least likely* and read the statement as *likely.* In this case, the false response (*d*) is the correct answer.

5. Most instructors should be primarily concerned about:
   a. Their ability to relate socially to their students.
   b. Their ability to present information to their students.
   c. Their research.
   d. Their ability to continue their own education.

Item 5: The question contains the word *most,* which you should note means not all but more than half. *Primarily* is a key word meaning first or most importantly. Answer (*a*) is important but probably not as important as other factors. Answer (*b*) is a good choice because instructors are in the classroom to help educate their students. Answers (*c*) and (*d*) may be important, but not primarily for most instructors. ■

Recall: Mental and Physical Strategies

Creating an error assessment form could help you properly analyze the types of errors you made while taking the practice test above. Taking a test without analyzing the results makes it impossible to learn from your mistakes. Carole Hyatt and Linda Gottlieb, in their book *When Smart People Fail,* make the following statement about learning from your mistakes:

> There are people who learn, who are open to what happens around them, who listen, who hear the lessons. When they do something stupid, they don't do it again. And when they do something that works a little bit, they do it even better and harder the next time. The question to ask is not whether you are a success or failure, but whether you are a learner or a nonlearner.

Use your test results as a learning device. Hear the lesson, and make some changes.

Recall: Mental Strategies

After taking a test, you should think about the kinds of mistakes you made and how to avoid repeating them on future tests. The suggestions below will show you how.

Analyze Your Difficulties. When you receive the results of your test, you must ask yourself, Were my errors the result of:

Format?
Anxiety?
Fatigue/pacing?

Reading errors?
Anger?
Studying in one direction only?
Second guessing?
Knowledge gaps?
Over- or underaccepting?

To answer these questions, devise an error assessment form.

Recall: Physical Strategies

To devise an error assessment form, use a sheet of notebook paper and make four columns:

Item No.	*Format*	*Topic*	*PYRAMID Level / Organizational Pattern*

Item Number. List the numbers of the test items you missed.

Format. Write the abbreviation of the type of test question you missed beside the proper number. Examples of such abbreviations are: T-F = true-false. FI = fill-in, SBA except = all of the above except, SBA = single best answer (regular multiple choice).

Topic of Question. Describe the material covered by the question with a word or a short phrase.

PYRAMID Level / Pattern of Organization. Determine whether the answer required you to memorize, translate, interpret, apply, analyze, synthesize, or evaluate. Also determine whether you were to define/describe, use time order, recall a simple list, know cause/effect, compare/contrast, or work a problem/solution.

A completed error assessment form is illustrated in Figure 9–3. See if you can detect patterns of errors made by analyzing information under each heading.

FIGURE 9–3
Completed error assessment form

Error Assessment Form

Item No. (30 total items)	Format	Topic	Level of PYRAMID Pattern of Organization
2	SBA	Credit	Memory: List
3	SBA except	Credit	Analyze: Cause/effect
10	SBA except	Cost ratio	Memory: Define
15	SBA except	Principal	Memory: Define
28	Essay	Credit/debit	Analyze: Compare/contrast
29	Essay	Assets	Analyze: Effects
30	Essay	Liabilities	Analyze: Effects

Sharing Your Ideas

Below is an example of a completed error assessment form. As a class, analyze the items, formats, topics, and PYRAMID levels/patterns of organization. List and discuss the patterns of errors that you find in format, possible anxiety, fatigue, possible anger, or knowledge gaps.

Item	*Format*	*Topic of Question*	*Level / Pattern*
1	SBA except	Hallucinogenic drugs	Memorize: List
2	SBA	Tranquilizers	Analyze: Cause/effect
3	SBA except	Narcotics	Evaluate: Cause/effect
10	SBA except	Tranquilizers	Analyze: Effect/cause
24	SBA	Tranquilizers	Analyze: Compare
25	SBA except	Drug abuse	Analyze: Effect/cause

To do a pattern summary, look at the items under each heading. Complete the statements below for each heading:

Item: Were several items missed at the beginning or end of the test?

____

Format: The question format missed most was ____________________

Topic: The topic(s) missed more than once was (were) ______________

____

Level/pattern: The PYRAMID level or organizational pattern missed most was ______________________________ ■

Correct Your Difficulties. After you have completed an error assessment form, you will have information about the types of problems you experienced on your test. Now you must devise ways of solving those problems before the next test. Here are some techniques you can use to strengthen each area of weakness.

1. *Format Problems.* If you seem to miss more of a certain type of test question than of other types, make up and take practice tests with that type of question. Remember, SBA except requires a switch from positive to negative thinking. Cross out the word *except,* and use the false answer as the correct response.

2. *Test Anxiety.* If you find that you made several errors at the beginning of a test, you may be having difficulty in relaxing and getting focused. Mentally recite your positive point card, and recall the positive visualization you practiced nightly. Make it a habit to recheck the first few items at the end of a test.

3. *Pacing or Fatigue.* If you find that you made several errors at the end of a test or that you ran out of time, time yourself while taking practice exams. Kinesthetic learners may become distracted and have difficulty in maintaining a good pace. Use a watch, and set goals for completing a certain number of questions. All students need to keep a proper study schedule and avoid staying up late the night before a test. Also, eating properly before taking tests can improve your ability to concentrate.

4. *Reading Errors.* To avoid misreading test items, underline key words and circle qualifying words. If you are an auditory learner, hear the items in your mind as you read them. Always mentally translate questions into your own words to be sure you understand them.

5. *Anger.* If a test item makes you mad, you may have difficulty in concentrating not only on that item but on several others after it. If this happens, use your visualization to stay focused. Circle the item, and plan to recheck it as well as several items after it.

6. *Studying in One Direction Only.* If you memorize your notes or study cards instead of understanding them, you could end up being able to recite their information in only one way. Then, if a test question asks for the information in another way, you may be unable to recall it. When studying, be sure to use levels of the PYRAMID beyond the memory stage for most learning. Practice reciting study cards in reverse order (front to back and back to front, cause to effect and effect to cause) and in your own words.

7. *Second Guessing.* Determine how many answers you changed during the exam. Changing a wrong answer to a wrong answer means that you didn't know the material. Luck accounts for changing a wrong answer to a right answer if the change was clearly a guess. You should change your answer only if you find that you misread something, that you were better able to analyze the test question/answers, or that you recalled more information while taking the test.

8. *Knowledge Difficulties.* If you find that you missed several items about the same topic, you must review that topic, especially if your final exam will be comprehensive (cover all that you learned).

9. *Over- or Underaccepting.* When reading test items that list *all of the above* or *none of the above* as possible answers, some students always want to mark one or the other. If you want to mark *all of the above* most of the time, read the possible answers with the intention of eliminating them. Be able to prove why they are right if you feel they are. If you want to mark *none of the above* most of the time, make yourself prove why each answer is incorrect. Circle questions of this type if they give you problems, and review them at the end of the test.

Putting It All Together

Test taking is the final stage of the learning process. If you have prepared and stored properly, this stage will represent what you know. If you have not used proper principles of learning and memory, this stage will represent what you don't know.

Preparing to take tests involves both mental and physical conditioning. Visualizing success should be paired with review of content on a daily basis. The practice of taking actual tests should be included in your preparation.

While taking tests, you must be able to pair good thinking and reasoning skills with your knowledge of the content. The CALM test taking approach will help you *C*alculate the time needed, *A*nalyze the test question, *L*ogically answer, and *M*ake sure you've checked your work.

The final step in good test taking is analyzing your errors. Identifying the kinds of mistakes you have made on an exam helps you avoid making them again. In this way, test taking becomes a learning experience.

Making the Connection

Check your understanding of the concepts presented in this chapter by completing the following activity. If you are unable to recall information in a particular area, go back and review that material before completing the rest of the exercises in this section.

1. Write one or two sentences to summarize what you recall about each of the following topics:

   How and why to visualize success ______________________________

   ____

   ____

   Devising a daily study plan ______________________________

   ____

   ____

   Mental strategies for preparing to take tests ______________________________

   ____

   ____

   Physical strategies for preparing to take tests ______________________________

   ____

   ____

   Mental strategies for taking tests ______________________________

   ____

   ____

   Physical strategies for taking tests: the CALM approach ______________

   ____

   ____

   Mental strategies for analyzing test errors ______________________________

   ____

   ____

   Physical strategies for analyzing test errors ______________________________

   ____

   ____

2. List one new idea you've gained about test taking as a result of this chapter. ______________________________

____

3. Describe one change you plan to make before test taking, one change you plan to make during test taking, and one change you plan to make after test taking. ______________________________

____

____

____

____

____

Thinking It Through

Read the following passage, and then answer the questions by applying what you've learned about test taking.

Edna is a perfectionist. She has always gone above and beyond what was required. As she enters college, she continues to strive for perfection. When given reading assignments, she reads, highlights, takes notes, and studies by rereading. When taking notes, she tries to make neat diagrams and to take down every word her instructors say. She uses Roman numerals for each heading and alphabetical listings of points. She recopies her notes after lectures and studies them for hours nightly by rereading them.

Edna is finding it difficult to stay awake in class. Her studying is taking her into the morning hours.

1. Based on information in the passage, what do you see as Edna's specific problem(s)? ______________________________

____

2. By using knowledge you already have, asking others, and perhaps doing a bit of research, list as many solutions to Edna's problem(s) as you can. ______________________________

____

____

3. List the pros and cons for each of these solutions from Edna's point of view.

4. Select the solution that appears to be the best in terms of pros and cons. List the steps necessary to carry out this solution. Be sure to describe the details, such as who, what, when, where, and how.

Applying Your Skills 1 *Creating a Study Plan*

Instructions: Use the study plan shown in Figure 9–1 and the study schedule you created in Chapter 2 to complete this activity.

1. Schedule time to recall your notes as soon after each class as possible. Write "Recall Notes" on your study schedule in those time slots.
2. Schedule time to read and mark your texts daily. Write "Read/Mark" on your study schedule in those time slots.
3. Schedule time daily to review and recite your note and text recalls. Write "Study Recalls" on your study schedule in that time slot.
4. Schedule time daily to prepare study aids for extra practice. Write "Study Aids" on your study schedule in that time slot.

Applying Your Skills 2 *Reasoning and Test Taking*

Instructions: Apply your reasoning and test taking skills to the following test. Remember to use the CALM approach to test taking as you Calculate the time needed, Analyze the questions, Logically answer, and Make sure your work is complete.

You will have five minutes to choose the one best answer to each of the following questions.

1. All of the following statements are true about college except:
   a. College is different from high school.
   b. It is possible to memorize your way through college.
   c. Most students fail college because they lack motivation.
   d. College students need to learn how to take control of their own learning.

2. An educated person:
   a. Knows how to learn.
   b. Has a college degree.
   c. Makes good money.
   d. Is always successful.

3. Good time management does not usually include:
   a. Leisure time.
   b. Time to study on weekends.
   c. One- to two-hour breaks.
   d. None of the above.

4. All of the following statements about learning styles are true except:
   a. Kinesthetic learners should move their bodies in order to learn effectively.
   b. Auditory learners should recite information out loud as they study.
   c. Visual learners do not have to attend class because they can learn by seeing the notes of others.
   d. We usually learn through a combination of learning styles.

5. During the storage process of memory:
   a. It takes 15–30 seconds to make a memory trace.
   b. Once you have stored information correctly, you will always be able to recall it with little effort.
   c. Memory traces are made only for completely new information.
   d. Old memory traces disappear as new ones are made.

6. All of the following statements about previewing or activating prior knowledge are true except:
   a. It helps tie new information to old.
   b. It creates an interest in the subject.
   c. It makes it easier to focus as you read.
   d. It causes memory traces to fade.

7. Critical thinking does not involve:
   a. Looking at all sides of an issue.
   b. Being able to identify obstacles to critical thinking in yourself and others.
   c. Being critical of others.
   d. Creativity.

8. Good problem solving involves:
   a. Knowing how to quickly find an answer.
   b. Being able to come to a solution without help.
   c. Precise and careful thinking.
   d. Precise and rapid thinking.

9. To take tests well:
   a. You must have knowledge of the content.
   b. You must have knowledge of the content and know how to use logic and reasoning when reading and when answering questions.
   c. You must put in many hours of study.
   d. You must not overstudy.

10. If a student finds that he always misses test items in which one of the possible answers is "All of the above," he should:
    a. Practice taking tests with that answer.
    b. Attempt to prove that each answer is truly correct.
    c. Read each answer with the intention of eliminating it.
    d. All of the above.

Applying Your Skills 3 *Error Assessment*

Instructions: Grade the test from Applying Your Skills 2 by using the answer key found below. Complete the error assessment form below for the items you missed.

Answers:

1. *c*	6. *d*
2. *a*	7. *c*
3. *d*	8. *c*
4. *c*	9. *b*
5. *a*	10. *d*

Item	*Format*	*Topic*	*Level / Pattern*

Pattern Summary

Item: Were several items missed at the beginning or end of the test?

____

Format: The question format missed most was ______________

____

Topic: The topic(s) missed more than once was (were) ________________

____

Level/pattern: The PYRAMID level or organizational pattern missed most was ______________________________

____

Applying Your Skills 4 *Using Your Resources*

Instructions: To know where to "radio for help," you will be asked to visit various school resources throughout this text. Keep this information so that you can refer to it when you are in need of help outside the classroom.

Complete the information below after meeting with your school's Counseling Services.

Location: ________________________________

Hours of operation: __________________________

Contact person: ____________________________

Phone: __________________________________

Services offered:

____

____

____

____

Personal comments:

Briefly discuss how you could use this resource.

____

____

____

____

____

C H A P T E R

10 The PPR Writing System

Apply the principles of thinking and learning to write effectively.

Chapter Goals

After you read this chapter, you will be able to:

- Use creative and critical processes when writing.
- Use mental and physical strategies for preparing to write.
- Use mental and physical strategies for processing information as you write.
- Use mental and physical strategies for evaluating material after you write.
- Use your learning style to enhance your ability to write.

Does the thought of a writing assignment make you break into a cold sweat? Are you afraid that you won't have good ideas or that you won't know how to express them? This book has shown you how to become aware of and direct your thinking processes as you take notes, read, and take tests. In this chapter you will learn how to tune in to your thinking and to express it on paper. You will discover that writing can be both a creative process and a process that requires critical thought. You will also discover that you have used these creative and critical processes since childhood.

Have you ever stretched the truth? Perhaps you've had to make up a story to cover up an actual occurrence that you knew would get you into trouble if it were known. For instance, suppose that after a night out with your friends you arrive home at 6 A.M. only to see your father picking up the morning paper from the doorstep. How would you account for your whereabouts? Before getting out of the car, you would probably come up with several creative ideas for explaining your late arrival. You might think: "What can I tell Dad? I can say I got lost. No, I've been out so late I've had time to hire a tour guide to find my way home. Maybe I can say I ran out of gas or had a flat tire. Yes, I can say that I had a flat tire and that the hubcap was stuck, so I had to walk somewhere to find a crowbar." Upon further thought, you might add: "I can say that the closest place I could find was my friend's house and that we ended up watching a movie and falling asleep."

In the above example, notice that you created a story line and then revised it to fit your purpose and to appeal to the audience, your father. During the presentation of your story you might make even more revisions to be sure it is believable. Thus, you are most likely quite practiced in the processes involved in writing: creatively brainstorming ideas, determining your purpose, considering your audience before you tell your story, organizing your story, revising it to make it better, and revising it one last time as you make your presentation.

PPR Writing

The PPR Writing System incorporates the principles of memory, learning, thinking, and time management in a process much like the one in the example above. It provides a framework for preparing to write, processing and refining information as you write, and revising your material after you write. It is illustrated in Table 10–1. Through the use of this system, writing can become an effective way of expressing your creative and critical thoughts.

Prepare: Mental and Physical Strategies

Many students think that the writing process begins with the actual production of a paper. When such students are assigned a paper, they will sit down and immediately try to write. If nothing happens, they often express their feelings of frustration in such statements as these: "I can't write"; "I don't know what to say"; "I don't have any good ideas." However, writing, like the academic tasks of notetaking, reading, and test taking, requires a warm-up period to activate the thinking processes. Both mental and physical activities can help you focus and organize your thoughts before you write.

Use your learning style to help you generate ideas before you write. If you are a visual learner, you can imagine ideas in your head. If you are an auditory learner, you can generate ideas out loud into a tape recorder or talk to yourself and others. If you are a kinesthetic learner, you can think of ideas as you walk or exercise. Just be sure to put your ideas on paper before you lose them.

TABLE 10–1 PPR Writing System

Stages	*Mental Strategies*	*Physical Strategies*
Before writing: *Prepare*	*Ask yourself:* • Where should I write? • What is my purpose? • Who is my audience? • What is my topic? • What do I already know? • How should I organize my ideas? • What is my focus? • What research is required? • How should I schedule my time?	• Read/analyze instructions. • Brainstorm/freewrite topics. • Outline ideas. • Create thesis. • Create time schedule.

While writing: *Process*	*Ask yourself:*
	• How should I introduce this topic?
	• What ideas should I present first, second, etc.?
	• What details should I include?
	• How should I conclude?
	• What needs to be revised?
		• Write first draft:
		  • Introduction
		  • Body
		  • Conclusion
		• Check:
		  • Clarity
		  • Flow
		  • Main ideas and details
		• Write second draft.

After writing: *Recall*	*Ask yourself:*
	• What errors need to be corrected?
		• Proofread:
		  • Spelling
		  • Punctuation
		  • Grammar

Prepare: Mental Strategies

Before you begin to write a paper, you must think about:

- A place to write free from distractions.
- Your purpose and your audience.
- Topics that interest you.
- Your background and how it relates to your topic.
- How to organize your ideas.
- How to schedule your time.

By preparing to write in this manner, you will be able to focus your attention and decide what, how, and when you're going to write. The suggestions below will help you mentally prepare to write.

Locate a Writing Area. Consider your learning style when you are looking for a place to write. The area you select should be free from distractions. If you are a visual learner, you should look for an uncluttered

Table 10–2 Types of Writing Assignments

Name	*Description*
Experience paper	A description of a personal experience
Response/reaction paper	A personal reaction or opinion
Critical essay	An in-depth analysis of theories, events, or another's work
Review/critique	A brief summary of a work's strengths and weaknesses
Factual report	Factual information on a topic
Research paper	An idea supported through research

area in which there are few windows and few people moving around. If you are an auditory learner, you should look for an area that is as quiet as possible. Because you will be reading and talking out loud as you write, you will want to select an area in which you won't distract others. If you are a kinesthetic learner, you should look for an area in which you can get up and walk around without bothering others. Your writing area should have the proper writing tools, such as paper, a pen or pencil, a dictionary, a thesaurus, and perhaps a computerized spelling device and a writer's handbook.

Using a word processor to write your paper can simplify the task of writing. Being able to easily make corrections and save your work can be a time-saver. Using a word processor may limit where you write, but adjustments can be made. Adapt your word processing area using the following suggestions:

- If you are visual, find a word processor that is away from the front of the room and in an area that few people will have to pass. Look for a machine away from windows or other visual distractions.
- If you are auditory, considering wearing headphones to block out noise. If the headphones alone do not work, you could play classical music quietly through them.
- If you are kinesthetic, locate a word processor near a door so that you can take frequent breaks without distracting others.

Determine Your Purpose. During your college career you may have to complete many types of writing assignments. Table 10–2 defines some of the common types. When you receive your instructions, ask yourself what type of writing assignment you are being asked to complete.

Once you determine the type of paper you are being asked to write, think about the pattern of organization that will help you write it. Determine whether you will be:

- Defining or describing a topic.
- Putting information in chronological order.
- Listing information about a topic.

- Showing cause and effect.
- Comparing and contrasting topics.
- Solving a problem.

Sharing Your Ideas

In pairs, read each of the writing assignments below. Use Table 10–2 to determine whether the assignment is asking for:

- An experience paper.
- A response/reaction paper.
- A critical essay.
- A review/critique.
- A factual report.
- A research paper.

Next, decide on the pattern of organization that you could use to complete the assignment. Use the organizational patterns listed above this activity to help you in your decision. Write your responses in the spaces provided. Discuss your answers as a class.

Assignment	*Type of Paper*	*Organizational Pattern*
1. Review a computer program.	____________	____________
2. Write a report on the findings of a telephone survey.	____________	____________
3. Write about a frightening experience you have had.	____________	____________
4. Describe your feelings on the president's health care proposal.	____________	____________
5. Write a paper on capital punishment.	____________	____________
6. Write a report on an experiment you performed in science lab.	____________	____________
7. Compare two computer programs.	____________	____________

Assignment	*Type of Paper*	*Organizational Pattern*
8. Write a letter to the editor of your school paper about an article in last week's issue.	________________	________________
9. Keep a personal journal on your progress in class.	________________	________________
10. Attend a play, and write a brief summary of its content.	________________	________________

■

Consider Your Audience. Have you ever had the experience of telling a joke or story that was viewed as very funny when you told it in one situation but as not funny at all when you told it in another situation? A joke well received by a friend at a Saturday night party might not be well received by your minister the following morning in church. The topic, language, and vocabulary of a story must be appropriate to its audience if the story is to be appreciated. For the same reason, you must think about the audience that will be reading and evaluating your writing. Before you begin to write, you must ask yourself who will be reading your work. Then think about how your topic, language, and vocabulary will affect that audience.

Develop a Topic. If your instructor permits you to select a topic, think about your interests and your background. It is usually easier to complete assignments in areas that you enjoy and find valuable. By asking yourself what you already know about various topics of interest, you will be able to develop many ideas to explore.

Organize Your Ideas. After you have selected a topic, ask yourself what ideas should be included in a paper on it. Think about a logical order for your ideas and about the organizational pattern that you will be using. This will guide you later as you begin the writing process.

Decide on Your Focus. Once you have organized your ideas, look at them and think about what area they focus on. By asking the question "What area do these ideas focus on?" you will be able to determine the main topic of your paper. Be sure that your focus matches the desired length of the paper. If your topic is too broad, you will have to cover too much information. If your topic is too narrow, you will have difficulty in finding enough information.

Suppose you want to do a 10-page paper on cigarette smoking. After you organize your ideas, you realize that this is a very broad topic. You could narrow it by dividing it into subtopics several times, as shown in the following example:

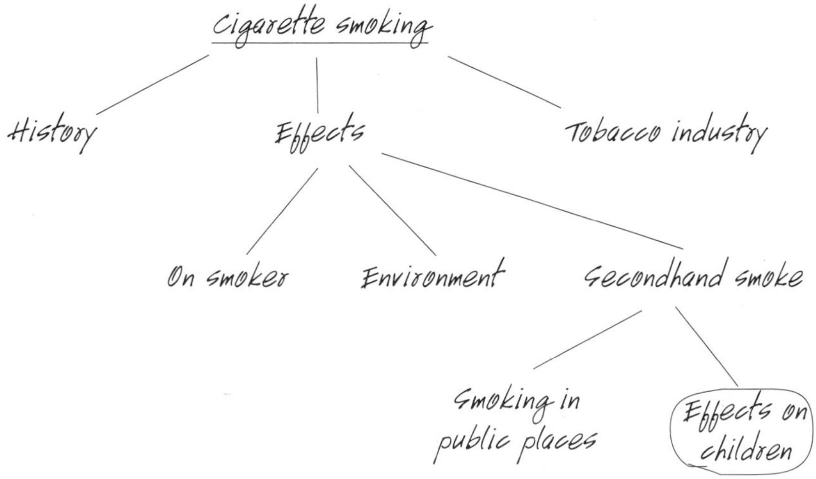

Determine Amount of Research. Once you have established your purpose, audience, focus, and topic, you must decide how much library research will be necessary. By looking at your organized ideas and asking the questions "What do I want to know about this?" and "How much do I already know?" you can gauge how much information you will have to research.

Schedule Your Time. When planning the time you will need to write your paper, think about the following questions:

- How long will it take to develop the ideas I want to cover?
- How much research do I need to do, and how long will it take?
- How much of my time is taken up with other commitments?
- When do I plan to begin writing my paper?
- When will I write the second draft?
- When will I type and proof the final copy?
- When is the paper due?

This information can be recorded on a term calendar. An example of such a record can be found at the end of the "Prepare: Physical Strategies" section.

Prepare: Physical Strategies

Before writing your paper, tune into your mental processes and take action.

Read and Analyze Your Assignment. Read your assignment carefully. Underline and circle key words that will help you focus on the purpose and content of the assignment. Make notes to yourself about the type of paper you will be writing and about the organizational patterns you think you might use. For example, the following advertising assignment has been analyzed using a student's notations.

Strengths & Weaknesses

Critique Compare two magazine advertisements.

List Determine the factors that make each effective.

Decide which one has more persuasive appeal.

Give reasons

Freewrite or Brainstorm Ideas. If you are permitted to select your own topic, relax. This is when you can use your creative efforts to have fun with the writing process. To freewrite, set aside 5 to 10 minutes to write without stopping. Write about anything that pops into your head. You can try to focus your thoughts on one general topic, or you can write about many different ideas. The important thing is to write continuously for a specified time without any concern for spelling, grammar, or content. If you get stuck, keep repeating the last words you wrote until you have a new idea. This is truly putting your thoughts on paper. An example of freewriting might look like Figure 10–1.

When you go back and read your freewriting, you may find thoughts and ideas you didn't know you had. You may also find that you've loosened up your mind as well as your hand.

To brainstorm, start with one topic and write down any idea you have that relates to it. Let one idea lead to another, even if this changes your topic. Don't worry about neatness or spelling. You can brainstorm alone or with others. Remember that this is a creative process. You should not judge your ideas yet. Figure 10–2 is an example of brainstorming.

The student who wrote this list began brainstorming about her children and ended up with ideas about what life was like for her grandparents. She went on to write a paper comparing her life with that of her grandmother.

FIGURE 10–1
Freewriting

I'm not sure what to write. I just know I have to keep writing. I don't have to worry about my spelling. I wish that was true all the time. I feel like I'd like to stop writing and have some fun. Today is such a beautiful day. I'd like to be at a beach in the sun. I need a vacation. I've been working too hard. I know I would be more productive if I had some time off. I know I would be more productive if I had time off.

FIGURE 10-2
Brainstorming

Problems with children
Spoiled
My fault?
Not like me
My childhood
My parents vs. my parenting
My grandparents vs. my parents
Different times
Women at home
Grandmother's life
My life
Differences
Compare/contrast

Sharing Your Ideas

Work in pairs to brainstorm a specific focus for a paper on the worst part of being a college student. List your combined ideas below. After five minutes, stop and decide what specific idea you would write about. Share your idea with the class.

Make an Outline. After you creatively select a topic for a paper, it is time to look at the topic critically and to determine its scope. List ideas you think should be included in a discussion of this topic. Try to put them in an order that seems appropriate. You can change the order later if necessary. Under each idea, list details for proof or support. The example below illustrates how one student feels he would develop the topic "The Mall."

The Mall

Things to do
- —Eat
- —Shop
- —Socialize

Things to see
- —Odd assortment of people
- —Store displays
- —Movies

By creating an outline, this student is able to see what areas he will be discussing in his paper. Moreover, the outline he has created provides him with a way of creating a thesis statement.

Develop a Thesis. The word *thesis* is another name for a general statement that tells what your entire paper will cover. To develop a thesis, look at your outline and make a general statement about the focus of your ideas. To create a thesis for his paper, the student discussed above read his outlined ideas about the mall. Then he made up this general sentence: "There are many things to do and see at the mall."

Sharing Your Ideas

Work with the same partner who helped you develop your list on the worst part of being a college student.

1. Organize your brainstormed list of ideas into an outline. You may add ideas to your original list or omit ideas from it. Under each idea, add information you might want to include.

____

____

____

____

2. Use your outline to create a thesis about the worst part of being a college student. Write it on the lines below.

3. Share your thesis with the class. ■

Create a Time Schedule. An important part of producing a good paper is giving yourself enough time to do your best work. On the day you receive your writing assignment, place the following items on your term calendar:

- The date your paper is due.
- The date you will begin topic selection.
- The date you plan to outline your ideas and develop a thesis.
- The dates you will go to the library if research is necessary.
- The dates you will be writing your first draft.
- The dates you will be revising your first draft.
- The dates you will begin writing/typing your second draft.
- The dates you will use for proofreading.
- The dates you will be writing/typing your final copy.

Be sure to allow yourself extra time so that you can deal with unexpected problems should they arise. Figure 10–3 illustrates a student's term calendar, with the steps of writing a research paper broken down into manageable parts.

Process: Mental and Physical Strategies

Once you have selected a topic, determined its focus, and created a thesis, you're ready to write. Because the act of writing is a physical process, you may forget that it is driven and guided by your thinking. To be a successful writer, however, you must be aware of both your mental activities and your physical activities.

FIGURE 10–3

Planning a writing assignment

Week #	Sunday	Monday	Tuesday	Wednesday	Thursday	Friday	Saturday
Sept Week 1	19	20	21	22	23	24	25
Sept/ Oct Week 2	26	27	28	29	30	1 Select topic	2 Outline/ thesis
Oct Week 3	3	4 Library research	5 Library research	6 Library research	7 Library research	8	9 Write 1st draft
Oct Week 4	10 Write 1st draft	11 Write 1st draft	12 Write 1st draft	13 Write 1st draft	14 Write 1st draft	15	16
Oct Week 5	17 Revise	18 Revise	19 Revise	20 Revise	21 Revise	22	23 Have friend read paper
Oct Week 6	24 Revise?	25	26	27	28	29 Type final copy	30 Type final copy
Oct/ Nov Week 7	31 Proof final copy	1 Type changes final copy	2	3	4	5 ☆ Paper due	6

It is also necessary for you to be aware of your learning style as you write. If you are a visual learner, you may be able to visualize the flow of ideas in your head as you write. If you are an auditory learner, you may have to say your thoughts out loud as you write. If you are a kinesthetic learner, remember to set goals or time limits for your writing and to reward yourself with several breaks while you write.

Process: Mental Strategies

The thinking part of writing is the motor that drives the machinery of the entire writing process. To keep your motor running smoothly, you must monitor its performance and tune it up when necessary. The following strategies will help you tune into and tune up your thinking processes as you write.

Decide How to Introduce Your Paper. The opening paragraph of your paper should introduce your topic, create an interest, and state your thesis. When thinking about how to do this effectively, consider using one of the strategies listed below:

- Open with a quote, statistics, or other evidence that will show the importance of your topic.
- Begin with a short definition.
- Combine a brief story with a quote or definition to introduce your topic.
- Open with a question that will arouse the readers' interest.
- Use a direct opening that discusses the topic in a general way and establishes a mood or scene.

Think about Main Points and Details. As you write your paper, refer to your outline to help your ideas flow logically into paragraphs. When creating each paragraph, remember to include a topic or main point and sentences that contain supporting points or details. All of the details should relate to the topic sentence. To be sure your details fit your topic sentence, read the topic sentence and each of the supporting sentences individually. Ask, "Does this sentence tell more about the topic sentence?" If it does not, omit it.

Sometimes students do not include enough detail in a paper to effectively communicate their information. Remember to give examples in your writing. When you use specific examples to develop your topic sentence, you make your writing more interesting and understandable.

Decide How to End Your Paper. When you have finished developing all the points in your outline, it is time to smoothly draw your paper to a close. Your ending should connect with all the ideas in your paper and give your readers a feeling of completion. Suggestions for ways to end a paper are:

- Summarize the main points.
- Use an appropriate quote.
- Make a recommendation for further action.
- Answer questions asked in the introduction, using information from your paper.
- Refer to points made earlier in the paper.
- Tell a brief story that relates to your thesis.

Tune Up Your Thoughts. After writing your paper for the first time, it's a good idea to take a break before trying to revise it. Time away from the thinking and writing process will give you a chance to review your writing with a fresh outlook. To revise your work, ask yourself the following questions:

- Is my introduction effective?
- Are my ideas clear?

- Are there better words I can use?
- Are my paragraphs in a logical order?
- Does each paragraph tie into my thesis?
- Does each sentence tie into a topic sentence?
- Did I include enough detail in the form of examples?
- Does my conclusion draw my ideas to a close?

Process: Physical Strategies

As you begin to physically write your paper, remember that good writing goes through many stages. You may have to write a paragraph or sentence many times before it is just the way you want it. The process of writing is an art that requires the writer to gather, shape, and create ideas. A work of art usually cannot be completed in a day.

Begin Your First Draft. Your paper should consist of an introduction, a body, and a conclusion. When you begin your first draft, focus on getting your ideas down on paper. You will refine your spelling, grammar, and punctuation later in the writing process. As you write, you may think of other ideas that you want to include in your paper. Jot them down in the margin, and refer to them later. If you find that you are beginning to lose your concentration, take a break. Removing yourself from the writing process can be refreshing and can help you return to the process with new ideas.

Sharing Your Ideas

Use the outline and thesis you created with a partner on the worst part of being a college student. Write your own short paper on that topic. Include an introduction, a body, and a conclusion. Use the information on pages 262 and 263 to guide your writing. ■

Check Your Work. After writing, take a break before you revise your work. Revising means improving the content of your writing. You will be looking more at the ideas in your writing than at the grammar, spelling, or punctuation. Use your learning style to read through your paper and make changes. Read each paragraph, and decide whether the ideas are clearly presented, whether they fit with the topic of the paragraph, and whether you have given enough details in the form of examples. If you are a visual learner, you may be able to visualize a better order for your ideas as you read through each paragraph. If you are an auditory learner, read your work out loud and decide whether it sounds logical, clear, and detailed. As a kinesthetic learner, you may feel more comfortable moving around as you read and revise your work. If you have trouble finding anything wrong with your work, ask someone whose opinion you value to read and critique it.

Sharing Your Ideas

Revise the paper you wrote on the worst part of being a college student.

1. Read through your introduction, body, and conclusion. To be sure your ideas are clear, organized, and detailed, ask yourself the questions listed under "Guidelines for Revising a Paper" below. Make needed changes.
2. Exchange your paper with a partner.
3. Read through your partner's paper. Offer suggestions, using the following guidelines:

Guidelines for Revising a Paper

- Is the introduction effective?
- Does the introduction contain a thesis?
- Are the ideas clear throughout the paper?
- Could better words be used?
- Are the paragraphs in logical order?
- Do the paragraphs tie into the thesis?
- Does each paragraph have a topic sentence, and do the other sentences in the paragraph tie into that sentence?
- Is enough detail included?
- Does the conclusion draw the ideas to a close? ■

Write Your Second Draft. After you have revised your first draft, rewrite your paper, making necessary changes. Although it is tempting to regard this as the final stage in the writing process, you may have to add some finishing touches after your second draft has been completed.

Recall: Mental and Physical Strategies

Students often forget the final step of the writing process. As a result, their writing does not reflect the time and effort they put into it. Your grade could be lowered by errors in typing, spelling, or grammar or by a poor overall appearance. You must think about and make final corrections before you turn your paper in.

Recall: Mental Strategies

After completing your final draft, you must proofread your paper. Proofreading means checking each word, sentence, punctuation mark, and capital letter to be sure it is correct. As you proofread, think about:

- Errors in sentence structure.
- Mistyped or misspelled words.
- Errors in grammar.
- Improper punctuation.
- Improper capital letters.
- Abbreviations that should be written out.
- Numbers that should be written out.

Recall: Physical Strategies

It is a good idea to take a break between revising your paper and proofreading. Because it is often difficult to find your own mistakes, use some of the strategies below to help you.

Read Slowly and Out Loud. This works especially well for auditory learners. When you read out loud, you may find that certain passages do not sound right.

Work Backward. Start at the end of your paper, and read each sentence from the last to the first. This will help you see what you actually wrote, not what you meant to write.

Proofread Several Times. Each time you go through your paper, you can look for a different type of error. Your first reading could focus on spelling, your second on punctuation, and so on.

Have a Friend Check Your Work. Sometimes it is difficult to read your own paper and spot errors. After you use some of the strategies suggested above, it might still be a good idea to have someone else proofread your paper. Think about having someone with a different learning style do your proofreading. A visual learner will see errors that an auditory learner might not notice, and an auditory learner will hear errors that a visual learner might not detect.

Writing a Research Paper

A research paper assignment can ask you to explore a topic in depth, analyze information collected, or research a topic and use your findings to develop your own ideas. Composing this type of paper requires additional work in the preparation stage of writing. After you read and analyze your instructions, brainstorm topics, outline ideas, create a thesis, and plan a time schedule, you must visit the library to collect information before you write. The following suggestions will help you efficiently gather the material you need in order to write a research paper.

Locate Your Library's Resources

A college library can be a very scary place. It often appears that everyone knows what he's doing except you. The truth is that most people do not know all there is to know about using a college library. Information is changing so rapidly that library procedures are constantly changing to keep up. Before you run for the safety of your public library, do what everyone else has to do and ask for help.

To make your research easier, you should locate the following resources:

- A library floor plan.
- The reference room.
- Card catalog or online card catalog.
- Periodical indexes (journals and magazines).
- Information on where periodicals are located.
- Information on where and how books are shelved.
- Information on CD-ROM.
- Microfilm.
- Information on interlibrary loan.
- Procedures for checking out material.
- Copying machines.

Locate Sources of Information

Several sources can be used to collect information about your topic. You can locate books by doing a subject search either in a card catalog or on a computer. If you have difficulty in finding listings under your topic, use *The Library of Congress Subject Headings.* This book lists subject headings under which various topics are filed.

To locate information in magazines and journals, use periodical indexes that are specific to your subject. For example, when doing research in education, instead of using *Reader's Guide,* use *Education Index,* which covers magazines and journals in the field of education. Most academic disciplines have a journal for their particular field.

Bibliographies at the end of books and journal articles provide an excellent means of finding additional information on a subject. A reference book titled *Bibliographic Index* can be used to locate bibliographies by subject heading.

FIGURE 10–4
A bibliography card for a book

FIGURE 10–5
A bibliography card for a journal

Record Your Sources

Locate as many sources as necessary, and use a separate 3″ × 5″ index card to record each reference. When your paper is completed, you will need to list all of the references you use in a bibliography. Because there are different ways to structure a bibliography, check with your instructor about the format. An example of the type of information to include for a book and a journal is illustrated in Figures 10–4 and 10–5.

Use a Notetaking System

Use 5″ × 8″ or 4″ × 6″ cards to take notes from your sources. Refer to your outline, and use a separate card for each topic. Use the PPR Notetaking System format to indent topics and subtopics as you record information. Be

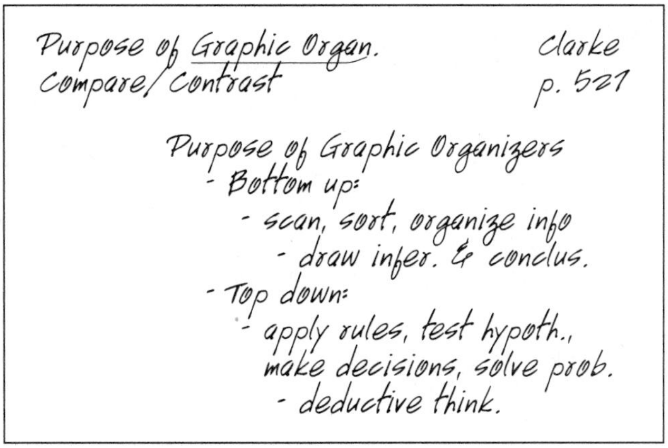

Purpose of Graphic Organ.
Compare/Contrast
Clarke
p. 527
Purpose of Graphic Organizers
- Bottom up:
- scan, sort, organize info
- draw infer. & conclus.
- Top down:
- apply rules, test hypoth., make decisions, solve prob.
- deductive think.

FIGURE 10–6
Notecard

sure to use your words unless you are quoting the author. If you are going to use a quote, be sure to copy it exactly, use quotation marks, and include the page number. In the upper right corner of each card, write the author's last name and the page(s) you used. Write the main topic of each card in the upper left corner and on the front of the card. Figure 10–6 illustrates a sample notecard.

Organize Your Notecards

After collecting information from all of your sources, separate your notecards into piles according to topic. Try to place them in an order that corresponds to the order of your original outline. If you found additional information while doing research, you may want to revise your outline at this time.

Use the PPR Writing System

Once you have arranged your notecards in a logical order, you are ready to begin the process stage of the PPR Writing System. You will write a first draft with an introduction, a body, and a conclusion. After revising the first draft, you will write a second draft. Refer to Table 10–1 for mental and physical strategies to guide you while you write and after you write.

Putting It All Together

Writing is a process that gives shape and form to thought. You must use creative and critical thought before, while, and after you write. Just as a sculpture takes many forms, so should your paper as you creatively brainstorm or freewrite ideas before writing. When writing for someone other than yourself, you must think critically about your purpose and your audience. As your work takes form, you can use creativity and critical thought to organize and revise your words. After writing, to ensure the best results for your time and effort, proofread your work. Writing a research paper requires additional steps in the preparation stage. You must locate your library's resources, locate sources of information, record your sources, use a notetaking system, and organize your notecards before you write.

Making the Connection

Check your understanding of the concepts presented in this chapter by completing the following activity. If you are unable to recall information in a particular area, go back and review that material before completing the rest of the exercises in this section.

1. Write one or two sentences to summarize what you recall about each of the following topics:

   Mental strategies for preparing to write ______________________

   Physical strategies for preparing to write ______________________

   Mental strategies while writing ______________________

   Physical strategies while writing ______________________

   Mental strategies after writing ______________________

   Physical strategies after writing ______________________

2. List one new idea you've gained about writing as a result of this chapter. ______________________

3. Describe one change you plan to make before writing, one change you plan to make during writing, and one change you plan to make after writing. ______

Thinking It Through

Read the following passage, and then answer the questions by applying what you've learned about writing.

Richard is a new student in a community college. He has never liked to write, and he dreads the day he will have to write a paper for one of his classes. When his history instructor announces that the class has a month to write a research paper on the Vietnam War, Richard immediately goes to the library to look up Vietnam. Under that topic he finds hundreds of books and articles. He selects the first book on the list and feels happy that he has completed his research.

After a week Richard begins to write his paper. He uses his book to summarize what the author says about Vietnam. He then adds his personal opinion about the Vietnam War. When he completes his paper, he reads it once and feels satisfied that it is done. Because he cannot type, Richard takes his paper to a typing service one week before it is due. A week later he picks up his paper on the way to class and hands it to his instructor.

1. Based on information in the passage, what do you see as Richard's specific problem(s)? ______

2. By using knowledge you already have, asking others, and possibly doing a bit of research, list as many solutions to Richard's problems as you can. ______

3. List the pros and cons for *each* of these solutions from Richard's point of view. ______

4. Select the solution that appears to be the best in terms of pros and cons. List the steps necessary to carry out this solution. Be sure to describe the details, such as who, what, when, where, and how.

Applying Your Skills 1 *Preparing to Write*

Instructions: Select a topic from the list below.

1. List some ideas that could be included in a one-page paper about this topic.
2. Organize your list into an outline that shows a logical order for discussing each of these ideas.

Topics

My happiest moment
The worst day of my life
Personal loss
My parents
Summer vacation
Childhood memories
My family
Goals for the future

List of Ideas

Outline of Ideas

Applying Your Skills 2 *Writing a Draft*

Instructions:

1. Use the outline produced in Applying Your Skills 1 to create a thesis. Write the thesis on the line below.

2. Decide whether you will be:
   - Describing your thesis.
   - Putting information in chronological order.
   - Listing information about your thesis.
   - Showing cause and effect.
   - Comparing and contrasting information.
   - Solving a problem.
3. Use your own paper to write a one-page draft based on your outline. Remember to include your thesis in the introduction, to develop your outline in the body, and to bring your ideas to a close in the conclusion.

Applying Your Skills 3 *Revising Your Work*

Instructions: Put your draft aside for a day. Then revise your work and rewrite it. Proofread your final copy for errors in spelling, grammar, and punctuation.

Applying Your Skills 4 *Using Your Resources*

Instructions: To know where to "radio for help," you will be asked to visit various school resources throughout this text. Keep this information so that you can refer to it when you are in need of help outside the classroom.

Complete the information below after touring your school's Writing Center.

Location: ______________________________

Hours of operation: ______________________________

Contact person: ______________________________

Phone: ______________________________

Services offered:

____

____

____

____

Personal comments:

Briefly discuss how you could use this resource.

____

____

____

____

Bibliography

Chapter 1

Biggs, J. B. "Learning Strategies, Student Motivation Patterns, and Subjectively Perceived Success." In *Cognitive Strategies and Educational Performance*, ed. R. Kirby. Orlando, Fla.: Academic Press, 1984.

Eanet, Marilyn, and Kay Camperell. "Students' Conceptions of Learning, Their Motivations and Their Approaches to Study." *Forum for Reading* 21, no. 1 (Fall–Winter 1989), p. 50.

Paul, Richard. "Toward a Critical Society." In *Critical Thinking: What Every Person Needs to Survive in a Rapidly Changing World*. ed. A. J. A. Binker. Rohnert Park, Calif.: Center for Critical Thinking and Moral Critique, 1990.

Snyder, Benson. *The Hidden Curriculum*. New York: Alfred A. Knopf, 1971.

Sternberg, Robert J. *Intelligence Applied: Understanding and Increasing Your Intellectual Skills*. San Diego, Calif.: Harcourt Brace Jovanovich, 1986.

Chapter 2

Donnelly, Rory. *Active Learning*. Fort Worth, Tex.: Holt, Rinehart & Winston, 1990.

McWhorter, Kathleen T. *College Reading and Study Skills*. 3rd ed. Boston: Little, Brown, 1986.

Miller, Lyle L. "Some Hints on Planning a Better Time Schedule." Developmental Reading Distributors.

Wood, Nancy V. *College Reading and Study Skills*. 3rd. ed. New York: Holt, Rinehart & Winston. 1986.

Chapter 3

McWilliams, John-Roger and Peter McWilliams. *Life 101*. Los Angeles, Calif.: Prelude Press, 1990.

Kanar, Carol C. *The Confident Student*. Boston: Houghton Mifflin, 1991.

Moses, Henry C. *Inside College*. New York: College Board Publications, 1990.

Rowh, Mark. *Coping with Stress in College*. New York: College Entrance Examination Board, 1989.

Throop, Robert K. *Reaching Your Potential: Personal and Professional Development*. New York: Delmar Publishing, 1993.

Chapter 4

Barbe, Walter, and H. Swassing, with Michael N. Milone. *Teaching through Modality Strengths: Concepts and Practices*. Columbus, Ohio: Zaner-Bloser, 1984.

Buzan, Tony. *Use Both Sides of Your Brain*. New York: E. P. Dutton, 1983.

Fleming, Neil D., and Colleen Mills. "Not Another Inventory, Rather a Catalyst for Reflections." *To Improve the Academy* 11 (1992), pp. 137–55.

Gibbs, Graham. "Changing Students' Approaches to Study through Classroom Exercises." In *Helping Adults Learn How to Learn*, New Directions for Continuing Education, no. 19. San Francisco: Jossey-Bass, September 1983.

McWhorter, Kathleen T. "Becoming a More Successful Learner: Principles of Learning and Memory." In Kathleen T. McWhorter, *College Reading and Study Skills*. 3rd ed. Boston: Little, Brown, 1986.

Scarr, Sandra, and James Vander Zanden. "Memory." In *Understanding Psychology*. 5th ed. New York: Random House, 1987.

Smilkstein, Rita. "A Natural Teaching Method Based on Learning Theory." *Gamut*, 1990–91.

Chapter 5

Bragstad, Bernice Jensen, and Sharyn Mueller Stumpf. *A Guideline for Teaching Study Skills and Motivation*. Boston: Allyn & Bacon, 1987.

Sanders, Norris M. *Classroom Questions: What Kinds*? New York: Harper & Row. 1966.

Schwenker, Judy A.; Steven R. Krogull; Janice S. Rudolph; and Deborah E. Simpson. *Mastering Medical Content: A Workbook for Entering Medical Students*. Milwaukee: Medical College of Wisconsin, 1989.

Stice, James E. "Learning How to Think." In *New Directions for Teaching and Learning,* no. 30 San Francisco: Jossey-Bass, Summer 1987.

Chapter 6

Lindzey, Gardner; Calvin S. Hall; and Richard Thompson. *Psychology*. New York: Worth Publishers, 1978.

Nosich, Gerald. "Educational Virtue: Becoming a Critical Thinker." In *Critical Thinking: What Every Person Needs to Survive in a Rapidly Changing World*, Richard W. Paul, ed. A. J. A. Binker. Rohnert Park, Calif.: Center for Critical Thinking and Moral Critique, 1990.

Parnes, Sidney J. *Creative Behavior Guidebook*. New York: Creative Education Foundation, 1967.

Paul, Richard W. "Bloom's Taxonomy and Critical Thinking Instruction." In *Critical Thinking: What Every Person Needs to Survive in a Rapidly Changing World*, Richard W. Paul, ed. A. J. A. Binker. Rohnert Park, Calif.: Center for Critical Thinking and Moral Critique, 1990.

Ruggiero, Vincent. *The Art of Thinking*. New York: Harper & Row, 1984.

________. *Beyond Feelings: A Guide to Critical Thinking*. New York: Alfred Publishing, 1975.

Whimby, Arthur, and Jack Lochhead. *Problem Solving and Comprehension*. 3rd ed. Philadelphia: Franklin Institute Press, 1982.

Chapter 7

Donnelly, Rory. *Active Learning*. Fort Worth, Tex.: Holt, Rinehart & Winston, 1990.

McWilliams, John-Roger, and Peter McWilliams. *Life 101*. (Los Angeles, California: Prelude Press, 1990).

Keller, Barbara. "Frontiersmen Are History." *Newsweek*, August 16, 1993, p. 10.

King, James R., and Norman A. Stahl. "Training and Evaluating Notetaking." *College Reading and Learning Assistance Technical Report* 85-06. Atlanta: Georgia State University, April 1985.

McWhorter, Kathleen T. *Study and Thinking Skills in College,* 2nd ed. New York: HarperCollins, 1992.

Sotiriou, Peter Elias. *Integrating College Study Skills*. Belmont, Calif.: Wadsorth Publishing, 1984.

Swift, E. M. "Dangerous Games." *Sports Illustrated*, November 18, 1991. p. 43.

Chapter 8

Cortina, Joe; Janet Elder; and Katherine Gonnet. *Comprehending College Textbooks*. 2nd ed. New York: McGraw Hill, 1992.

Megginson, William L.; Mary Jane Byrd; Charles R. Scott; and Leon C. Megginson. *Small Business Management: An Entrepreneur's Guide to Success*. Burr Ridge, Ill. Richard D. Irwin, 1994.

Parker, Rosemary. "Learning by Intimidation." *Newsweek*, November 8, 1993, p. 14.

Wood, Nancy. *Strategies for College Reading and Thinking*. New York: McGraw Hill, 1991.

Wootton, James. "Lessons of Pop Jordan's Death." *Newsweek*, September 13, 1993, p. 12.

Chapter 9

Huang, Chungliang Al, and Jerry Lynch. *Thinking Body, Dancing Mind*. New York: Bantam Books, 1992.

Hyatt, Carole, and Linda Gottlieb. *When Smart People Fail*. New York: Simon & Schuster, 1987.

McWhorter, Kathleen T. *Study and Thinking Skills in College*. 2nd ed. New York: HarperCollins, 1992.

Schwenker, Judy A.; Steven R. Krogull; Janice S. Rudolph; and Deborah E. Simpson. *Mastering Medical Content*. Milwaukee: Medical College of Wisconsin, 1989.

Willey, Miriam S., and Barbara M. Jarecky. *Analysis and Application of Information*. Maryland School of Medicine, Baltimore: Miriam S. Willey and Barbara M. Jarecky, 1979.

Wood, Nancy V. *College Reading and Study Skills*. 3rd ed. New York: Holt, Rinehart & Winston, 1986.

Chapter 10

McWhorter, Kathleen T. *Study and Thinking Skills In College*. 2nd ed. New York: Harper Collins, 1992.

Pemberton, Carol. *Writing Essays*. Boston: Allyn & Bacon, 1993.

Schor, Sandra, and Judith Summerfield. *The Random House Guide to Writing*. 3rd ed. New York: Random House, 1986.

Troyka, Lynn Quitman. *Handbook for Writers*. Englewood Cliffs, N.J.: Prentice Hall, 1987.

I N D E X

7:00
808 So Rt 57